RE... FOR
DAILY PRAYER

ADVENT **2021** TO
EVE OF ADVENT **2022**

JUSTINE ALLAIN CHAPMAN
JOANNA COLLICUTT
STEPHEN COTTRELL
AZARIAH FRANCE-WILLIAMS
GULI FRANCIS-DEHQANI
MALCOLM GUITE
ISABELLE HAMLEY
COLIN HEBER-PERCY
CHRISTOPHER HERBERT
DAVID HOYLE
JOHN INGE
RACHEL MANN
ANNA MATTHEWS
PETER MOGER
PHILIP NORTH
KAREN O'DONNELL
BROTHER SAMUEL SSF
ANGELA TILBY
RACHEL TREWEEK
CATHERINE WILLIAMS
ROWAN WILLIAMS

Church House Publishing
Church House
Great Smith Street
London SW1P 3AZ

ISBN 978 0 7151 2383 6

Published 2021 by Church House Publishing
Copyright © The Archbishops' Council 2021

The opinions expressed in this book are those of the
authors and do not necessarily reflect the official policy of
the General Synod or The Archbishops' Council of the
Church of England.

Liturgical editor: Peter Moger
Series editor: Hugh Hillyard-Parker
Designed and typeset by Hugh Hillyard-Parker
Copy edited by Ros Connelly
Printed by CPI Group (UK) Croydon CR0 4YY

What do you think of *Reflections for Daily Prayer*?

We'd love to hear from you – simply email us at

publishing@churchofengland.org

or write to us at

Church House Publishing, Church House,
Great Smith Street, London SW1P 3AZ.

Visit **www.dailyprayer.org.uk** for more
information on the *Reflections* series, ordering
and subscriptions.

Contents

Table of contributors

About the authors

Justine Allain Chapman has served as a parish priest and in theological education specializing in mission and pastoral care. She is currently Archdeacon of Boston in the Diocese of Lincoln committed to the wellbeing of clergy, congregations and churches. She is the author of *The Resilient Disciple*.

Joanna Collicutt has a professional background in clinical psychology, but her current area of academic interest is psychology of religion, which she teaches at Oxford University. She is also an associate priest in an Oxfordshire parish. She is the author of several books on the interface between psychology and faith.

Stephen Cottrell is the Archbishop of York. He was formerly Bishop of Chelmsford and is a well-known writer and speaker on evangelism, spirituality and catechesis. He is one of the team that produced *Pilgrim*, the popular course for the Christian Journey.

Azariah France-Williams is Rector of Ascension Church Hulme in Manchester, a member of the HeartEdge Network. He is a broadcaster with BBC Radio and author of *Ghostship: Institutional Racism and the Church of England* published by SCM Press. He is also a Visiting Scholar with Sarum College.

Guli Francis-Dehqani was born in Iran but moved to England following the events of the 1979 Islamic Revolution. Having studied music as an undergraduate, she worked at the BBC for a few years before training for ordination and completing a PhD. She was ordained in 1998 and has served as Bishop of Loughborough since 2017.

Malcolm Guite is a life fellow of Girton College, Cambridge, a poet and author of *What do Christians Believe?; Faith, Hope and Poetry; Sounding the Seasons: Seventy Sonnets for the Christian Year; The Singing Bowl; Word in the Wilderness; Mariner: A voyage with Samuel Taylor Coleridge*, and *David's Crown: Sounding The Psalms*. He also writes the 'Poet's Corner' column for the *Church Times*.

Isabelle Hamley is currently Theological Adviser to the House of Bishops; her previous posts included being chaplain to the Archbishop of Canterbury, parish priest, Old Testament lecturer and university chaplain. Her two main passions in life are the Old Testament and chocolate, which go very well together!

Colin Heber-Percy is an Anglican priest serving in the Salisbury Diocese. Before ordination, he was a screenwriter. His films and works for television won many awards and are shown all over the world. His publications include *Perfect in Weakness*, on the cinema of Andrei Tarkovsky, and *A Wing and a Prayer*, reflections on life in a country parish during the pandemic.

Christopher Herbert was ordained in Hereford in 1967, becoming a curate and then Diocesan Director of Education. He was an incumbent in Surrey and later, Archdeacon of Dorking. Appointed Bishop of St Albans, he retired in 2009.

David Hoyle is the Dean of Westminster. His ministry has embraced a Cambridge College, a London parish and both Gloucester and Bristol Cathedrals. His early academic work was as a Church historian, but more recently *The Pattern of Our Calling* was about ministry, and *A Year of Grace* is a book about the Christian year.

John Inge read chemistry at university and taught before ordination. He served in a variety of contexts before becoming the 113th Bishop of Worcester. He loves God, the Scriptures, the Church, his family and his friends – not always in that order. His most esoteric role is that of Lord High Almoner.

Rachel Mann is an Anglican priest, writer and scholar. Author of eleven books, including her debut novel, *The Gospel of Eve*, and the Michael Ramsey Prize shortlisted, *Fierce Imaginings*, she is Visiting Fellow at the Manchester Writing School. She regularly contributes to *Pause For Thought* on BBC Radio Two, as well as other radio programmes. More info: www.rachelmann.co.uk

Anna Matthews has been vicar of St Bene't's, Cambridge since 2012, prior to which she spent six years as a Minor Canon at St Albans Cathedral. From 2012–19, she was also Director of Ordinands for the Diocese of Ely, and she retains an interest and involvement in vocations work and spirituality.

Peter Moger is a priest in the Scottish Episcopal Church based at Stornoway on the Isle of Lewis. Until 2019 he was Canon Precentor of York Minster and, prior to that, Secretary of the Church of England Liturgical Commission. He has been liturgical editor of *Reflections for Daily Prayer* since its inception in 2007.

Philip North is the Bishop of Burnley. He has spent much of his ministry in urban and estates parishes in the Dioceses of Durham and London, and has also served as Priest Administrator of the Shrine of Our Lady of Walsingham. He is a member of the Company of Mission Priests.

Karen O'Donnell leads the programmes in Christian Spirituality at Sarum College. Her research is focused on the intersection of bodies and theology, with a particular emphasis on trauma experiences. Her book *Broken Bodies* was published with SCM Press in 2019.

Brother Samuel SSF is a member of The Society of St Francis (an Anglican Franciscan religious order) and lives in a community of Franciscan brothers in East London, sharing a rhythm of daily prayer and reading the Scriptures, and offering a welcome to people living on the margins.

Angela Tilby is a Canon Emeritus of Christ Church Cathedral, Oxford, and Canon of Honour at Portsmouth Cathedral. Prior to that she served in the Diocese of Oxford following a period in Cambridge, where she was at Westcott House and St Bene't's Church. Before ordination she was a producer for the BBC, and she still broadcasts regularly.

Rachel Treweek is the Bishop of Gloucester and the first female diocesan bishop in England. She served in two parishes in London and was Archdeacon of Northolt and later Hackney. Prior to ordination she was a speech and language therapist and is a trained practitioner in conflict transformation.

Catherine Williams, a former National Adviser for Selection, has a portfolio ministry as a Spiritual Director, Retreat Leader and Writer. Licensed to the Bishop of Gloucester as a Public Preacher, Catherine lives in Tewkesbury. Her passions include prayer, poetry, theatre, music and butterfly conservation.

Rowan Williams was born and brought up in Wales, and worked in pastoral and academic settings in Cambridge and Oxford before becoming Bishop of Monmouth in 1992. He was Archbishop of Canterbury from 2002 to 2012, and is the author of over 30 books on theology, spirituality, literature and current issues.

About *Reflections for Daily Prayer*

Based on the *Common Worship Lectionary* readings for Morning Prayer, these daily reflections are designed to refresh and inspire times of personal prayer. The aim is to provide rich, contemporary and engaging insights into Scripture.

Each page lists the Lectionary readings for the day, with the main psalms for that day highlighted in **bold**. The collect of the day – either the *Common Worship* collect or the shorter additional collect – is also included.

For those using this book in conjunction with a service of Morning Prayer, the following conventions apply: a psalm printed in parentheses is omitted if it has been used as the opening canticle at that office; a psalm marked with an asterisk may be shortened if desired.

A short reflection is provided on either the Old or New Testament reading. Popular writers, experienced ministers, biblical scholars and theologians all contribute to this series, bringing with them their own emphases, enthusiasms and approaches to biblical interpretation.

Regular users of Morning Prayer and *Time to Pray* (from *Common Worship: Daily Prayer*) and anyone who follows the Lectionary for their regular Bible reading will benefit from the rich variety of traditions represented in these stimulating and accessible pieces.

This volume also includes both a simple form of *Common Worship* Morning Prayer (see inside front and back covers) and a short form of Night Prayer – also known as Compline – (see pp. 326–7), particularly for the benefit of those readers who are new to the habit of the Daily Office or for any reader while travelling.

Building daily prayer into daily life

In our morning routines, there are many tasks we do without giving much thought to them, and others that we do with careful attention. Daily prayer and Bible reading is a strange mixture of these. These are disciplines (and gifts) that we as Christians should have in our daily pattern, but they are not tasks to be ticked off. Rather they are a key component of our developing relationship with God. In them is *life* – for the fruits of this time are to be lived out by us – and to be most fruitful, the task requires both purpose and letting go.

In saying a daily office of prayer, we make the deliberate decision to say 'yes' to spending time with God – the God who is always with us. In prayer and attentive reading of the Scriptures, there is both a conscious entering into God's presence and a 'letting go' of all we strive to control: both are our acknowledgement that it is God who is God.

> *… come into his presence with singing.*
>
> *Know that the Lord is God.*
> *It is he that has made us, and we are his;*
> *we are his people, and the sheep of his pasture.*
>
> *Enter his gates with thanksgiving…*
>
> (Psalm 100, a traditional Canticle at Morning Prayer)

If we want a relationship with someone to deepen and grow, we need to spend time with that person. It can be no surprise that the same is true between us and God.

In our daily routines, I suspect that most of us intentionally look in the mirror; occasionally we might see beyond the surface of our external reflection and catch a glimpse of who we truly are. For me, a regular pattern of daily prayer and Bible reading is like a hard look in a clean mirror: it gives a clear reflection of myself, my life and the world in which I live. But it is more than that, for in it I can also see the reflection of God who is most clearly revealed in Jesus Christ and present with us now in the Holy Spirit.

This commitment to daily prayer is about our relationship with the God who is love. St Paul, in his great passage about love, speaks of now seeing 'in a mirror, dimly' but one day seeing face to face: 'Now I know only in part; then I will know fully, even as I have been fully known' (1 Corinthians 13.12). Our daily prayer is part of that seeing in a mirror dimly, and it is also part of our deep yearning for an ever-clearer vision of our God. As we read Scripture, the past and the future converge in the present moment. We hear words from long ago – some of which can appear strange and confusing – and yet, the Holy Spirit is living and active in the present. In this place of relationship and revelation, we open ourselves to the possibility of being changed, of being reshaped in a way that is good for us and all creation.

It is important that the words of prayer and Scripture should penetrate deep within rather than be a mere veneer. A quiet location is therefore a helpful starting point. For some, domestic circumstances or daily schedule make that difficult, but it is never impossible to become more fully present to God. The depths of our being can still be accessed no matter the world's clamour and activity. An awareness of this is all part of our journey from a false sense of control to a place of letting go, to a place where there is an opportunity for transformation.

Sometimes in our attention to Scripture, there will be connection with places of joy or pain; we might be encouraged or provoked or both. As we look and see and encounter God more deeply, there will be thanksgiving and repentance; the cries of our heart will surface as we acknowledge our needs and desires for ourselves and the world. The liturgy of Morning Prayer gives this voice and space.

I find it helpful to begin Morning Prayer by lighting a candle. This marks my sense of purpose and my acknowledgement of Christ's presence with me. It is also a silent prayer for illumination as I prepare to be attentive to what I see in the mirror, both of myself and of God. Amid the revelation of Scripture and the cries of my heart, the constancy of the tiny flame bears witness to the hope and light of Christ in all that is and will be.

When the candle is extinguished, I try to be still as I watch the smoke disappear. For me, it is symbolic of my prayers merging with the day. I know that my prayer and the reading of Scripture are not the smoke and mirrors of delusion. Rather, they are about encounter and discovery as I seek to venture into the day to love and serve the Lord as a disciple of Jesus Christ.

+ Rachel Treweek

Monday 29 November

Matthew 12.1-21

'Here is my servant, whom I have chosen' (v.18)

Today's reading tells two stories of Jesus stretching and challenging the Jewish understanding of the Sabbath. He explains to them that the Sabbath is a gift from God, not just a narrow rule about abstention from work, and good and necessary work can be done.

However, the climax of the passage lies beyond the stories. Matthew quotes the prophet Isaiah, saying: 'Here is my servant, whom I have chosen, my beloved, with whom my soul is well pleased.' These words echo the words that Jesus heard at his baptism. His ministry begins with, and is fuelled by, the affirmation of God's love for Jesus and God's pleasure in him. This affirmation is available to all of us.

The Advent season also has these stories and proclamations at their heart. We are getting ready not just to celebrate the birth of Jesus, but to prepare for that day when we see God face to face. That is the endless Sabbath of God's kingdom, where we enjoy God's company and only do work that is good.

The religious establishment is confounded by Jesus, but because he reinterprets and fulfils the teaching of Judaism in such a compelling and life-giving way, the crowds follow him. But Isaiah takes us one step further. He says that what we see and experience in Jesus is for the whole world. The season of Advent is about the coming of Christ as ruler and judge of everything.

COLLECT

Almighty God,
give us grace to cast away the works of darkness
and to put on the armour of light,
now in the time of this mortal life,
in which your Son Jesus Christ came to us in great humility;
that on the last day,
when he shall come again in his glorious majesty
    to judge the living and the dead,
we may rise to the life immortal;
through him who is alive and reigns with you,
in the unity of the Holy Spirit,
one God, now and for ever.

| *Reflection by* **Stephen Cottrell**

Psalms 47, 147.1-12
Ezekiel 47.1-12
or Ecclesiasticus 14.20-end
John 12.20-32

Tuesday 30 November

Andrew the Apostle

John 12.20-32

'... where I am, there will my servant be also' (v.26)

In today's' reading on the Feast Day of St Andrew, we build on some of the words and ideas we looked at yesterday. Quoting Isaiah, 'Here is my servant, whom I have chosen,' Matthew was making an editorial point about Jesus. Today, Jesus says of those who follow him: '... where I am, there will my servant be also'.

Judgement is one of the great Advent themes. There will be a day of reckoning, that day when we see God face to face. Things that are in darkness will be brought to light. We will say more about this as we travel through the Advent season. But Jesus tells us that the main criterion by which we will be judged is whether we served others. And it's no good saying that we didn't see Jesus hungry or naked or suffering. When we serve others, we serve him (see Matthew 25.37-40).

He also says that he will be present, serving others through us. Therefore, when we find people wanting to see Jesus, like the Greeks who came to Philip, we don't need to go through the same chain of command – Philip went to Andrew; Andrew went to Jesus. Jesus himself is present through us. And Jesus will be encountered in the people we meet, especially those in need.

Almighty God,
who gave such grace to your apostle Saint Andrew
that he readily obeyed the call of your Son Jesus Christ
and brought his brother with him:
call us by your holy word,
and give us grace to follow you without delay
and to tell the good news of your kingdom;
through Jesus Christ your Son our Lord,
who is alive and reigns with you,
in the unity of the Holy Spirit,
one God, now and for ever.

COLLECT

Reflection by **Stephen Cottrell**   11

Wednesday 1 December

Matthew 12.38-end

'... pointing to his disciples, he said, "Here are my mother and my brothers!"' (v.49)

To be the ones through whom Jesus is known today, to be his hands and heart in the midst of the world's hurt, is an awesome and privileged vocation. It is shared by everyone who is baptized into Christ.

Jesus is not callously snubbing his mother and his family in this reading. He is pointing us to realities of belonging and identity that transcend even bonds of human family.

Water is thicker than blood. This is the audacious Christian claim. We have a new belonging with each other and with God through Jesus Christ. The story of his birth that we are preparing to celebrate is the advent of the fulfilment of God's heart, and leads through cross and resurrection to a new humanity. This promise of eternal life with God and new relationship with each other is another of the great Advent themes. The sign that is even greater than the sign of Jonah is the sign of Jesus' death and resurrection, the promise of a new humanity and of life lived with God.

Judgement, in this sense, isn't about being weighed in the scales and found wanting – this is a contest no one can win and the reason Christ came in the first place! – but about being judged ready for glory.

COLLECT

Almighty God,
give us grace to cast away the works of darkness
and to put on the armour of light,
now in the time of this mortal life,
in which your Son Jesus Christ came to us in great humility;
that on the last day,
when he shall come again in his glorious majesty
    to judge the living and the dead,
we may rise to the life immortal;
through him who is alive and reigns with you,
in the unity of the Holy Spirit,
one God, now and for ever.

Reflection by **Stephen Cottrell**

Psalms **42**, 43 *or* 14, **15**, 16
Isaiah 28.14-end
Matthew 13.1-23

Matthew 13.1-23

'... blessed are your eyes, for they see, and your ears, for they hear'
(v.16)

Any farmer listening to the parable of the sower – and of course most of the people listening were farmers – would be outraged at the injustice of what was being said. Seed is precious. It doesn't fall on the path unless you've been stupid enough to drop it. It isn't planted in rocky ground unless you've been too lazy to have cleared and tilled the soil before you sow. Birds don't eat up. You provide a scarecrow. This feckless sower doesn't seem to know much about sowing. He doesn't deserve such an abundant harvest.

We don't hear the story this way, not just because most of us, today, are not farmers and get our food from supermarkets, but because we have the interpretation that follows, directing us to understand the story in a very particular way: it's all about the snares and temptations that we the followers of Jesus face in our discipleship. Not really about seed at all. But only the disciples get that explanation. Everyone else just had the story. A story of profligate abundance, despite failure.

'Blessed are your eyes, for they see, and your ears, for they hear', says Jesus after he has again quoted Isaiah. What we learn here is that there is more than one interpretation. We encounter both the dangers and snares of discipleship and the extravagant generosity of God. His judgement seems to be that, despite failure, blessing is given.

Almighty God,
as your kingdom dawns,
turn us from the darkness of sin to the
light of holiness,
that we may be ready to meet you
in our Lord and Saviour, Jesus Christ.

COLLECT

Reflection by **Stephen Cottrell**

Friday 3 December

Psalms **25**, 26 *or* 17, **19**
Isaiah 29.1-14
Matthew 13.24-43

Matthew 13.24-43

'... without a parable he told them nothing' (v.34)

These words of Jesus are extremely beautiful and somewhat irritating. He teaches us in stories. Just stories. Nothing else. And as we discovered yesterday, stories can have more than one meaning. To understand the story, you have to get inside it. There is rarely a simple takeaway message, only a sit-down-and-chew-it-over invitation to dinner. What's more, Jesus tumbles one story upon another, showing us that God's kingdom can be seen and known from many different angles.

Advent is a time for us to consider what the Church calls the last things: death, judgement, heaven and hell. Eternal life.

These parables give us pictures and stories of what eternal life in God's kingdom is like. They invite us to see God's kingdom breaking in around us now – like yeast leavening the dough. Or growing among us from tiny beginnings – like mustard seeds.

Most challenging of all, Jesus tells us that the weeds and the wheat grow up alongside each other. I think we know this. We know that there is good and evil in our world. We know that the world is not divided up into angels and demons. Only frail human beings, with a great capacity for good and a terrible capacity to get it wrong.

We get ready for judgement by acknowledging this reality and asking for God's mercy, not by pretending we are just wheat.

COLLECT

Almighty God,
give us grace to cast away the works of darkness
and to put on the armour of light,
now in the time of this mortal life,
in which your Son Jesus Christ came to us in great humility;
that on the last day,
when he shall come again in his glorious majesty
   to judge the living and the dead,
we may rise to the life immortal;
through him who is alive and reigns with you,
in the unity of the Holy Spirit,
one God, now and for ever.

Reflection by **Stephen Cottrell**

Psalms **9** (10) *or* 20, 21, **23**
Isaiah 29.15-end
Matthew 13.44-end

Saturday 4 December

Matthew 13.44-end

'... they took offence at him' (v.57)

The greatest story Jesus tells is the story of his own life. He is the treasure in the field for which we would give up everything. He is the pearl of great price we seek.

Let us then move from this rich harvest of stories about God's kingdom to Jesus himself and the terrible story of how he is misunderstood, rejected, abandoned and ultimately killed by the very people he came to help.

'They took offence at him' is the terrible sentence that shouts out from this passage. Who is he to say and do these things! Just the carpenter's son.

The story of Jesus that begins in Bethlehem, a helpless baby crying out in need, ends on a cross, a crucified man crying out in pain. Those two images are the most prevalent in Christian art: Christ at his birth and Christ on the cross. They frame his life. They also frame ours. We are born, and one day we will die. We know our birthday, but each year in the calendar the day of our death, not yet known to us, passes by.

Without people's belief, Jesus isn't able to do much. After all, he's not a magician; he's God's son. But *with* belief, knowing that, in Jesus, God shares our birth and shares our death, God can do so much, leading us through death to resurrection, just as he led Jesus. This is the Advent hope.

Almighty God,
as your kingdom dawns,
turn us from the darkness of sin to the
light of holiness,
that we may be ready to meet you
in our Lord and Saviour, Jesus Christ.

COLLECT

Monday 6 December

Psalm **44** or 27, **30**
Isaiah 30.1-18
Matthew 14.1-12

Matthew 14.1-12

'At that time Herod the ruler heard reports about Jesus' (v.1)

We ended last week acknowledging that the greatest story Jesus told was his own life. We begin this week by seeing how the story of Jesus continues in our stories, and in all the stories of those who follow him, beginning with John the Baptist.

John was the forerunner of Jesus, the one who prepares the way. Those words – 'Prepare a way for the Lord' – echo through the Advent season. John's life and witness straddle the Old and New Testaments. He is the last of the prophets, but, in many ways, the first disciple, for John is also a follower. He famously says at Jesus' baptism that he must decrease so that Jesus can increase (John 3.30).

This is a pattern for all who follow Jesus. We follow him, and we invite others to follow. But we point to Jesus, not ourselves.

It is costly, though. John the baptizer had dared to question Herod's morality. Herod wanted to get rid of him, but was frightened of the crowds who followed John. Now that John has been put to death following a most macabre manipulation of events, Herod is frightened again. Like all weak leaders, he tries to please everyone, but ends up pleasing no one. And though he has got rid of John, Jesus is still very much alive. Thus the life of Jesus continues in all who follow him and point to him.

COLLECT

O Lord, raise up, we pray, your power
and come among us,
and with great might succour us;
that whereas, through our sins and wickedness
we are grievously hindered
in running the race that is set before us,
your bountiful grace and mercy
may speedily help and deliver us;
through Jesus Christ your Son our Lord,
to whom with you and the Holy Spirit,
be honour and glory, now and for ever.

16 | *Reflection by* **Stephen Cottrell**

Psalms **56**, 57 *or* 32, **36**
Isaiah 30.19-end
Matthew 14.13-end

Tuesday 7 December

Matthew 14.13-end

'... he had compassion for them' (v.14)

If we think about judgement at all, we tend to be frightened of the prospect. Basil Hume, the former Roman Catholic Cardinal, once described judgement like this: he said that to be judged was to whisper the story of your life into the ear of an all-loving Father.

If judgement is about being made ready for glory, for eternal life with God, then the God who is revealed to us by Jesus as the merciful Father will have compassion on us in the same way that we see Jesus have compassion in these stories. Jesus has compassion on the crowds because they are hungry. The disciples want to send them away; Jesus wants them to stay and eat.

He takes the small offerings that are available and he feeds the crowd. He even has mastery over the storm. He pulls Peter out of the depths. His presence is a blessing; people reach out to touch the fringe of his cloak.

The compassion we see in Jesus flows from God the Father. That is why Jesus who is so compassionate to Peter and so compassionate to the crowds, also withdraws from them, so that he can be replenished by the Father's love.

We need to do the same. When we are hungry. When we are sinking. When we are in pain. Jesus' judgement is this: we are worthy; worthy of his love and welcome at his table. Worth listening to.

Almighty God,
purify our hearts and minds,
that when your Son Jesus Christ comes again as
judge and saviour
we may be ready to receive him,
who is our Lord and our God.

COLLECT

Reflection by **Stephen Cottrell**   17

Wednesday 8 December

Psalms **62**, 63 *or* **34**
Isaiah 31
Matthew 15.1-20

Matthew 15.1-20

'... what comes out of the mouth proceeds from the heart' (v.18)

In John's Gospel, Jesus says that the judgement is this: 'light has come into the world, and people loved darkness rather than light because their deeds were evil' (John 3.19).

The scribes and Pharisees are again trying to trap Jesus, pointing to the ways his disciples allegedly fail to follow every little point of the law. Jesus, who is always compassionate to those who acknowledge their need and know where they have gone wrong, is also quick to condemn those who judge others. Quoting Isaiah, he accuses them of only honouring God with their lips, not their lives. Making fun of their pompous hypocrisy, he entertains the crowds by ridiculing this obsession with what is eaten or not eaten. After all, says Jesus to the disciples, we all know where what we have eaten ends up: down the sewer!

No, says Jesus, it is not what goes into your mouth, but what comes out that truly matters. Therefore, as Jesus says in Luke's Gospel: 'Be merciful, just as your Father is merciful' (Luke 6.36).

We, too, must pay attention to what comes out of our mouths, praying that our words and actions may be merciful and compassionate. Just as Jesus is quick to condemn those who are quick to condemn, he is quick to forgive those who seek forgiveness and who are ready to forgive others.

COLLECT

O Lord, raise up, we pray, your power
and come among us,
and with great might succour us;
that whereas, through our sins and wickedness
we are grievously hindered
in running the race that is set before us,
your bountiful grace and mercy
may speedily help and deliver us;
through Jesus Christ your Son our Lord,
to whom with you and the Holy Spirit,
be honour and glory, now and for ever.

Reflection by **Stephen Cottrell**

Thursday 9 December

Matthew 15.21-28

'Woman, great is your faith!' (v.28)

Now here is an interesting story because, it seems, Jesus is the one being judged ... The Canaanite woman asks Jesus for mercy, but he ignores her. The disciples urge him to send her away because she is badgering them as well. Jesus doesn't show compassion; he just rather rudely reminds everyone present that he has come for the 'lost sheep of the house of Israel' (and therefore not for foreigners like her). But she persists. She kneels before Jesus and pleads for help.

Jesus appears unmoved. 'It isn't fair to take the children's food and throw it to the dogs,' he replies. Her answer is brilliant. 'Yes, Lord, yet even the dogs eat the crumbs that fall from their masters' table.' It turns Jesus around. He is astounded by her faithfulness. Her daughter is healed. What's going on here?

Might it be this? Jesus himself is learning and refining his vocation to be the one through whom God's merciful judgement is going to be made available to everyone, not just Israel. For Jesus, this journey of fully understanding his vocation to be the light of the world reaches its climax in Gethsemane and Calvary. This woman helps him get there.

Vocation is learned, not just received. Judgement is also a journey of becoming. On the way we all need challenge – as it turns out, even Jesus. So, therefore, we definitely do too!

Almighty God,
purify our hearts and minds,
that when your Son Jesus Christ comes again as
judge and saviour
we may be ready to receive him,
who is our Lord and our God.

COLLECT

Reflection by **Stephen Cottrell**   19

Friday 10 December

Matthew 15.29-end

'... they praised the God of Israel' (v.31)

In Luke's Gospel, the followers of John the Baptist come to Jesus asking whether he is the one promised from God, or whether they should wait for another. Jesus answers by pointing to the things he does: 'the blind receive their sight, the lame walk, the lepers are cleansed, the deaf hear, the dead are raised, the poor have good news brought to them' (Luke 7.22).

In today's reading, the crowds come to Jesus again. They bring with them 'the lame, the maimed, the blind, the mute, and many others'. They put them at Jesus' feet, and he cures them.

In Jesus, God's promises and God's future break into our present. If Advent is about getting ready to see God clearly and to enjoy eternal life with God, then these are the signs of what the reign of God will be like: tears wiped away and the sick healed.

It is hard for us to imagine this. Our world is besieged by sickness, poverty and injustice. Yet still we need to bring ourselves and bring others to Jesus. Then we will be able to see God clearly and see clearly where our world needs to change.

God's Church will be most like Jesus when we turn outwards to feed and heal and teach, and when we remember the poor. It is our willingness to do this – or otherwise – that will be the criterion of judgement. Then people will praise God.

COLLECT

O Lord, raise up, we pray, your power
and come among us,
and with great might succour us;
that whereas, through our sins and wickedness
we are grievously hindered
in running the race that is set before us,
your bountiful grace and mercy
may speedily help and deliver us;
through Jesus Christ your Son our Lord,
to whom with you and the Holy Spirit,
be honour and glory, now and for ever.

| *Reflection by* **Stephen Cottrell**

Psalm **145** *or* 41, **42**, 43
Isaiah 35
Matthew 16.1-12

Saturday 11 December

Matthew 16.1-12

'Then he left them and went away.' (v.4)

We end this week with these hard words: Jesus left them and went away.

The Pharisees and Sadducees want signs. As if what Jesus has said and done is not already enough! The disciples are covered in confusion and muddle. Isn't that always the case? Now, as well as then.

The only sign that is given is the sign of Jonah. But what is the sign of Jonah? Is it the sign of redemption: Jonah spewed out of the whale after three days, an anticipation of Jesus' resurrection? Or is it the message of Jonah to Nineveh: repent or die?

Or is it that we need to work out our own discipleship? That God has given us freedom and responsibility to carry forward the mission of Jesus in the world today? Is it like Jesus saying to Mary Magdalene, do not cling to me?

Like the first disciples, maybe the main problem is that we forget to bring bread; forget to depend on the living bread of God's word, the sacramental bread of God's presence?

As the thoughts of Advent that look to the last things, turn towards Christmas, and God's first things, let us receive the vocation to be God's presence in the world, shining as brightly as the star over Bethlehem, sustained by the bread of God's continuing presence with us. Until that day when we see him face to face.

Almighty God,
purify our hearts and minds,
that when your Son Jesus Christ comes again as
judge and saviour
we may be ready to receive him,
who is our Lord and our God.

COLLECT

Reflection by **Stephen Cottrell** 21

Monday 13 December

Matthew 16.13-end

'But who do you say that I am?' (v.15)

Today we encounter Peter, both at his brightest and his dimmest – he catches a glimpse of the reality that yes, this man Jesus is the long-awaited Messiah, yet fails to recognize the truth about the nature of Christ's identity. He gets it badly wrong and is reprimanded severely.

The gap between Peter's rise and fall, as it were, is his lack of understanding about the place of suffering in the journey of faith. He had visions of a powerful political Messiah come to overthrow the oppressive Roman rule but instead was confronted by talk of taking up his cross and losing his life. Over 2000 years later, I wonder if we too are still sometimes caught in the horns of exactly the same dilemma, acknowledging Jesus as Lord but not fully grasping the significance of that for our lives and for the Church.

This passage makes crystal clear the implications of following Christ and lays bare the cost of discipleship. As church communities and as individuals seeking to understand who Jesus is for us, we do well to remember we have not been promised prosperity and success, power and position. Rather we are called to witness faithfully to a saviour whose obedience took him even to death on a cross. We are to offer ourselves in humble service of others confident that, though we may lose everything, in Christ we are made whole.

COLLECT

O Lord Jesus Christ,
who at your first coming sent your messenger
to prepare your way before you:
grant that the ministers and stewards of your mysteries
may likewise so prepare and make ready your way
by turning the hearts of the disobedient to the wisdom of the just,
that at your second coming to judge the world
we may be found an acceptable people in your sight;
for you are alive and reign with the Father
in the unity of the Holy Spirit,
one God, now and for ever.

Reflection by **Guli Francis-Dehqani**

Psalms **70**, 74 *or* **48**, 52
Isaiah 38. 9-20
Matthew 17.1-13

Tuesday 14 December

Matthew 17.1-13
'This is my Son, the Beloved' (v.5)

Do you recognize that feeling of being in an unexpected situation, not of your own making, unsure what to do or say, and eventually covering your awkwardness with a rush of words or activity?

I wonder whether Peter, James and John felt something of that as they witnessed Jesus' transfiguration and the appearance of Moses and Elijah. In this highly charged and emotional scene, it's hardly surprising they were utterly bewildered and, to fill the silence and make themselves feel useful, they started talking about building shelters. God then literally interrupted their busyness with an echo from Jesus' baptism in Matthew 3, 'This is my Son, the Beloved, with him I am well pleased'. Words of love and affirmation, and a reminder that the most important thing about Jesus' ministry was not all the activity but the relationship with his father. Everything he said and did emanated from his identity as the Beloved of God.

As God in human form, Jesus invites us to recognize something of this patterning in our own lives too. It is perhaps the greatest gift and yet the hardest to receive – to know that you are a beloved child of God, to feel at the core of your being that this is what gives you value, over and above your greatest successes and achievements. It can take a lifetime to fully understand this truth, but once grasped, its power is transformative.

God for whom we watch and wait,
you sent John the Baptist to prepare the way of your Son:
give us courage to speak the truth,
to hunger for justice,
and to suffer for the cause of right,
with Jesus Christ our Lord.

COLLECT

Reflection by **Guli Francis-Dehqani**

Wednesday 15 December

Matthew 17.14-21

'... the disciples came to Jesus' (v.19)

This is one of those difficult incidents that at first sight can be confusing and disheartening. It's worth remembering that the verses follow immediately on from the account of Jesus' transfiguration. As such we can't help but notice two striking contrasts that need to be held in tension. The glory of God's presence evident in the transfiguration does not remove the reality of suffering in the world (exemplified here by the boy with epilepsy), nor does experiencing that glory (as the disciples did) guarantee success even in matters of faith. Put another way, pain and anguish will always be with us, as will our failures and weaknesses but neither can undermine the splendour, mercy or compassion of God.

If that's our starting place, what positive message can we take from this passage? Here are three brief thoughts to reflect on. First, despite their failure and the disappointment that must have stung badly, the disciples *stay with Jesus*. They remain alongside him, eager to learn and deepen their faith – sometimes that's all we can manage, and that's OK. Second, together with the disciples, perhaps we come to see that faith is not so much about specific beliefs or intellectual understanding but about *trust* in a growing relationship. And finally, faith – even in small amounts – enables and empowers, whereas its lack weakens and diminishes.

COLLECT

O Lord Jesus Christ,
who at your first coming sent your messenger
to prepare your way before you:
grant that the ministers and stewards of your mysteries
may likewise so prepare and make ready your way
by turning the hearts of the disobedient to the wisdom of the just,
that at your second coming to judge the world
we may be found an acceptable people in your sight;
for you are alive and reign with the Father
in the unity of the Holy Spirit,
one God, now and for ever.

Reflection by **Guli Francis-Dehqani**

Psalms **76**, 97 *or* 56, **57** (63*)
Zephaniah 1.1 – 2.3
Matthew 17.22-end

Thursday 16 December

Matthew 17.22-end

'... so that we do not give offence' (v.27)

Fearless and outspoken as Jesus is on occasions, he can also be the master of diplomacy, avoiding traps or refusing to cause unnecessary offence. This curious episode is one such occasion providing an abject lesson to those of us eager to ensure that our way wins or that our point is loudly made.

The temple tax mentioned in verse 24 probably refers to a tax imposed either for the upkeep of the temple or specifically to maintain the sacrificial system in Jerusalem. Either way, Jesus is against the tax, arguing that just like a king would never tax his own family, so God would not tax his people Israel. However, Jesus also recognizes that for some, the tax is considered a religious duty and so he pays it, notably not from his own pocket, but using a lost coin found in a fish.

How wedded are you to particular forms of worship and spirituality? What is your response and how do you act when you are in a church different from your own, with traditions and conventions you don't understand and maybe even disagree with? It's so easy to take the moral high ground, refuse to participate or look down on the practices of others. Jesus reminds us that our actions, even those we hold dear, should always take into account the feelings of others. Sometimes we are on holy ground and we do well to tread carefully and gently.

God for whom we watch and wait,
you sent John the Baptist to prepare the way of your Son:
give us courage to speak the truth,
to hunger for justice,
and to suffer for the cause of right,
with Jesus Christ our Lord.

COLLECT

Friday 17 December

Psalms 77, **98** or **51**, 54
Zephaniah 3.1-13
Matthew 18.1-20

Matthew 18.1-20

'... these little ones' (v.6)

A large portion of today's passage reads rather like a manifesto for children and young people. It puts them centre stage, giving them their rightful place as cherished human beings within the community of believers – and this at a time when children had little value and few rights. Jesus' sentiments are entirely counter-cultural and he uses some of his harshest words for those who would harm or hurt children, and it is spine-chilling.

In these weeks leading up to Christmas, children are often more in our minds than usual: the stars of all those nativity plays, the purest expression of Christmas joy, the sounds of singing and laughter. But we do well to remember that our responsibility towards the welfare of children is an all-year requirement. The Church has often fallen gravely short in this area, but, in truth, the safety and protection of children should be at the heart of all we do. This is not just a moral imperative but a theological one, central to our faith and how we build communities.

If this is true for children, it is also true of other vulnerable people – those undermined and undervalued by society. Ultimately, the Church will be judged by how we treat those who are weakest and most powerless, and lest we forget, the baby whom we wait to greet on Christmas morning is our ever present reminder.

COLLECT

O Lord Jesus Christ,
who at your first coming sent your messenger
to prepare your way before you:
grant that the ministers and stewards of your mysteries
may likewise so prepare and make ready your way
by turning the hearts of the disobedient to the wisdom of the just,
that at your second coming to judge the world
we may be found an acceptable people in your sight;
for you are alive and reign with the Father
in the unity of the Holy Spirit,
one God, now and for ever.

Reflection by **Guli Francis-Dehqani**

Psalm **71** *or* **68**
Zephaniah 3.14-end
Matthew 18.21-end

Saturday 18 December

Matthew 18.21-end

*'... out of pity for him, the lord of that slave released him
and forgave him' (v.27)*

You could argue that the thorny topic of forgiveness hasn't always
been served well in the Church. It can all too easily be used flippantly,
leading to the accusation that Christians don't take justice seriously,
or it can be imposed on those who have suffered harm and abuse,
making them feel guilty if they are unable to forgive. Forgiveness, far
from being a simple equation, is a messy process and immensely
complex. It should be handled with great care and with concern for
the safety and welfare of the most vulnerable.

That said, forgiveness remains a central Christian tenet and one we
can't circumvent. That we must each recognize our own need of
forgiveness and in turn extend it to those who cause us hurt is at the
heart of our faith, and we are called to practise it in smaller and
larger ways. This is far from easy, but the rewards are precious:
forgiveness offers redemption to the offender and freedom from
anger and bitterness for the one wronged.

The *desire to forgive* is often the starting place for what can be a
long journey with twists and turns. The story in today's Bible passage
helps us understand that in order to forgive, first we need
compassion – the ability to put ourselves in another's shoes and see
the world from their perspective. With compassion in our hearts and
with God's grace, we can find the way towards, 'father forgive'.

God for whom we watch and wait,
you sent John the Baptist to prepare the way of your Son:
give us courage to speak the truth,
to hunger for justice,
and to suffer for the cause of right,
with Jesus Christ our Lord.

COLLECT

Reflection by **Guli Francis-Dehqani** | 27

Monday 20 December

Psalms **46**, 95
Malachi 1.1, 6-end
Matthew 19.1-12

Matthew 19.1-12

'Let anyone accept this who can' (v.12)

Today, we encounter Jesus once more in the company of the Pharisees who are wanting to catch him out over a controversial issue of the day. In Jewish law, divorce was permitted, but arguments continued over whether or not it was only permissible on some legitimate grounds.

Jesus responds by doing two things. First, and typically for him, he reframes the debate from the negative (grounds for divorce) to the positive (grounds for marriage): God made them male and female so they may become one flesh. Second, he distinguishes between the perfect will of God and the Commandments, which allowed for human sin. He thereby shifts from what may be legally possible towards a radical demand for conformity to God's will as expressed in the beginning. Arguably, however, this purity of heart that Jesus envisions is an impossible ideal for mere mortals and hence our need of God's grace and forgiveness in all our shortcomings and failings.

Still, it's possible to see from these verses why the question of divorce and remarriage remains difficult for some Christians today. But most have concluded that, in some cases, it is not only permissible but maybe even preferable – the lesser of two evils. And lest we be tempted to judge, perhaps we should call to mind those other words of Jesus uttered when the woman was caught in adultery: let the one without sin cast the first stone.

COLLECT

God our redeemer,
who prepared the Blessed Virgin Mary
to be the mother of your Son:
grant that, as she looked for his coming as our saviour,
so we may be ready to greet him
when he comes again as our judge;
who is alive and reigns with you,
in the unity of the Holy Spirit,
one God, now and for ever.

Reflection by **Guli Francis-Dehqani**

Psalms **121**, 122, 123
Malachi 2.1-16
Matthew 19.13-15

Tuesday 21 December

Matthew 19.13-15

'Let the little children come to me' (v.14)

Like most parents, I'd easily say my children always come first. As they've grown older and my working life has become busier, I still remind them that when push comes to shove, I'd gladly drop everything to be there if they need me. And I mean it ... except that sometimes I fall short.

Over the years there have been occasions when one or other of them has been ill on a particularly inconvenient day. I've begrudgingly cancelled appointments or made my excuses for meetings I should have attended, feeling guilty about not fulfilling my responsibilities or letting people down.

But without fail, on each occasion, I've come to realize soon enough that I made the right decision. Not just because I did what a mother should do, but because the unexpected time has been a precious gift and a reminder of all the blessings my children have given me and the way in which they continue to enrich my life.

This Christmas season, who are the treasured people in your life that you need to make time for – those whom you might sometimes think of as an inconvenience, just as the disciples did with the little ones who came to Jesus? Who are those who can all too easily get squeezed out of your life by the pressure of all your other responsibilities? Who knows what blessings await you if you make time just to be with them.

Eternal God,
as Mary waited for the birth of your Son,
so we wait for his coming in glory;
bring us through the birth pangs of this present age
to see, with her, our great salvation
in Jesus Christ our Lord.

COLLECT

Reflection by **Guli Francis-Dehqani**   29

Wednesday 22 December

Psalms **124**, 125, 126, 127
Malachi 2.17 – 3.12
Matthew 19.16-end

Matthew 19.16-end

'... you will have treasure in heaven' (v.21)

With my family I left our homeland of Iran suddenly and unexpectedly after traumatic events around the 1979 Islamic Revolution. We left behind all we owned, each bringing just one suitcase hurriedly packed. My parents lost their home and everything they possessed. Soon, however, they began rebuilding their lives and I noticed how they still took pleasure in the material things that filled their home. But what I noticed too was their disposition towards these belongings. Though they still valued and enjoyed them, there was a lightness in the attachment. They were generous to a fault and lived as those who knew what the really important things in life are. Had they lost everything a second time, they would still have remained the joyful, faith-filled people they always were.

Today's passage is more about priorities than about how rich or poor we are per se. The young man was challenged by Jesus to sell all his possessions not so much because he was too rich but because he had grown too attached to his belongings. They were damaging his relationship with God and his capacity to be generous. Jesus' words are a reminder of how easy it is to lose sight of our priorities.

In the busyness of preparing for Christmas, it might be helpful to take a moment to consider what things get in the way of our relationships, both with God and with others.

COLLECT

God our redeemer,
who prepared the Blessed Virgin Mary
to be the mother of your Son:
grant that, as she looked for his coming as our saviour,
so we may be ready to greet him
when he comes again as our judge;
who is alive and reigns with you,
in the unity of the Holy Spirit,
one God, now and for ever.

| *Reflection by* **Guli Francis-Dehqani**

Psalms 128, 129, **130**, 131
Malachi 3.13 – end of 4
Matthew 23.1-12

Thursday 23 December

Matthew 23.1-12

'They tie up heavy burdens … and lay them on the shoulders of others' (v.4)

The American author and Unitarian Minister Robert Fulghum is reputed to have said, 'Don't worry that children never listen to you; worry that they're always watching you'. Wise words, and an object lesson for parents and all who have dealings with children and young people. Similarly, Jesus tells his disciples to do as the scribes and Pharisees teach but not as they do, for they are hypocrites and there is disparity between their words and actions.

I recall hearing my father preach a sermon in the early days of the revolution in Iran as the Christian community was facing the very real possibility of suffering and persecution. It was early 1979 and I was 12 years old, but it's remained with me ever since. 'I have been speaking about forgiveness for many years', he said, 'but now the time is coming when I will have to learn to live it.'

The disparity between words and actions is a perennial problem for the Church generally. Over the centuries, Jesus' words of love and welcome, of compassion, generosity and reconciliation have been preached far and wide. And yet so often as Christian communities we struggle to embody the radical inclusion that the message demands. Practising what we preach can be demanding and sometimes costly, but it's worth reminding ourselves that ultimately we will be remembered for how we behaved and we will be judged more by our actions than our words.

COLLECT

Eternal God,
as Mary waited for the birth of your Son,
so we wait for his coming in glory;
bring us through the birth pangs of this present age
to see, with her, our great salvation
in Jesus Christ our Lord.

Reflection by **Guli Francis-Dehqani** | 31

Friday 24 December
Christmas Eve

Matthew 23.13-28
'... the altar that makes the gift sacred' (v.19)

It might at first seem like we can relax a little on reading today's passage, despite its harsh tone and recurring chorus of 'woe to you'. After all, it's not you and me being addressed, but the scribes and Pharisees. We, on the other hand, are seeking to live the life of faith honestly and devotedly. Well, I invite you to look deep into your heart and reflect more searchingly.

The entire extract sounds for me like a warning bell, a reminder of how easy it is to get religion wrong. The scribes and Pharisees were probably trying their best, following the law and teaching the tenets of faith. But repeatedly they got it wrong. For us too, I wonder if it's all too easy to live as those constrained by the rules, bound by the doctrines, trying to do the right thing but missing the real point, the weightier matters of justice, mercy and faith. How much time and energy do we spend, even as Christians, disagreeing with one another over details of the law instead of building relationships across our differences, seeking the face of Christ in each other.

This Christmas Eve, let's pause for a moment and pray for the Church. Let's remember the gift we are offered in the Christ child who did not come for us to argue and fall out over but as the gracious and loving cause of our worship and wonder.

COLLECT

Almighty God,
you make us glad with the yearly remembrance
    of the birth of your Son Jesus Christ:
grant that, as we joyfully receive him as our redeemer,
so we may with sure confidence behold him
when he shall come to be our judge;
who is alive and reigns with you,
in the unity of the Holy Spirit,
one God, now and for ever.

Reflection by **Guli Francis-Dehqani**

Psalms **110**, 117
Isaiah 62.1-5
Matthew 1.18-end

Saturday 25 December
Christmas Day

Matthew 1.18-end

'[Joseph] did as the angel of the Lord commanded him' (v.24)

Throughout the Gospel narratives around the birth of Jesus, there's a phrase that reappears several times, running like a thread throughout the season. And here it is today too in verse 20: 'Do not be afraid'. On other occasions, the angel appears to Zachariah, Mary, and of course the shepherds; today it is to Joseph. But each time the angel utters the same words of comfort, 'Do not be afraid'.

Whoever we are and whatever our circumstances, there are likely to be things this Christmas Day, beneath the tinsel and celebrations, that cause fear and anxiety. Fear of failing in our responsibilities or facing the future, fear of illness, loss and all the other things we cannot control.

Whatever it is, God understands our fears and our propensity to be anxious and worried, which is why the angels are sent to reassure and soothe. Joseph was fearful of taking Mary for his wife – of what it would do to her reputation, and perhaps his own. Fearful of how they would cope and of what the future might hold. But once his fears were named and acknowledged, he was able to embrace the angel's message and play his part in the story of the incarnation.

I pray that today you too will place your fears before God and in doing so will hear the message of the angel; that it will gladden your heart and give strength for the future.

COLLECT

Almighty God,
you have given us your only-begotten Son
to take our nature upon him
and as at this time to be born of a pure virgin:
grant that we, who have been born again
and made your children by adoption and grace,
may daily be renewed by your Holy Spirit;
through Jesus Christ your Son our Lord,
who is alive and reigns with you,
in the unity of the Holy Spirit,
one God, now and for ever.

Reflection by **Guli Francis-Dehqani** | 33

Monday 27 December

John, Apostle and Evangelist

Psalms **21**, 147.13-end
Exodus 33.12-end
1 John 2.1-11

1 John 2.1-11

'... the true light is already shining' (v.8)

The writings ascribed to John the Evangelist have a very particular tone and vocabulary. So much depends on the repetition, exploration and contrast between simple but profound words. Think of words such as 'abide', 'walk', 'darkness', 'light' and, of course, 'love'. The commandment to love God is nothing new. It has been with us 'from the beginning'. There are two ways of being human, the one that leads to death and the other that leads to life; it is for us to watch how we walk. Sin is serious but not fatal. The death of Jesus has more than atoned for our personal and particular sins. The consequences of Christ's sacrifice reach far beyond us to embrace the whole world. We live in the light.

At this dark time of the year (at least for those in the Northern Hemisphere), we need to be grounded again and again in these simple but enormous realities. By abiding in Christ we belong to the light. The practice of sitting still with a single word such as 'light' or 'love' can make faith real to us.

The word 'abide' is the clue here. How do we rest, remain and dwell in God? We practise our faith through practice, by a conscious calling to mind that we dwell in God's presence. Failure to do so does not mean we should stop trying. The chance to 'abide' in God is new every morning.

COLLECT

Merciful Lord,
cast your bright beams of light upon the Church:
that, being enlightened by the teaching
of your blessed apostle and evangelist Saint John,
we may so walk in the light of your truth
that we may at last attain to the light of everlasting life;
through Jesus Christ your incarnate Son our Lord,
who is alive and reigns with you,
in the unity of the Holy Spirit,
one God, now and for ever.

| *Reflection by* **Angela Tilby**

Psalms **36**, 146
Baruch 4.21-27
or Genesis 37.13-20
Matthew 18.1-10

Tuesday 28 December
The Holy Innocents

Matthew 18.1-10

'... change and become like children' (v.3)

To see children as examples of greatness would have struck Jesus' contemporaries as bizarre. In a peasant society, children were mouths to feed, a potential burden, mini-adults as soon as they could be useful. Yet they are the future. Jesus' linkage of children to the kingdom of heaven reflects this. The kingdom is not given to those who think they have earned it, but to those who long for it.

One of the most shocking things about the tragic story of the Holy Innocents is the way Herod's actions are an attempt to set back God's future. He hopes to destroy a rival king, but in murdering small children he not only takes young life, he also robs innocent parents of their hope.

It is not only the children who are his victims. The story of the Holy Innocents comes home to us in our time as we reflect on the way children are so often the victims of adult greed, exploitation and carelessness. It is our own life that we destroy when we treat children as disposable. We need to mourn our narrow vision, our careless violence. The command to cut off a hand or foot or to cast away an eye is scary hyperbole, but it reminds us that we will never be free to greet the kingdom until we repent of 'me first'.

Heavenly Father,
whose children suffered at the hands of Herod,
though they had done no wrong:
by the suffering of your Son
and by the innocence of our lives
frustrate all evil designs
and establish your reign of justice and peace;
through Jesus Christ your Son our Lord,
who is alive and reigns with you,
in the unity of the Holy Spirit,
one God, now and for ever.

COLLECT

Reflection by **Angela Tilby**

35

Wednesday 29 December

Psalms 19, 20
Jonah 1
Colossians 1.1-14

Jonah 1

'... the word of the Lord came to Jonah' (v.1)

Jonah is a comedy and, in the season of pantomime, we should read it as such. Jonah is a reluctant prophet. As soon as he hears the word of the Lord, he runs away. We are meant to smile and recognize ourselves in this unflattering portrait. An artist friend of mine once painted a black-and-white picture of Jonah fleeing through the back streets of Tarshish with his fingers in his ears, a dark wheel of fire pursuing him.

Christians are often more reluctant to acknowledge the darkness of God than Jews, who are more candid about their love/hate relationship with the divine. Sometimes we simply make God too nice. Yet, it is 'a fearful thing to fall into the hands of the living God' (Hebrews 10.31).

Jonah hopes to hide from God in a pagan crowd, only to find that his very presence brings near-disaster. He cannot escape his connection with the crew of the stricken ship any more than he can escape God's call. Wherever he goes, he is in God's eyeline. Yet even as he is thrown into the sea, God is waiting for him, having provided a large fish (a whale?) to swallow him.

Comedy can be cruel, but it can also show up the sometimes vast gap between what we pretend and what we are. What does it mean today that God is inescapable?

COLLECT

Almighty God,
who wonderfully created us in your own image
and yet more wonderfully restored us
through your Son Jesus Christ:
grant that, as he came to share in our humanity,
so we may share the life of his divinity;
who is alive and reigns with you,
in the unity of the Holy Spirit,
one God, now and for ever.

Reflection by **Angela Tilby**

Psalms 111, 112, **113**
Jonah 2
Colossians 1.15-23

Thursday 30 December

Jonah 2

'I remembered the Lord; and my prayer came to you' (v.7)

Lost in the fish's innards, Jonah turns to the prayers of his ancestors. This is a formal prayer, very similar in tone and structure to some of the psalms (see Psalms 42.5-7, 130). By praying for deliverance in traditional liturgical language, Jonah somewhat cringingly acknowledges what he has tried to deny: that he is indeed one of God's people, called to be God's prophet and messenger. It is a comic touch that God, as soon as he hears Jonah's prayer, has a quiet word with the fish, who obligingly vomits the unwilling prophet up onto land.

Jonah is heard not for his sincerity – anyone stuck in the bowels of a fish is likely to pray for deliverance – but because he is forced under pressure to remember who he is. The anguish of the prayer reflects the spiritual experience of a people who know what it is like to feel abandoned by God. In their own memory they have known God's punishment and God's salvation.

Desperate though the prayer is, it is also a confession of faith. God is not bound by suffering or even by death. He is able to save to restore communion with himself even when our sense of being abandoned by him is a reflection of our own disloyalty.

God in Trinity,
eternal unity of perfect love:
gather the nations to be one family,
and draw us into your holy life
through the birth of Emmanuel,
our Lord Jesus Christ.

COLLECT

Friday 31 December

Jonah 3 – 4

'... should I not be concerned about Nineveh, that great city?'
(4.11)

Jonah fulfils his mission, but the outcome – the repentance of the Ninevites – leaves him with a sense of injustice. We now learn that Jonah's initial reluctance to obey God was because he was more afraid of God's mercy than he was of his wrath. It is worth looking back to the point in the first chapter where the sailors who threw Jonah overboard were more frightened of God when the storm ceased than when it was at its height (1.15-16).

The terrifying nature of God's mercy is echoed in Psalm 130.3: 'There is forgiveness with you, *so that* you shall be feared'. God's willingness to forgive demonstrates what God's people are always inclined to fear: that God acts independently of his messengers, that he is beyond our control and understanding. Obeying him does not bring us special treatment. This is what moves Jonah to despair.

God rubs Jonah's misery in further by the trick of the bush. At first this shades him from the heat, but then it is destroyed, leaving him exposed. The book ends asking the painful question of whether the faith of God's people is really an investment in our own advantage or a genuine and humble concern for the wellbeing of others.

At the end of what has been another challenging year, we remember that we are always in need of God's mercy.

COLLECT

Almighty God,
who wonderfully created us in your own image
and yet more wonderfully restored us
through your Son Jesus Christ:
grant that, as he came to share in our humanity,
so we may share the life of his divinity;
who is alive and reigns with you,
in the unity of the Holy Spirit,
one God, now and for ever.

Reflection by **Angela Tilby**

Psalms **103**, 150
Genesis 17.1-13
Romans 2.17-end

Saturday I January

Naming and Circumcision of Jesus

Genesis 17.1-13

'I will establish my covenant between me and you' (v. 7)

The sign of circumcision is given to Abraham as a mark of his covenant relationship with God, a mark to be made on all Jewish males in perpetuity. It is hard to think of anything quite so irreversible; a Jewish man bears this intimate mark for the rest of his life.

Jesus comes into the world as one of Abraham's descendants, a Jewish man, and yet in the way he lives out the covenant, the meaning of mark undergoes a transformation. In Christian understanding, the mark of circumcision now points to sacrifice, to the shedding of blood that will redeem the world.

Today's New Year reading spells out continuity and faithfulness. God's covenant is for ever, but it is not a contract in which two sides negotiate to their own mutual advantage; it is a gift. God underwrites the covenant, which should free us from anxiety, though not from responsibility. God knows that Israel's vocation will come under strain, that faithfulness will be hard, that there will be backsliding and the need for repentance.

As we read of Abraham and his descendants, we look ahead to Jesus 'the mediator of a new covenant' (Hebrews 12.24). We can start this new year in the light of his promise. He will never leave us or forsake us. We are his.

Almighty God,
whose blessed Son was circumcised
in obedience to the law for our sake
and given the Name that is above every name:
give us grace faithfully to bear his Name,
to worship him in the freedom of the Spirit,
and to proclaim him as the Saviour of the world;
who is alive and reigns with you,
in the unity of the Holy Spirit,
one God, now and for ever.

COLLECT

Reflection by **Angela Tilby**

Monday 3 January

Psalms **127**, 128, 131
Ruth 2
Colossians 3.1-11

Ruth 2

'... a full reward from the Lord, the God of Israel' (v. 12)

The book of Ruth, like Jonah, is concerned with God's relationship with the gentiles. While Jonah is the reluctant prophet to Nineveh, Ruth is a gentile who seeks refuge under the wings of Israel's God. Jonah is the bad Jew who is converted through the gentiles; Ruth is the good gentile who brings salvation to the Jews. They lead us in different ways to Epiphany, the manifestation of Christ to the gentiles.

As so often, God's acts of salvation unfold through an ordinary human story, this time a story of great poignancy. Ruth is the widow of a man from Bethlehem whose father had migrated to Moab. Now she struggles to provide security for herself and her mother-in-law. Her courage leads to blessing for all the participants in the story, as Naomi discovers her prosperous relative, Boaz, shows kindness to the young foreign girl and sets in motion the reversal of her fortunes. Ruth herself becomes part of God's people.

Today, we should be grateful that we are not called to God in isolation. The human threads that bind us together are always sources of potential blessing, for ourselves as well as others. We should remember this especially when we are thinking of those who are migrants, whose welfare often depends on the quality of welcome they receive.

COLLECT

Almighty God,
in the birth of your Son
you have poured on us the new light of your incarnate Word,
and shown us the fullness of your love:
help us to walk in his light and dwell in his love
that we may know the fullness of his joy;
who is alive and reigns with you,
in the unity of the Holy Spirit,
one God, now and for ever.

Reflection by **Angela Tilby**

Psalm **89.1-37**
Ruth 3
Colossians 3.12 – 4.1

Tuesday 4 January

Ruth 3

'All that you tell me, I will do' (v.5)

Though the destiny of Ruth is in God's hands, Naomi's encouragement helps it along. She sees Ruth's potential to make a good marriage, bringing security to both of them. Here is a very different standpoint from that of the Book of Ezra, in which foreign wives are forbidden.

The advice Naomi gives to Ruth, mother-in-law to daughter-in-law, is both daring and prudent. She is to take the risk of approaching Boaz at night when he will be mellow with food and drink in the hope that he will find her attractive and want to marry her. It is an old ruse, but in this story, seduction takes on a kind of blessed innocence. Everyone comes out enriched.

A good outcome, though, is not to be taken for granted. First, Boaz must deal with the potential claim of an even closer relative. But Ruth is encouraged by his present of new harvested grain. The whole story speaks of courage, initiative and solidarity. And also of tact.

In legitimately pursuing our own security and wellbeing, we need to anticipate the consequences for others and try to ensure that what is good for us is good for them too. Blessings are not to be hoarded. When they are shared, they tend to multiply, if we keep them to ourselves, they tend to run out.

God our Father,
in love you sent your Son
that the world may have life:
lead us to seek him among the outcast
and to find him in those in need,
for Jesus Christ's sake.

COLLECT

Reflection by **Angela Tilby** | 41

Wednesday 5 January

Ruth 4.1-17

'Then all the people ... said, "We are witnesses"' (v.11)

Boaz enables Ruth to marry him by dealing with the stronger claim of the nearer relative. The details of this agreement are described along with the legal processes. The point being made here is that Boaz was scrupulous. Before he could have what he wanted, the legalities had to be attended to according to custom and order. Detail matters. Legalities matter.

In an age of reckless individualism, we need to remember that there are proper curtailments on our own personal desires, especially where sexual relations are involved. Personal choices have public implications. But in the story of Ruth, personal choices also have implications for the history of Israel and for human salvation. This concern for propriety is important because it shows that when God acts, the vulnerable have a voice and are protected.

The birth of Ruth's son completes a cycle of blessing for the two women. Through the very human qualities of faith, loyalty, obedience and discretion, God comforts and restores Ruth and Naomi after their bereavement. But the ending shows that their personal story goes beyond themselves and opens a new chapter in the history of salvation. Obed is the grandfather of King David. The Messianic line actually runs through a gentile woman, revealing the good news that the hope that God has rested in the Jews is indeed for all people.

COLLECT

Almighty God,
in the birth of your Son
you have poured on us the new light of your incarnate Word,
and shown us the fullness of your love:
help us to walk in his light and dwell in his love
that we may know the fullness of his joy;
who is alive and reigns with you,
in the unity of the Holy Spirit,
one God, now and for ever.

Reflection by **Angela Tilby**

Thursday 6 January
Epiphany

John 1.29-34
'... this is the Son of God' (v.34)

A wonderful sculpture from Chartres Cathedral shows John the Baptist cradling the Lamb of God in his arms as a kind of medallion, as though at one and the same time to protect him and to proclaim him. In John's Gospel, the Baptist names Jesus specifically as 'the Lamb of God' pointing ahead to his sacrifice for sin. John is always seen as the herald, the one who points beyond himself.

Epiphany marks the end of the Christmas season. Christ is no longer the child in the manger but the anointed one, the human being in whom God will act to save us all. So John stands on the threshold of salvation, pointing out to us the way ahead. He also stands on the threshold between the Old Testament and the New; Jewish hope and gentile fulfilment.

As we enter this new year, the challenge for us is simply to point to Jesus by what we say, by what we do not say, and by what we do. It is not just a matter of holding the 'correct' opinions, or siding with those we already agree with. A true prophet is primarily accountable to God. The loneliness of John's vocation suggests that only when we have taken the Lamb of God to our hearts will we know what form our witness and proclamation must take.

O God,
who by the leading of a star
manifested your only Son to the peoples of the earth:
mercifully grant that we,
who know you now by faith,
may at last behold your glory face to face;
through Jesus Christ your Son our Lord,
who is alive and reigns with you,
in the unity of the Holy Spirit,
one God, now and for ever.

COLLECT

Reflection by **Angela Tilby**

Friday 7 January

Psalms **99**, 147.1-12 *or* **55**
Jeremiah 23.1-8
Matthew 20.1-16

Matthew 20.1-16

'... are you envious because I am generous?' (v.15)

Deep within us lies a sense of fair play. One of the instinctive complaints of childhood is, 'It's unfair'. We cannot help sympathizing with the complaint of the labourers who have worked all day and are getting the same wage as the latecomers.

Jesus' parables are meant to surprise and disturb us, drawing out our instinctive responses and helping us to question them. We can rationalize the story of the labourers in the vineyard and ask whether perhaps the latecomers were those who were poor or disadvantaged and so worthy recipients of the landowner's generosity. And yet, this does not quite fit the spirit of the story. The point seems to be that the generosity of the landlord was random. He picked anyone and everyone available. The kingdom is not limited to those who share its values or who choose to follow the way of Jesus. It is not limited to the 'deserving' poor. Those who get caught up in the work of the vineyard are as likely to be lazy and undeserving as much as they are virtuous.

Sometimes we need to be shaken out of our moral rectitude by God's generosity. He does not play the game of life by our rules. See if you can spot God's work today in someone you least expect to be doing it.

COLLECT

O God,
who by the leading of a star
manifested your only Son to the peoples of the earth:
mercifully grant that we,
who know you now by faith,
may at last behold your glory face to face;
through Jesus Christ your Son our Lord,
who is alive and reigns with you,
in the unity of the Holy Spirit,
one God, now and for ever.

Reflection by **Angela Tilby**

Psalms **46**, 147.13-end *or* **76**, 79
Jeremiah 30.1-17
Matthew 20.17-28

Saturday 8 January

Matthew 20.17-28

'Jesus answered, "You do not know what you are asking."' (v.22)

The road to Jerusalem marks the turn of the Gospel towards the passion story. This solemn transition is interrupted by James' and John's request for special recognition in the kingdom. In Mark's Gospel, the two brothers ask this for themselves, but here in Matthew, it is their mother who presses their case.

Part of the moral revolution that comes with Christianity is its critique of the usual obligations of kinship. It was normal in the ancient world, and still is in many societies, to seek advantage for one's family and friends. These obligations run deep. When Christianity fades from society, we see them return, not just in serving the interests of our relatives but in the widespread cronyism that now infects Western society. Jesus insists that requests for such favours come from ignorance. The solidarity of the Gospel does not allow for special treatment on the basis of kinship except in the sharing of suffering.

We should reflect on how far our lives are dominated by a craving for recognition, by the desire to be treated as exceptional. Do we seek advantages for close friends and neighbours, and who pays the price when we do? The Church speaks a lot about 'servant' ministry. Being a servant means being 'disposable' in the old-fashioned sense of being available to God for whatever God desires – costly, but ultimately creative.

COLLECT

Creator of the heavens,
who led the Magi by a star
to worship the Christ-child:
guide and sustain us,
that we may find our journey's end
in Jesus Christ our Lord.

Reflection by **Angela Tilby**   45

Monday 10 January

Psalms **2**, 110 *or* **80**, 82
Genesis 1.1-19
Matthew 21.1-17

Matthew 21.1-17

' ... they brought the donkey' (v.7)

During the course of my ministry, quite a few Palm Sunday services have involved a donkey. For various reasons, some unmentionable, the donkey tends to be the most memorable thing about them. That's as it should be, it seems to me, since the fact that Jesus chose to enter Jerusalem not using a regal mode of transport but seated on a donkey is surely significant. It is a clear sign that his kingship is not like that of earthly rulers.

That is because the only power he wields is the power of love. Those who greeted him so ecstatically on Palm Sunday expected him to take up arms, but he refused and so, it seemed at the time, let evil triumph. In fact, Jesus defeated evil the godly way. He showed us that God wins by going on loving. As they knocked in the nails, Jesus prayed for the forgiveness of his tormentors.

Jesus made clear that love, though it might seem to us to be a weak force, is in fact the strongest in all creation. It lies at the heart of everything that is, for God is Love. It was Love that created the world, Love that fashioned you and me, and it was Love that raised Jesus from the dead. And the donkey is the sign. Will we follow that sign in our lives?

COLLECT

Eternal Father,
who at the baptism of Jesus
revealed him to be your Son,
anointing him with the Holy Spirit:
grant to us, who are born again by water and the Spirit,
that we may be faithful to our calling as your adopted children;
through Jesus Christ your Son our Lord,
who is alive and reigns with you,
in the unity of the Holy Spirit,
one God, now and for ever.

46 | *Reflection by* **John Inge**

Psalms 8, **9** *or* 87, **89.1-18**
Genesis 1.20 – 2.3
Matthew 21.18-32

Tuesday 11 January

Matthew 21.18-32

'What do you think?' (v.28)

This passage reminds us that Jesus was forever asking questions. In this passage alone he asks, 'What do you think?'; 'Which of the two did the will of his father?'; 'What will he do to those tenants?' They are the tip of the proverbial iceberg. Jesus asks a total of 307 questions in the Gospels. That's nearly twice the number he was asked, 183. Not only did he ask a large number of questions, he did not seem very keen on answering the ones he was asked. Of the 183, he only answers three straightforwardly. To the others he either gives no response, changes the subject, asks another question, tells a story or says that it is the wrong question.

Why is this? It is surely because he is not interested in communicating information; his goal is transformation. That necessitates deep reflection and will involve asking ourselves questions. It was once observed that we are formed by the questions we ask. Jesus knew that well.

'What do you think?' is the fundamental question Jesus asks in this passage. The scriptures are not an instruction manual. They are something much more rich and profound. The questions they pose – and imply – are crucial to their transformational potential. Jesus surely wants us to keep reflecting prayerfully on what it means to follow him. May we keep asking questions as we seek to do so.

Heavenly Father,
at the Jordan you revealed Jesus as your Son:
may we recognize him as our Lord
and know ourselves to be your beloved children;
through Jesus Christ our Saviour.

COLLECT

Reflection by **John Inge**   47

Wednesday 12 January

Matthew 21.33-end

'He will put those wretches to a miserable death' (v.41)

As a 'religious leader', I find Jesus' denunciations of those of his day rather disconcerting. I fear I might discover on Judgement Day that I have been leading people away from rather than towards God. The warning to leaders in this passage – that they will be treated like the dishonest tenants and put to a 'miserable death' – is stark, to put it mildly.

Before you relax if you are not a 'religious leader', note that it's also ordinary people of faith who are criticized by Jesus. Again and again, as in this passage, he tells us that the 'bad' people – those on the edges, the tax collectors and prostitutes – will be going to the kingdom of heaven before the upright, honest and godly.

Maybe this is a reminder to all of us who are 'religious', not just leaders, that nothing that we do, or say, will ever justify us. Only God's grace will save us. If we see ourselves as 'good' and 'godly' people, maybe we need God's grace more than anyone. Put another way, what we need is the faith of which Jesus speaks, that can move mountains.

If we worry, as Jesus' disciples did, that our faith is not sufficient, we should take heart from Jesus' words that 'all things are possible for God' as we pray for grace and mercy.

COLLECT

Eternal Father,
who at the baptism of Jesus
revealed him to be your Son,
anointing him with the Holy Spirit:
grant to us, who are born again by water and the Spirit,
that we may be faithful to our calling as your adopted children;
through Jesus Christ your Son our Lord,
who is alive and reigns with you,
in the unity of the Holy Spirit,
one God, now and for ever.

Reflection by **John Inge**

Psalms **21**, 24 *or* 90, **92**　　　　**Thursday 13 January**
Genesis 3
Matthew 22.1-14

Matthew 22.1-14

'Friend, how did you get in here without a wedding robe?' (v.12)

This is a difficult passage to understand: it has caused much puzzlement down the centuries. What message is Jesus wanting to convey? The most helpful and imaginative commentary on it I have read is a poem, 'The Wedding Garment' by Charles Williams. He tells how 'the Prince Emmanuel gave a ball', a fancy-dress ball in which everyone had to come dressed in the virtues of another. So, heeding the instructions:

> *'This guest his brother's courage wore / That, his wife's zeal, while, just before, / She in his steady patience shone; / There a young lover had put on / The fine integrity of sense / His mistress used; magnificence. / A father borrowed of his son, / Who was not there ashamed to don / His father's wise economy.'*

In the poem, only one person dared to turn up in his own virtue and stuttered as he tried to enter:

> *'I have not strictly . . . an old friend . . . / His Highness . . . come, let me ascend. / My family has always been / In its own exquisite habit seen. / And, courteous as such beings are, / The Angels bowed him to his car.*

I find it a very helpful reminder of what Jesus' teaching constantly tells us – that we should not rely on our own righteousness and we certainly should not boast of it. What a good thing it would be if we were able constantly to rejoice in other people's virtues. Perhaps we could learn from them in the process.

Heavenly Father,
at the Jordan you revealed Jesus as your Son:
may we recognize him as our Lord
and know ourselves to be your beloved children;
through Jesus Christ our Saviour.

COLLECT

Reflection by **John Inge**　　49

Friday 14 January

Psalms **67**, 72 *or* **88** (95)
Genesis 4.1-16, 25-26
Matthew 22.15-33

Matthew 22.15-33

'Whose head is this, and whose title?' (v.20)

The sheer brilliance of Jesus shines through the pages of the Gospel, and gloriously in the two encounters described here. 'Whose head is this, and whose title?', Jesus asks. It's a brilliant question, which silenced those who were hoping to trap him. More than that, it enabled Jesus to assert the sovereignty of God over all things while appearing superficially to support the emperor. The image on the coin was that of Caesar, so he was able to tell them to give to the emperor the things that are the emperor's and to God the things that are God's.

There is another level to what Jesus says, though: an unspoken message being conveyed. Caesar's head is that of a human being. Human beings, Jesus' hearers were well aware, are made in the image of God: '... in the image of God he created them; male and female he created them' (Genesis 1.27). So, in a very subtle and subversive manner, which they could not challenge, he was telling them that *all* things are God's.

There is an important reminder for us all here that God is sovereign over all things. That being the case, do we ensure that God is sovereign of our hearts and lives, that our allegiance to God takes precedence over anything else in our lives? Do we put God first?

COLLECT

Eternal Father,
who at the baptism of Jesus
revealed him to be your Son,
anointing him with the Holy Spirit:
grant to us, who are born again by water and the Spirit,
that we may be faithful to our calling as your adopted children;
through Jesus Christ your Son our Lord,
who is alive and reigns with you,
in the unity of the Holy Spirit,
one God, now and for ever.

Reflection by **John Inge**

Psalms 29, **33** *or* 96, **97**, 100
Genesis 6.1-10
Matthew 22.34-end

Saturday 15 January

Matthew 22.34-end

'On these two commandments hang all the law and the prophets'
(v.40)

This passage, which includes Jesus' summary of the law, will be very familiar to most Christians. The two commandments, to love God (Deuteronomy 6.5) and love your neighbour (Leviticus 19.18), appear separately in the Hebrew Scriptures. Although there is some precedent in pre-Christian Judaism for bringing them together, Jesus seems to have done something new in referring to them as a summary of all the requirements of the law (Mark 12.29-31).

Expressed together, they are the hallmark of healthy Christianity. When one or other takes priority to the detriment of the other, trouble ensues. Exclusive concentration on the first leads to a pietism that tends to ignore the plight of those around us who are made in the image of God, a sect-like separation from the world that forgets that in serving the least of humanity we are serving Christ. Concentration on the second to the detriment of the first leads to what used to be called a 'social gospel' approach that reduces the Church to just another agent of social responsibility. The Church and the gospel flourish when attention is given to both; they belong together. Each is dependent on the other, the one flows from and to the other.

The same is true of us as individuals. Do we neglect God because we're too busy worrying about our fellow human beings or do we neglect our fellow human beings because we're too busy worrying about God?

Heavenly Father,
at the Jordan you revealed Jesus as your Son:
may we recognize him as our Lord
and know ourselves to be your beloved children;
through Jesus Christ our Saviour.

COLLECT

Reflection by **John Inge** | 51

Monday 17 January

Matthew 24.1-14

'... they will hand you over to be tortured' (v.9)

The words of this passage are chilling and horribly relevant to today's world. We see 'nation rise against nation, and kingdom against kingdom' as Jesus prophesied. Christians today are being handed over to be tortured and put to death, just as Jesus predicted they would, more than ever before. Terribly, there is widespread evidence showing that persecution of Christians now is worse than it has ever been in terms of numbers, and that Christians constitute by far the most widely persecuted religion in today's world. In its comprehensive study for 2018, the respected Pew Research Center concluded that Christians were targeted in 145 countries – a rise from 125 in 2015.

It is easy enough for those of us who enjoy freedom to practise our faith to read the words the one 'who endures to the end will be saved', but they are hugely costly ones for millions of our fellow Christians. What should we do? The first thing is surely to give heartfelt thanks for the freedom we enjoy and never take it for granted. Our experience is not the norm – quite the opposite – and we are very blessed.

The second is to give our support, prayerful and financial, to organizations that work for the rights of Christian minorities. One such, Open Doors, states on its website: 'Over 340 million Christians are persecuted. They follow Jesus, no matter the cost. With your help, we're bringing them hope and resources.'

COLLECT

Almighty God,
in Christ you make all things new:
transform the poverty of our nature by the riches of your grace,
and in the renewal of our lives
make known your heavenly glory;
through Jesus Christ your Son our Lord,
who is alive and reigns with you,
in the unity of the Holy Spirit,
one God, now and for ever.

Reflection by **John Inge**

Psalms **132**, 147.1-12 *or* **106*** (*or* 103) **Tuesday 18 January**
Genesis 7.11-end
Matthew 24.15-28

Matthew 24.15-28

'So when you see the desolating sacrilege ...' (v.15)

There has been a great deal of speculation over the centuries about what Jesus is referring to in the term 'desolating sacrilege'. It can't be a future desecration of the Temple since he has just stated that the Temple will be torn down: a ruined Temple cannot be desecrated. The theologian Stanley Hauerwas argues persuasively that Jesus is the great high priest and he is the temple (Hebrews 8 – 9), so his crucifixion is the desolating sacrilege: the death of the Son of God that is the sacrilege that desecrates the cosmos. Jesus tells the disciples that at that time there will be suffering that has not been known since the beginning of the world and will be never known again. Jesus is trying to teach his disciples how to live in the light of his cross.

Jesus calls us to leave behind things that might seem important – or even indispensable – because nothing is important in the light of the cross. We are called, with St Paul to 'regard everything as loss because of the surpassing value of knowing Christ Jesus my Lord' regarding all things as 'rubbish, in order that [we] may gain Christ' (Philippians 3.8).

Days of crisis invite vultures to feed on the corpse of the age-old, false messiahs. There are plenty of those around at present. How can we recognize them in our own lives? And how will we reassess our priorities?

Eternal Lord,
our beginning and our end:
bring us with the whole creation
to your glory, hidden through past ages
and made known
in Jesus Christ our Lord.

COLLECT

Reflection by **John Inge** 53

Wednesday 19 January

Psalms **81**, 147.13-end
or 110, **111**, 112
Genesis 8.1-14
Matthew 24.29-end

Matthew 24.29-end

'Keep awake therefore ...' (v.42)

Jesus quotes the prophet Isaiah to demonstrate that the sun and moon and stars will herald the coming of Jesus again, and on that day, the prophecy of Daniel – that he will come on the clouds with power and great glory – will be fulfilled.

Jesus is not inviting his hearers to think ahead but to understand the meaning of the present. His followers are not to speculate on when this will happen – only the Father knows that. Our role is to wait with a purpose, awake and ready. I think one good way of thinking of repentance is to see it as 'staying awake' while reorientating one's life towards Jesus. We are to be prepared, as Noah was when he built an ark even when it was not raining, whilst others were going about their business as normal. The name of our ark is 'Church'.

'Apocalyptic' names the time that requires waiting. It is not just any kind of waiting but the waiting made possible by a hope made real. Jesus says plainly that 'this generation will not pass away' without the things he prophesies taking place, for in him eternity is disrupted, in him heaven and earth will pass away but his words will not. How could they? He is, after all, the Word of God. Can we wait expectantly, in faith and hope?

COLLECT

Almighty God,
in Christ you make all things new:
transform the poverty of our nature by the riches of your grace,
and in the renewal of our lives
make known your heavenly glory;
through Jesus Christ your Son our Lord,
who is alive and reigns with you,
in the unity of the Holy Spirit,
one God, now and for ever.

| *Reflection by* **John Inge**

Psalms **76**, 148 *or* 113, **115**
Genesis 8.15 – 9.7
Matthew 25.1-13

Thursday 20 January

Matthew 25.1-13

'No! there will not be enough for you and for us ...' (v.9)

The parable of the wise and foolish bridesmaids gives more clues of how Jesus wants his followers to live in the light of his death and resurrection. When you do not know when something is going to happen, you have to prepare for it to do so at any time. The wise bridesmaids were ready, and the foolish were not. How were they prepared? There has been much discussion over the centuries about what the oil in the lamps represent. Is it faith? Is it good works?

A more interesting aspect of this parable for me is the clear indication it gives that sometimes it is perfectly acceptable to say 'no'. The wise bridesmaids say 'no' to the foolish ones when they ask for help. Jesus said 'no' – sometimes to those who wanted to follow him, for example. In the Gospels, one of the striking things about Jesus is his radical unavailability, his withdrawing from the crowds. One of my favourite encounters is in Mark chapter 1. Jesus' disciples look for him all night and, when they find him, exclaim: 'Everyone is looking for you.' His response? 'Let's go somewhere else!'

As Christians, we sometimes feel that we must always be available to others, offering help whenever it is asked for. That's not only a recipe for burnout, it also risks neglecting our relationship with God. If the wise bridesmaids had said 'yes' to the foolish ones, would they have run the risk of losing their relationship with Jesus? Are there times when our 'yes' to others can undermine our relationship with God?

Eternal Lord,
our beginning and our end:
bring us with the whole creation
to your glory, hidden through past ages
and made known
in Jesus Christ our Lord.

COLLECT

Friday 21 January

Psalms **27**, 149 *or* **139**
Genesis 9.8-19
Matthew 25.14-30

Matthew 25.14-30

' ... see, I have made five more talents' (v.20)

Jesus' attitude to money seems to have been that it is a dangerous thing – camels and the eyes of needles and all that. His ambivalence has meant that preachers have tended to ignore the money side of this parable: the original Greek, *talanton*, a weight or sum of money, has come to mean a natural aptitude or gift. If we are to understand the *manner* in which we are to use our gifts, though, there is something about the approach of the successful entrepreneur that the Lord is commending: the taking of risk.

The sum given to the first servant was huge – equivalent to more than fifteen years' wages of a labourer. That might have led the servant to believe that it was enough and that he could just keep it safe. But that, of course, is not the way of the entrepreneur: enough is never enough.

If you want to make serious money, you need be prepared to take risks with what you already have: you must be ready to lose the lot. The reason why money and possessions can become a prison and make it so hard for us to enter the kingdom of heaven is partly that those who have them can be consumed by wanting to hang on to them in exactly the opposite approach to that of the successful entrepreneur. It is risk taking that Jesus is commending here. Will we risk everything for God?

COLLECT

Almighty God,
in Christ you make all things new:
transform the poverty of our nature by the riches of your grace,
and in the renewal of our lives
make known your heavenly glory;
through Jesus Christ your Son our Lord,
who is alive and reigns with you,
in the unity of the Holy Spirit,
one God, now and for ever.

Reflection by **John Inge**

Psalms **122**, 128, 150
or 120, **121**, 122
Genesis 11.1-9
Matthew 25.31-end

Saturday 22 January

Matthew 25.31-end

'Lord, when was it that we saw you hungry ...?' (v.37)

At first reading, this parable appears to be a straightforward direction to care for the needy. There's more to it than that, though. One of the most striking things about this passage is the astonishment that the righteous express. They don't know their good deeds. Their left hand doesn't seem to know what their right hand is doing (Matthew 6.3).

The most important moral choices we make are those we don't even stop to think about. If I go to help someone who has been knocked over by a car, I do so without a thought. I probably don't even think of it as a 'good deed'. Heroic deeds are often dismissed by those who do them as 'just what anyone would do'. They are not. Immersion in a Christian moral framework helps us to see and perform good deeds as a natural part of life.

The unrighteous know their deeds and are quite confident about their righteousness. Maybe that's always the case with humanly crafted righteousness. Maybe those who measure their righteousness on human scales are in for a shock at the day of judgement.

Again and again, Jesus warns us about being presumptuous and this parable is no exception. Which of us can truly say we have been as loving, thoughtful and charitable as God calls us to be? We can rely only on the grace of God, hoping and praying that the surprise we receive on Judgement Day will be a happy-making one.

Eternal Lord,
our beginning and our end:
bring us with the whole creation
to your glory, hidden through past ages
and made known
in Jesus Christ our Lord.

COLLECT

Reflection by **John Inge** | 57

Monday 24 January

Psalms 40, **108** or 123, 124, 125, **126**
Genesis 11.27 – 12.9
Matthew 26.1-16

Matthew 26.1-16

'Why this waste?' (v.8)

This passage offers a meditation on the difference between true value and mere valuation, an illustrating and undergirding of Oscar Wilde's famous dictum that a cynic is someone who knows the price of everything and the value of nothing.

Here we are shown two distinct instances of valuation. The costly ointment is valued, a little vaguely, at 'a large sum', and the disciples ask in horror: 'Why this waste?' (In John's version, it is not 'the disciples' but, more poignantly and sharply, Judas himself who makes the objection and values the ointment very precisely at 300 denarii.) Then the second valuation is of Christ himself, the price of his life, and Judas again gives an exact valuation of the priceless, at the rather smaller sum: 30 pieces of silver.

But running counter to the tabulation of this worldly accounting is the current of the gospel, the currency of grace. Jesus sees not the mere price of the ointment but the infinite value of the love that lavished it – the extravagant response to his own extravagant love. For he knows that the breaking of the precious jar whose fragrance richly fills the room anticipates the breaking open of his wounded side, the release of his heart's blood and, with it, the love at the heart of God for the heart of humanity, a love whose fragrance and beauty still richly fill the world.

COLLECT

Almighty God,
whose Son revealed in signs and miracles
the wonder of your saving presence:
renew your people with your heavenly grace,
and in all our weakness
sustain us by your mighty power;
through Jesus Christ your Son our Lord,
who is alive and reigns with you,
in the unity of the Holy Spirit,
one God, now and for ever.

| *Reflection by* **Malcolm Guite**

Psalms 66, 147.13-end
Ezekiel 3.22-end
Philippians 3.1-14

Tuesday 25 January
Conversion of Paul

Philippians 3.1-14
'I have more' (v.4)

Of all the paradoxes of Paul, this flourishing of his impeccable CV only to scrunch it up and throw it in the bin is one of the most striking. It must have been galling to Paul when the so-called super-apostles were bigging themselves up and insisting on their spiritual credentials, implying that he was far less 'qualified' than they, and implying that we will find favour with God only if we have the right qualifications, the right 'heritage' and, of course, the old school tie of circumcision.

As it happens, Paul has all of these and more, and for a moment it all bursts out of him in an impressive checklist. And then he remembers himself, and comes to the great 'Yet' of verse 7: 'Yet whatever gains I had, these I have come to regard as loss because of Christ.' He sees, in a moment of prophetic insight that has not yet dawned on some parts of the Church, that it might just be your impeccable CV that's keeping you from Christ. You might have become so self-confident, so 'entitled', so reliant on applause for your justification that you entirely miss the only thing that justifies any of us: the all-surpassing love of God in Christ, lavished alike on the least as on the greatest.

Paul prefaced his CV with the boast 'I have more' but he concludes it by knowing it's better to have nothing, if that way we can have Christ.

COLLECT

Almighty God,
who caused the light of the gospel
to shine throughout the world
through the preaching of your servant Saint Paul:
grant that we who celebrate his wonderful conversion
may follow him in bearing witness to your truth;
through Jesus Christ your Son our Lord,
who is alive and reigns with you,
in the unity of the Holy Spirit,
one God, now and for ever.

Reflection by **Malcolm Guite** | 59

Wednesday 26 January

Matthew 26.36-46

'... your will be done' (v.42)

There is so much in this harrowing passage that speaks of Jesus' humanity: the anguish of a man who is about to suffer horribly, but who still trembles as it were in the waiting room, before the torture starts.

There's the desperate need to have his friends with him for this last hour, to know that they are there to witness the struggle, though that intensely private agony has drawn him apart for a while. There's the sense of the unsustainable: the collapse of the physical frame even as the mental frame sustains an unbearable burden, as he 'threw himself on the ground'. There is the desperate desire to escape, which only brings him sooner to the intimate and inexorable moment of choice. Whose will is to be done? And perhaps barely in a whisper, unheard by the sleeping disciples, the resolution: 'My Father, if this cannot pass unless I drink it, your will be done.'

And so the central petition of the Lord's Prayer is fulfilled: 'your will be done'. Had the disciples been alert, they would have seen what their daily prayer meant and what it cost, and the gift of Christ's self sacrifice disclosed at the heart of it. But they were asleep, and so, quite often, are we. But sometimes, God willing, drowsily mumbling the Lord's Prayer in a draughty church, we will open our eyes and see what Christ has done for us.

COLLECT

Almighty God,
whose Son revealed in signs and miracles
the wonder of your saving presence:
renew your people with your heavenly grace,
and in all our weakness
sustain us by your mighty power;
through Jesus Christ your Son our Lord,
who is alive and reigns with you,
in the unity of the Holy Spirit,
one God, now and for ever.

Psalms **47**, **48** *or* **143**, 146
Genesis 15
Matthew 26.47-56

Thursday 27 January

Matthew 26.47-56

'The one I will kiss is the man' (v.48)

In the kiss of Judas, we encounter a terrible fusion of intimacy and irony. The kiss of greeting, the kiss of peace, becomes the kiss of betrayal. But that's how it is in the broken world that Jesus came to save. We always take the deepest hurt from the ones we love.

We have learned alas, to put up shields and barriers to most people, to defend ourselves from the stranger by keeping them strange. We defend ourselves with distance or with the carefully fashioned armour of formality, but somehow, somewhere, with someone, we have to let our guard down, or there would be no intimacy or tenderness at all.

The range of the word 'tender' says it all. Tentatively, we tender love to one another and that love, to be love at all, must be tender. But if we fall and hurt ourselves, if our exposed skin is grazed or broken, we speak of it as 'tender to the touch'. We cannot have the one tenderness without the other, for we cannot love through callouses. In order to touch tenderly, we must risk becoming tender to the touch. We must take off the armour, take off our shoes and risk the thorns. So God in his invulnerable heaven, in tenderness towards us, empties himself, takes on our tender flesh, exposes himself and his love to every wound, even the wound of betrayal, that he might search and heal those wounds in us.

COLLECT

God of all mercy,
your Son proclaimed good news to the poor,
release to the captives,
and freedom to the oppressed:
anoint us with your Holy Spirit
and set all your people free
to praise you in Christ our Lord.

Reflection by **Malcolm Guite**   61

Friday 28 January

Psalms 61, **65** or 142, **144**
Genesis 16
Matthew 26.57-end

Matthew 26.57-end

'Who is it that struck you?' (v.68)

It's an almost unbearable moment. The one who gives us our freedom is bound. The one who took spittle and made of it a healing salve for the blind is spat upon with blind fury. The one who knows us intimately, who knows who we are far better than we do ourselves, is struck in the face and asked by that lost violator: 'Who is it that struck you?'

He knows who that tormentor is better than he knows himself in that moment. For that abuser, drunk on violence, has forgotten himself, but Jesus knows and remembers, and will soon speak words of forgiveness from the cross and value the lives of his enemies at the price of his own heart's blood.

'Who is it that struck you?' Peter will have to answer that question too, for he is about to deliver to Jesus a slap in the face far more hurtful than those outer blows: the stinging slap of betrayal. 'Who is it that struck you?' When Peter goes out to weep bitterly, he thinks he knows the answer: Peter – the rock who turned out to be no more than quicksand, Peter the weak, Peter the coward, Peter the traitor. But that is not the final answer to that question, for Jesus has a better one. And Peter will only know himself as Jesus knows him when each betrayal is undone by love.

COLLECT

Almighty God,
whose Son revealed in signs and miracles
the wonder of your saving presence:
renew your people with your heavenly grace,
and in all our weakness
sustain us by your mighty power;
through Jesus Christ your Son our Lord,
who is alive and reigns with you,
in the unity of the Holy Spirit,
one God, now and for ever.

Reflection by **Malcolm Guite**

Psalm **68** *or* **147**　　　　　　**Saturday 29 January**
Genesis 17.1-22
Matthew 27.1-10

Matthew 27.1-10

'... he went and hanged himself' (v.5)

This strange story with its particular concern for what happened to the 30 pieces of silver takes us back to Monday's story of the two false valuations: the great sum for the perfume and the paltry price on Jesus' head, and how that extravagance of love lived on, when all the sums of money mentioned were spent. Judas threw down the 30 pieces in the temple and then went out to throw away something far more precious: his own life.

I remember in theological college once, someone asked a visiting speaker: 'What was Jesus doing when he descended into hell?' And he answered, without hesitation, 'Looking for Judas!' A powerful answer. Peter, for all his bitterness, at least had the patience to wait for Jesus, and Jesus found him, as he had once before, by the sea, and asked him the three loving questions whose answers undid the three denials. But Judas prematurely took judgement into his own hands and fled beyond the gates of life, so Christ descended deeper, 'to preach to the spirits in prison', as Peter later said, and surely asked Judas the same loving question and held out the same possibility of redemption.

It is not for us to know how that question was answered, only to know that it will be asked of us too, as it was of Peter and Judas: 'Do you love me?'

> God of all mercy,
> your Son proclaimed good news to the poor,
> release to the captives,
> and freedom to the oppressed:
> anoint us with your Holy Spirit
> and set all your people free
> to praise you in Christ our Lord.

COLLECT

Reflection by **Malcolm Guite**　　　63

Monday 31 January

Psalms **57**, 96 *or* 1, 2, 3
Genesis 18.1-15
Matthew 27.11-26

Matthew 27.11-26

'... Jesus Barabbas or Jesus who is called the Messiah?' (v.17)

What was Pilate thinking? A man in office but not in authority, who has already been manipulated and cajoled into trying and condemning the innocent Jesus, suddenly making a last desperate bid to the crowd for his life because he happens to have another (presumably) guilty 'Jesus' waiting in the stocks. And like all Pilate's other little stratagems, this one also fails, and he resorts to the guilty pantomime of public hand-washing, not the first or last politician to do so.

But what are we to make of this strange exchange of one Jesus for another: Jesus Christ for Jesus Barabbas, the one condemned and the other released? Jesus was a common name, Joshua, 'Yahweh Saves', and Bar Abbas, curiously enough means 'son of the father'. I have no doubt Barabbas was a real person, a notorious prisoner, perhaps the first person to wake up to freedom knowing that Jesus Christ had taken his place, but I also believe his name is significant: Jesus Barabbas: 'Yahweh saves a son of the father'! In one sense we are all Barabbas: everyone of us unexpectedly released from condemnation because Christ suffers in our stead. But with this difference: it was a fickle crowd who called for Barabbas' release, but it is Yahweh himself, who calls for our release, and, in the person of his son, suffers in our stead.

COLLECT

God our creator,
who in the beginning
commanded the light to shine out of darkness:
we pray that the light of the glorious gospel of Christ
may dispel the darkness of ignorance and unbelief,
shine into the hearts of all your people,
and reveal the knowledge of your glory
in the face of Jesus Christ your Son our Lord,
who is alive and reigns with you,
in the unity of the Holy Spirit,
one God, now and for ever.

| *Reflection by* **Malcolm Guite**

Psalms **93**, 97 *or* **5**, 6 (8)
Genesis 18.16-end
Matthew 27.27-44

Tuesday 1 February

Matthew 27.27-44

'... twisting some thorns into a crown' (v.29)

As so often in the Gospels, even the hurts and insults hurled at Jesus are strangely redeemed and carry truer meanings than the mockers intend. As with the pejorative title 'friend of sinners' (Matthew 11.19), so with the sadistic mock coronation depicted here. For Jesus really is the king, and the mocking and painful coronation with the *'corona spinea'*, the crown of thorns, goes to the heart of that kingship, for Jesus is a king who is crowned with the pain of his people rather than elevated above it. During the first peak of the coronavirus pandemic, I reflected poetically on Psalms 21 and 22, the psalms of coronation and crucifixion, and wrote:

> *Our Lord comes down*
> *Into the heart of all our hurts to wear*
> *The sharp corona spinea, the crown*
> *Of thorns, and to descend with us to death.*
> ....
> *Before he shares with us the golden crown,*
> *He comes to share with us the crown of thorns.*
> *Our hurts and hates close in and hem him round*
> *Mock and humiliate him. All the scorns*
> *With which we blaspheme God in one another*
> *Are concentrated here among 'the horns*
> *Of unicorns', the lions' mouths, the slather*
> *Of our devouring wickedness. He takes*
> *It all and turns it into love.*

(Malcolm Guite, *David's Crown*, Canterbury Press 2021)

God of heaven,
you send the gospel to the ends of the earth
and your messengers to every nation:
send your Holy Spirit to transform us
by the good news of everlasting life
in Jesus Christ our Lord.

COLLECT

Reflection by **Malcolm Guite**   65

Wednesday 2 February

Presentation of Christ
in the Temple

Romans 12.1-5

'... present your bodies' (v.1)

On this feast of the Presentation, I take some comfort in the stark simplicity of Paul's request: 'present your bodies'. At least we *can* do that, and there are days when it feels as though that's all we can do: show up, sit down, be at least physically present, for the length of the service, the office, the meditation. We may feel that our minds are elsewhere; we may feel that our hearts are empty and our spirits vacant, even as we take the prayers on our lips, and yet Paul assures us that this bodily obedience, presenting our bodies, moving our lips, is itself our spiritual worship. That if we present our bodies, God himself will be at work helping us not to be merely conformed to habit but rather transformed by the renewing of our minds.

It was much the same for Mary and Joseph, I imagine, when they showed up physically and presented Jesus at the temple. They, too, had a lot more on their minds than just their allotted slot in the rituals of the day: how to pay for the two young doves, how to get better housing, how – eventually – to get safely out of Jerusalem. Yet when they presented themselves to the priest, they made present to Simeon, to Anna, to the temple, to the whole world, the saving body of Christ, in whom God is made present to us.

COLLECT

Almighty and ever-living God,
clothed in majesty,
whose beloved Son was this day presented in the Temple,
in substance of our flesh:
grant that we may be presented to you
with pure and clean hearts,
by your Son Jesus Christ our Lord,
who is alive and reigns with you,
in the unity of the Holy Spirit,
one God, now and for ever.

| *Reflection by* **Malcolm Guite**

Psalms 14, **15**, 16
Genesis 21.1-21
Matthew 27.57-end

Thursday 3 February

Matthew 27.57-end

'... and laid it in his own new tomb' (v.60)

This is the second time in this passion narrative that a figure has stepped forth and provided for the burial of the unburied, but what a contrast between the two figures! It was Judas who inadvertently, unknowingly, posthumously, provided for the burial of strangers when the 30 pieces of silver he threw down in the temple were taken up and used to buy the potter's field. But now, in steps Joseph of Arimathea, deliberately, consciously, offering the tomb he had prepared for himself for another, and so the deep motif of substitution and exchange in this Gospel continues.

According to Roman Law, relatives of a criminal might claim his body for burial and, though there is no evidence that Joseph's act was anything more than the kindness of a stranger, there is the lovely Glastonbury legend that he was actually Mary's uncle and so had the claim of kinship to the body, having known Jesus since he was a boy. Whether that or any of the subsequent speculations of poets Malory or Blake are true or not, it is true that we who have been, in one sense, Barabbas, can also be, in another sense, Joseph of Arimathea, and sing with Samuel Crossman in his lovely hymn 'My song is love unknown':

What may I say?
Heaven was his home,
But mine the tomb wherein he lay.

Friday 4 February

Psalms 17, **19**
Genesis 22.1-19
Matthew 28.1-15

Matthew 28.1-15

'... do not be afraid' (vv.5,10)

'Do not be afraid' is always the message of the angels. They said it to the shepherds at his birth and now they say it to the women at his resurrection. And here we see the 'angel' in *Evangelium*, for 'do not be afraid' is indeed the beginning of the good news. Christmas means we need no longer be afraid that we are alone, for Emmanuel has come, God is with us, and Easter means we need no longer fear our death for death itself has been defeated. 'Do not be afraid' has been a message on the lips of angels, human and divine, from that day to this. It was, for example, the very last message of the Nobel Laureate Seamus Heaney as he lay dying in hospital and texted it to his wife, pithily in Latin: *'Noli timere'*.

It's interesting to note that it was the supposedly courageous soldiers who were too terrified even to hear this message, but it was the supposedly 'weaker' women, who could look the bright angel in the face and hear the good news, and that it was the women who brought it to the men, thus becoming apostles to the apostles and evangelists to the evangelists.

Now we too must hear it from them, and whatever our fears may have been or still are, we can go out, like them, to proclaim it 'with fear and great joy'.

COLLECT

Almighty God,
by whose grace alone we are accepted and called to your service:
strengthen us by your Holy Spirit
and make us worthy of our calling;
through Jesus Christ your Son our Lord,
who is alive and reigns with you,
in the unity of the Holy Spirit,
one God, now and for ever.

| *Reflection by* **Malcolm Guite**

Psalms 20, 21, **23**
Genesis 23
Matthew 28.16-end

Saturday 5 February

Matthew 28.16-end

'I am with you always' (v.20)

Matthew's Gospel is a good instance of poet T. S. Eliot's dictum 'In my end is my beginning', both because it ends with the beginning of the Church and our whole mission to share good news with the world, but also because the last words of Jesus, as Matthew reports them, circle back to the first chapter of his Gospel when he quotes Isaiah: 'and they shall name him Emmanuel, which means, God is with us'. And now we come full circle as Jesus takes on the full meaning of his name and says, 'remember, I am with you always'.

Some years ago, in *Parable and Paradox* (Canterbury Press 2016), I put my reflection on that into this poem, which is also a prayer:

> *Your final words fulfil your ancient name,*
> *A promise hidden in Emmanuel,*
> *A promise that can never fade or fail:*
> *I will be with you till the end of time;*
> *I will be with you when you scale the height,*
> *And with you when you fall to earth again,*
> *With you when you flourish in the light,*
> *And with you through the shadow and the pain.*
> *Our God with us, you leave and yet remain*
> *Risen and hidden with us everywhere;*
> *Hidden and flowing in the wine we share,*
> *Broken and hidden in the growing grain.*
> *Be with us till we know we are forgiven,*
> *Be with us here till we're with you in heaven.*

COLLECT

God of our salvation,
help us to turn away from those habits
which harm our bodies and poison our minds
and to choose again your gift of life,
revealed to us in Jesus Christ our Lord.

Reflection by **Malcolm Guite**   69

Monday 7 February

Psalms 27, **30**
Leviticus 19.1-18, 30-end
I Timothy 1.1-17

1 Timothy 1.1-17

'... the aim of such instruction is love' (v.5)

The Letters of Paul to Timothy are often referred to as the Pastoral Epistles, their subject being guidance for pastoring Christ's flock, nurturing the life of Christians and building up the Church. Addressed to Timothy, Paul's 'loyal child in the faith', the letter is concerned with instruction for good practice that Timothy is to uphold and to teach within the life of the congregation in Ephesus. The instruction ranges over a variety of subjects: from prayer for secular rulers, to the character of Church leaders, the care of the elderly and the avoidance of false ascetic practices.

Some of the instruction, notably on the submissive role of women in the Church and the proper behaviour of slaves towards their masters, is challenging to read, reflecting a time and a culture very different from ours. Many find these particular verses hard to square with our present understanding of the gospel of Jesus Christ.

However, the aim of Christian instruction, says Paul, is 'love that comes from a pure heart, a good conscience, and sincere faith'. This is not instruction by rote nor the imposition of an external rule. The ultimate guide for Christian behaviour is the disposition of the heart, the integrity of conscience and the sincerity of faith. Paul's own heart, conscience and faith have been transformed and shaped by the 'faith and love that are in Christ Jesus'. He urges the same for us.

COLLECT

O God,
you know us to be set
in the midst of so many and great dangers,
that by reason of the frailty of our nature
we cannot always stand upright:
grant to us such strength and protection
as may support us in all dangers
and carry us through all temptations;
through Jesus Christ your Son our Lord,
who is alive and reigns with you,
in the unity of the Holy Spirit,
one God, now and for ever.

Reflection by **Brother Samuel SSF**

Psalms 32, **36**
Leviticus 23.1-22
1 Timothy 1.18 – end of 2

Tuesday 8 February

1 Timothy 1.18 – end of 2

'God our Saviour, who desires everyone to be saved' (2.3-4)

The instructions that Timothy has been given to pass on to the church at Ephesus are founded on the faith that God's purpose in Christ is to bring all to salvation. This was a remarkable claim at the time of writing. The Christian churches founded by Paul were still tiny minorities in a diverse religious culture of many gods, where worship of the Roman Emperor was an expectation of good citizenship throughout the Empire. Christians were seen by those around them as belonging to a strange sect of Judaism, suspected of atheistic subversion, and sometimes persecuted and repressed. Yet in this letter they are told to pray for everyone, including 'kings and all who are in high positions'.

This is not simply a precautionary injunction to prove to outsiders that they were peaceable subjects of the established order; it issues from the conviction and confidence that the gospel of Jesus is good news for all, including those big people on the world stage who may well be known as oppressors. Jesus taught his disciples to 'love your enemies and pray for those who persecute you' (Matthew 5.44). I wonder how faithful we are at doing this today with those whose policies and practices we find ourselves deeply opposed to – not just praying that they see the truth as we see it, but praying for them that they might come to know that they, like us, are 'children of the same heavenly father'.

Lord of the hosts of heaven,
our salvation and our strength,
without you we are lost:
guard us from all that harms or hurts
and raise us when we fall;
through Jesus Christ our Lord.

COLLECT

Wednesday 9 February

1 Timothy 3

*'... if someone does not know how to manage his own household,
how can he take care of God's church?' (v.5)*

Wise management is as necessary a part of Church leadership, as it is of looking after an extended household or running a business, and a considerable part of this pastoral letter is devoted to establishing some basic norms for the sound ordering of the Church. However, the guidance is not about structures, meetings and training courses, but about character, the sort of person the leader – in this case the bishop or deacon – should be.

Later in the letter, Timothy is warned not to 'ordain anyone hastily' (5.22). We rightly look for gifts – of leadership, pastoral care, teaching, communication and insight – when discerning whether or not someone should be entrusted with a role of authority in the Church. Such gifts can be enhanced and developed through good training. But 'character' is something different. Respect, humility, faithfulness in relationships, temperance, discretion, simplicity of life – all of which are referred to here – are virtues that are acquired, formed, in relationship with others. They are gained and nurtured through the experiences of life – practical engagement, love and friendship, coping with differences, adversity, failure and repentance – all situations through which God shapes and draws us to himself.

These virtues of character are the essential building-blocks of every 'household', whether that is a school, a football team, a business, a family or a congregation.

COLLECT

O God,
you know us to be set
in the midst of so many and great dangers,
that by reason of the frailty of our nature
we cannot always stand upright:
grant to us such strength and protection
as may support us in all dangers
and carry us through all temptations;
through Jesus Christ your Son our Lord,
who is alive and reigns with you,
in the unity of the Holy Spirit,
one God, now and for ever.

Reflection by **Brother Samuel SSF**

Psalm 37*
Leviticus 24.1-9
1 Timothy 4

Thursday 10 February

1 Timothy 4

'For everything created by God is good ...' (v.4)

For the second time in this letter (the first at 1.4), Timothy is warned about false teachings that lead people astray from that which he himself has received and has been following. These seem to have included ascetic practices that have become ends in themselves and speculations about mythical esoteric knowledge, both of which are diversions from 'hope set on the living God'. Counterparts of such distractions in our contemporary culture might be the excessive preoccupation with achieving the ideal physical body that is promoted through advertising, the cult of celebrity that often dominates our public life, and the widespread fascination on social media with conspiracy theories.

Following the one who 'was revealed in flesh' (1 Timothy 3.16) involves a healthy materialism, which rejoices in the fundamental goodness of every aspect of creation and the whole of our human life. If God in Jesus Christ has fully inhabited our humanity in order to redeem it, it's through our redeemed embodied life that we come to know the fullness of God's love. While there is a place for fasting and celibacy as means of growing in self-discipline, nothing of the body in itself is to be despised or rejected. Likewise, spiritualized speculation that turns attention away from the physical reality of our humanity is to be avoided. Gratitude brings us back to our dependence on the essential giftedness of our existence.

COLLECT

Lord of the hosts of heaven,
our salvation and our strength,
without you we are lost:
guard us from all that harms or hurts
and raise us when we fall;
through Jesus Christ our Lord.

Reflection by **Brother Samuel SSF**

73

Friday 11 February

Psalm 31
Leviticus 25.1-24
1 Timothy 5.1-16

1 Timothy 5.1-16

*'Do not speak harshly to an older man, but speak to him
as to a father' (v.1)*

It is significant that, in these instructions on good order in the Church, attention is given to the subject of family relationships. Many local churches today describe themselves as 'family friendly' – by which they usually mean they advertise that families with children are welcome. But in these instructions to Timothy, the message is not just that 'we want families to join', but that the Church itself is a family, a household. The members of the congregation are to show the same honour and respect for one another as they hold for members of their own families. As children should provide for elderly parents, and relatives have a responsibility to care for family members who fall on hard times, so the Church must care for the needs of its own members, especially those who are alone and without support – though with the caveat that the need should be recognized as genuine.

While there's a valid concern today to grow congregations, and in particular to attract children and young people into the life of the Church, it's important that the elderly and vulnerable should not be overlooked. The domestic vision of the Church given in this passage, with its emphasis on the kindness, care and respect due to all its members, is a powerful witness to the world of today in which the bonds of family life are often eroded by individualism and the cultural and market pressures that go with it.

C O L L E C T

O God,
you know us to be set
in the midst of so many and great dangers,
that by reason of the frailty of our nature
we cannot always stand upright:
grant to us such strength and protection
as may support us in all dangers
and carry us through all temptations;
through Jesus Christ your Son our Lord,
who is alive and reigns with you,
in the unity of the Holy Spirit,
one God, now and for ever.

74   *Reflection by* **Brother Samuel SSF**

Psalms 41, **42**, 43
Numbers 6.1-5, 21-end
1 Timothy 5.17-end

Saturday 12 February

1 Timothy 5.17–end

'... take a little wine for the sake of your frequent ailments' (v.23)

Having read the instruction that the bishop should not be a drunkard (1 Timothy 3.3), it's something of a relief to know that an occasional glass of wine is not only permitted but is actively encouraged. Despite the cultural dissonance in the letter between our world and that of the first century AD, which rightly offends our own world view – particularly the instruction about slaves honouring their masters – there's a gentle humaneness that runs throughout the letter. The elders who lead, preach and teach should be sufficiently honoured and compensated for their labour. Accusations of wrongdoing should be treated seriously but cautiously; partiality in judgement is to be set aside. The sins of others should be a stimulus to the purity of one's own life rather than an encouragement to participation. Good works tend to be a witness to good character.

Christians are sometimes viewed by those outside the Church as hypocrites who fail to practise the strict injunctions that they preach. In fact, those who follow faithfully in the way of Christ are usually acutely aware of their failure always to live faithfully and lovingly according to the gospel. In these verses, while there is an acknowledgement that, when people fall into sin, there sometimes needs to be public rebuke and resistance, harsh punishments are not recommended and expulsion from the Church is not prescribed. Here is a practical wisdom that acknowledges failure and recognizes virtue as its own reward.

Lord of the hosts of heaven,
our salvation and our strength,
without you we are lost:
guard us from all that harms or hurts
and raise us when we fall;
through Jesus Christ our Lord.

COLLECT

Reflection by **Brother Samuel SSF**   75

Monday 14 February

1 Timothy 6.1-10

'For the love of money is a root of all kinds of evil' (v.10)

Living as we do in a market economy for which money is an essential medium of exchange, these words may come across as rather a heavy warning. Most of us wouldn't own to loving the lucre. Yet the acquiring of money to keep a roof over our heads, pay the bills and buy those luxuries that we count essential can be a major concern – one that easily slips over into something of an obsession with money. There never seems to be enough of it!

It may especially appear so in the life of a congregation in which financial matters often play a dominant role in discussions and decisions. How to hold and use money without being possessed by it is even more of a challenge in the world of today than it was in first-century Ephesus.

Here and in the next section of the chapter, we are reminded that we live in God's economy of gift. We come into the world with nothing in terms of monetary value. Everything that we receive throughout our lives, including what we may think of as hard-earned cash rewards and all that money may buy, is in fact given to us only on loan. It doesn't actually belong to us and we can't take it with us when we die. Rejoicing in life's abundant giftedness can unburden us of anxiety, free us from envy and liberate us for generosity.

COLLECT

Almighty God,
who alone can bring order
to the unruly wills and passions of sinful humanity:
give your people grace
so to love what you command
and to desire what you promise,
that, among the many changes of this world,
our hearts may surely there be fixed
where true joys are to be found;
through Jesus Christ your Son our Lord,
who is alive and reigns with you,
in the unity of the Holy Spirit,
one God, now and for ever.

Reflection by **Brother Samuel SSF**

Psalms **48**, 52
Genesis 24.29-end
1 Timothy 6.11-end

Tuesday 15 February

1 Timothy 6.11-end

'Fight the good fight of the faith ...' (v.12)

Military metaphors occur a number of times in the two letters to Timothy and elsewhere in the Pauline writings ('take up the whole armour of God ...' Ephesians 6.13). They have become incorporated into the imagery and hymnody of the Church and have shaped several Church institutions. Over the centuries, the idea of fighting for the faith has sometimes been taken literally; terrible religious wars have been fought both against people of other faiths and also between Christians of different traditions. Blood has been shamefully shed in the name of Christ.

But the true fight of faith, alluded to here, is always that which is within us – the interior struggle to remain faithful to the confession made in our baptism to the one who, by making 'the good confession' before Pontius Pilate, has stayed faithful for us. Often the fight is against our demons: those thoughts, fears and obsessions that can dominate, control and bind us, and that become a rampart against the mercy and love of God, which is always seeking to break through to us. In this warfare, a certain robustness is necessary. Note the active verbs used in these verses: '... shun all this; pursue righteousness, ... take hold of the eternal life, to which you were called'.

The letter ends with the words 'Grace be with you' – a reminder that the battle is won not just by our own strenuous efforts, resolutions and arguments, but through the life that is found and given to us in Jesus Christ.

Eternal God,
whose Son went among the crowds
and brought healing with his touch:
help us to show his love,
in your Church as we gather together,
and by our lives as they are transformed
into the image of Christ our Lord.

COLLECT

Reflection by **Brother Samuel SSF** | 77

Wednesday 16 February

Psalm 119.57-80
Genesis 25.7-11, 19-end
2 Timothy 1.1-14

2 Timothy 1.1-14

'Guard the good treasure entrusted to you ...' (v.14)

In the Gospels, Jesus speaks of the kingdom of God as 'treasure hidden in a field' (Matthew 13.44), worth selling everything to gain. Here, Timothy is told to guard that treasure with which he has been entrusted. He has grown up surrounded and nurtured by the faith of his grandmother Lois and his mother Eunice. How important those two women were in passing on to him the treasure that they themselves had received through the teaching of Paul, who himself had come to know the inexhaustible riches of Christ.

Although life in Jesus Christ is a first-hand discovery, we come to that life not through a vacuum, but because of the faithfulness of others who, through their witness, have pointed us to where treasure is to be found. It's worthwhile considering those who have been signposts to us – family members, friends, chance-encountered strangers perhaps – and to give thanks for these treasure bearers. Some we may not have known personally, but we will have heard or read of them. Some we may know only through their work – the building of a church many generations back, the nurture of a congregation or the offering of loving service; the gift of their theology, technology or teaching; the creativity of their music, poetry or painting. These and others will have had a hand in the treasure being entrusted to us.

Tradition, 'handing-on', is sometimes dismissed as unnecessary in the life of faith – but without it we wouldn't know where to start digging.

COLLECT

Almighty God,
who alone can bring order
to the unruly wills and passions of sinful humanity:
give your people grace
so to love what you command
and to desire what you promise,
that, among the many changes of this world,
our hearts may surely there be fixed
where true joys are to be found;
through Jesus Christ your Son our Lord,
who is alive and reigns with you,
in the unity of the Holy Spirit,
one God, now and for ever.

Reflection by **Brother Samuel SSF**

Thursday 17 February

2 Timothy 1.15 – 2.13
'... if we are faithless, he remains faithful' (2.13)

In these verses, the demanding nature of the task ahead of Timothy is spelled out. A number of times in this second letter, Paul refers to his suffering in prison and to his chains. He has struggled with setbacks and has been let down by fellow Christians. He has learnt the necessity of endurance in proclaiming the gospel and he urges Timothy to 'be strong'. But the strength required is that which comes not simply from his own resolve. Timothy is told to 'remember Jesus Christ, raised from the dead'. That is, he is reminded of the one whose suffering has revealed the love and forgiveness of God, which endures and overcomes even death itself.

There are many around the world today who are facing oppression and persecution on account of their faith in Christ. Churches are burned or bombed; individuals suffer violence and imprisonment. Their faithful endurance witnesses powerfully to that love and forgiveness that is Jesus' life laid down for the world. For others of us, the opposition we experience may be less brutal and the difficulties we encounter more subtle – a culture of indifference and cynicism can be discouraging, can sap our energy and cloud our vision, but it calls for the same steadfastness. The life of the Church depends ultimately on the one who 'remains faithful' to us and who 'cannot deny himself'.

COLLECT

Eternal God,
whose Son went among the crowds
and brought healing with his touch:
help us to show his love,
in your Church as we gather together,
and by our lives as they are transformed
into the image of Christ our Lord.

Reflection by **Brother Samuel SSF**

Friday 18 February

2 Timothy 2.14-end

'Remind them ... to avoid wrangling over words' (v.14)

People sometimes speak of the early days of the Church, imagining that they were full of zeal and unity, and comparing them wistfully with the contentions and disputes of today. These verses, however, reveal that the congregation in Ephesus suffered from the same arguments over minor issues as are often experienced in an average church council meeting. It's strange how small items – the placing of a vase of flowers, the choice of music, or the clothes worn by the priest or minister – can cause a storm of argument quite disproportionate to the rest of a church's business, let alone the life of witnessing to the kingdom of God. It's usually because these apparently insignificant matters represent deeper conflicts of personality and power, and are the tip of an iceberg of hurt and fear.

Community life can be challenging in these circumstances, especially for those in positions of leadership. Gentleness, kindness, courtesy and patience are much the best tools for bringing people together and resolving conflict. Generosity – bucketloads of it – is essential if a community of any kind is to live and work together. There's a real skill in recognizing and including people's different gifts and temperaments – likened here to the various utensils of a household – in service for the ultimate purpose of the community's existence. Keeping in mind who the community is, and what it is for, is the best way of avoiding becoming ensnared and tangled over inessentials.

COLLECT

Almighty God,
who alone can bring order
to the unruly wills and passions of sinful humanity:
give your people grace
so to love what you command
and to desire what you promise,
that, among the many changes of this world,
our hearts may surely there be fixed
where true joys are to be found;
through Jesus Christ your Son our Lord,
who is alive and reigns with you,
in the unity of the Holy Spirit,
one God, now and for ever.

Reflection by **Brother Samuel SSF**

Saturday 19 February

2 Timothy 3

'... from childhood you have known the sacred writings' (v.15)

The scriptures with which Timothy is so well acquainted are not what we know as the 'New Testament', for the gospels and the epistles were in the process of being written in his day. It was the Hebrew scriptures in which he was steeped – the Torah (the five books of Law), the prophets and the wisdom literature – which contained the story of God with his people and which shaped his world view.

Until a century ago, it could be assumed that the majority of people in countries where Christian faith has long been established would have at least some familiarity with the scriptures, both Old and New Testaments. The family Bible was a treasured possession. Today, sadly, it is more a museum piece; our culture has become biblically illiterate. Even within churches there's often a shallow and selective reading of scripture that focuses on particular verses to prove a point of view, rather than a deep engagement with the whole.

There's a story of a keen young Jewish man who went to his rabbi. 'Rabbi' he said, 'I have been through the Torah a thousand times.' To which the rabbi replied: 'My son, it's not how many times you have been through the Torah that counts, but how many times the Torah has been through you.' The scriptures only come alive for us when we inhabit them so that they shape our imagination, challenge our expectations and form us in the likeness of Christ.

Eternal God,
whose Son went among the crowds
and brought healing with his touch:
help us to show his love,
in your Church as we gather together,
and by our lives as they are transformed
into the image of Christ our Lord.

COLLECT

Monday 21 February

Psalm **71**
Genesis 29.31 – 30.24
2 Timothy 4.1-8

2 Timothy 4.1-8

'... always be steady' (v.5 RSV)

'He's a bit of a Steady Eddie.' That well-known expression is often read as a bit of an insult. Steady Eddies are reliable and dependable but perhaps they are also a little dull and unimaginative. If you want some fresh thinking, you'd turn to an entrepreneur, not to a Steady Eddie. We undervalue our Steady Eddies.

In the Second Letter to Timothy, Paul is doing what all the best leaders do, which is to train up his successor prior to his own departure, and as we approach the end of the Epistle his advice to this young evangelist is surprising. Not, 'Be imaginative, be dynamic, think outside the box', or any of the usual hackneyed lexicon of inspirational phrases. Paul simply tells Timothy to 'be steady' (translated as 'be sober' in the NRSV). As people 'wander away to myths' in seeking the truth, be a fixed point, Paul advises. Hold firm to the gospel that has been revealed in Jesus Christ.

Maybe we need to rethink our perception of steadiness and see it as a strength. In a world where new ideas can flash from one end of the globe to another in a few seconds and where a confused generation will look in almost any direction to find a narrative that makes sense of their lives, it can be tempting to think that gospel is something we need constantly to re-engineer to capture the latest mood.

But Paul reminds us that what matters is not transient popularity, but a deep-rooted faithfulness that endures to eternity. Be steady.

COLLECT

> Almighty God,
> you have created the heavens and the earth
> and made us in your own image:
> teach us to discern your hand in all your works
> and your likeness in all your children;
> through Jesus Christ your Son our Lord,
> who with you and the Holy Spirit reigns supreme over all things,
> now and for ever.

| *Reflection by* **Philip North**

Tuesday 22 February

2 Timothy 4.9-end

'To him be the glory for ever and ever' (v.18)

Who's getting on your nerves right now? Or to use a more colloquial expression, who's doing your head in?

We all have an image of the perfect church, where the community is strong, the worship idyllic, the outreach dynamic, and where everyone dwells in harmony and friendship. The only problem is, that church does not exist; nor has it ever existed. Because the thing about Christians is that we're all sinners. There will always be someone who gets on your nerves.

The last sentences of St Paul's Second Letter to Timothy are wonderfully authentic as suddenly the author's humanity is laid bare. He longs to see his young protégé before he dies. He wants his cloak and his books. He mentions the people who are pleasing him, and he lays into Alexander the coppersmith who is getting on his nerves. This is the real Paul living in a real church where things are not all as he would like, because everyone is a sinner.

And yet in the midst of it all, there is salvation. Amidst all those complex situations and relationships, the Lord gave Paul strength and rescued him. To him be the glory.

Even these very last words of the epistle have a rich message. We don't live out the Christian life in the midst of some imaginary Christian theme park. We do it in the real world and in the context of authentic relationships where things go right and things go wrong. Even those people who get on your nerves are playing a part in your salvation.

> Almighty God,
> give us reverence for all creation
> and respect for every person,
> that we may mirror your likeness
> in Jesus Christ our Lord.

COLLECT

Reflection by **Philip North**   83

Wednesday 23 February

Psalm **77**
Genesis 31.25 – 32.2
Titus 1

Titus 1

'... for the sake of the faith of God's elect' (v.1)

Good writing always has a clear and well-defined purpose. We come now to the third of St Paul's pastoral epistles (letters written not to whole churches but to individual leaders). This one is to Titus, Paul's trouble-shooter who brought reconciliation in Corinth and now has the equally unenviable task of choosing bishops for the church in Crete. Fortunately, Paul knows exactly why he's writing: 'for the sake of the faith of God's elect.' It is this clear purpose that steers the content of the whole letter.

The criteria that Paul lays down for the leaders Titus is to appoint are by anyone's standards tough ones. Titus is to find elders who are blameless, upright, holy and self-controlled. Why is he quite so strict?

It all comes back to Paul's stated purpose. If leaders are to act 'for the sake of the faith' of those whom they lead, they must role-model that faith in their own lives. Recent child abuse scandals demonstrate all too clearly the fatal damage that is done by Church leaders whose lifestyles are at odds with their calling.

All those in Christian leadership, lay or ordained, are called to further the faith of others. Their primary role is to help people to understand more richly the mystery of our salvation in Christ. So Paul's words ask them, and indeed all of us, an awkward question. In what areas do we need to amend our own lifestyles in order to build up others in the faith of Jesus Christ?

COLLECT

Almighty God,
you have created the heavens and the earth
and made us in your own image:
teach us to discern your hand in all your works
and your likeness in all your children;
through Jesus Christ your Son our Lord,
who with you and the Holy Spirit reigns supreme over all things,
now and for ever.

| *Reflection by* **Philip North**

Psalm **78.1-39***
Genesis 32.3-30
Titus 2

Thursday 24 February

Titus 2

'... that the word of God may not be discredited' (v.5)

'Top tips for Christian living' would be a good subheading for chapter 2 of the letter to Titus, as Paul turns his attention to the Christian home. Much of this chapter comprises sound advice for different groups of people on how they can put their faith into practice in their daily lives.

Whilst there is much wisdom here, some of the content grates to the modern ear. The women are to be reverent and obedient. The men must be serious and sensible. Hardest of all is the instruction that slaves should be submissive to their masters. How do we make sense of this teaching today?

It is critical to remember Paul's intended audience. The Church at this stage was, in the eyes of the establishment, a small and dangerous sect. Even in addressing slave and free as equals in the Church, Paul was on dangerous ground and could have been accused of undermining the ordering of society. Paul wanted people to live the faith distinctively but not in a way that would bring needless oppression or endanger lives. It was a tricky balancing act.

So, imagine prayerfully that you have the task of rewriting chapter 2 for today in a context in which we take for granted freedom of religious expression. What would be your advice for the men, the women, the children? What would you say to younger people, older people and employees? How can we live distinctively, that the word of God may not be discredited?

Almighty God,
give us reverence for all creation
and respect for every person,
that we may mirror your likeness
in Jesus Christ our Lord.

COLLECT

Reflection by **Philip North**   85

Friday 25 February

Psalm **55**
Genesis 33.1-17
Titus 3

Titus 3

'For we ourselves were once foolish ...' (v.3)

The great preacher John Stott suggested that the three chapters of Paul's letter to Titus point us to the three contexts for Christian living: the Church, the home and the world. And so, as this letter reaches its conclusion, Paul advises how Christians can live the gospel in their dealings with the world.

Once again there is plenty of stern advice on Christian living. But this time Paul goes a little further to explain why it is important for Christians to pay attention to their lifestyle, and he does so by referring to his own life story and indeed that of Titus himself.

They were both once slaves to various passions, living foolishly and disobediently. But the forgiveness they came to experience in their own lives pointed to the power of God to forgive through the saving work of Jesus Christ. Their life stories became therefore parables of the gospel.

In the same way, the reason that we seek to live out our faith through our actions and decisions is not to merit or earn salvation. That is a gift we have already received through faith in the grace that flows from the cross. Rather, we pay attention to our lifestyles so that our own lives can be a parable of the gospel. The fresh start that we have received from Jesus Christ points others to the abundant grace and generosity of God. Your story can tell God's story.

COLLECT

Almighty God,
you have created the heavens and the earth
and made us in your own image:
teach us to discern your hand in all your works
and your likeness in all your children;
through Jesus Christ your Son our Lord,
who with you and the Holy Spirit reigns supreme over all things,
now and for ever.

| *Reflection by* **Philip North**

Psalms **76**, 79
Genesis 35
Philemon

Saturday 26 February

Philemon

'... no longer as a slave but as more than a slave, a beloved brother'
(v.16)

'Shy bairns get nowt,' they used to say in the North East of England. (Or put another way, 'Shy children get nothing'.) It's a cruel expression, but it contains a truth. If you don't ask for something, you're unlikely to get it. Paul's letter to Philemon, gentle in tone but revolutionary in content, could not be accused of shyness. It asks for Philemon's generosity not once, but twice. And as it does so, it points us to the extraordinary graciousness of God.

Things looked bleak for Onesimus, Philemon's runaway slave to whom Paul had offered sanctuary. In the laws of the day, he could expect severe punishment, even execution. Paul's first request, that Philemon accept Onesimus back unpunished, may seem pretty daring on its own. But the apostle goes even further and asks the slave-owner to have him back as 'a beloved brother'. That is a subversive request. He was inviting Philemon to see Onesimus as his equal, maybe even asking him to set him free.

And the basis of so outrageous a request? The saving work of Jesus. Philemon himself had been set free from slavery to sin through the grace of God in Christ. Now Paul was asking him to respond through his own graciousness.

So this short letter about household affairs takes us to the heart of the gospel. It reminds us first that everyone, no matter what their status, is our brother and sister. But even more richly, it points to the abundance of God's grace, so generous and free, and challenges us to respond through our own gracious generosity.

Almighty God,
give us reverence for all creation
and respect for every person,
that we may mirror your likeness
in Jesus Christ our Lord.

COLLECT

Reflection by **Philip North**

Monday 28 February

Psalms **80**, 82
Genesis 37.1-11
Galatians 1

Genesis 37.1-11

'Israel loved Joseph more than any other of his children' (v.3)

Over the next few weeks, we can delight in one of the great narratives of the scriptures. The Joseph story has it all – compelling characters, a fast-moving plot, deadly rivalries, false accusations and beautiful reconciliations.

And yet it starts with something as simple and human as a father's favouritism. Joseph's brothers find themselves on the receiving end of a great deal of criticism as the story unfolds, but in this opening episode it's easy to feel sorry for them.

How stupid of Jacob to make his special love for Joseph so widely known. How ill-judged to give him an expensive coat with long sleeves, a sign that he was excused from the back-breaking labour of farming, unlike his brothers. No wonder Joseph grew smug in his 'special one' status, infuriating the rest of the family by boasting embarrassingly about the dreams that foretold his future power.

Yet it is these mistakes that lie behind the events that will take first Joseph and then Jacob's family to Egypt, that lead us to the Exodus and so anticipate for us the whole saving work of God in Jesus Christ.

At the very end of the story, Joseph will say to his brothers, 'Even though you intended to do harm to me, God intended it for good, in order to preserve a numerous people' (Genesis 50.20). That conclusion is anticipated here as a foolish father's favouritism is used by God to his eventual glory. God's grace is such that human sin becomes the means of human salvation. This is a story that carries us all the way to the cross.

COLLECT

Almighty Father,
whose Son was revealed in majesty
before he suffered death upon the cross:
give us grace to perceive his glory,
that we may be strengthened to suffer with him
and be changed into his likeness, from glory to glory;
who is alive and reigns with you,
in the unity of the Holy Spirit,
one God, now and for ever.

Reflection by **Philip North**

Psalms 87, **89**.1-18
Genesis 37.12-end
Galatians 2.1-10

Tuesday 1 March

Genesis 37.12-end

'Come now, let us kill him ...' (v.20)

What a grotesque sequence of squalid, violent events in the wilderness near Dothan. And for Joseph, the trauma must have been appalling. He travels 50 or 60 miles on foot to check up on his brothers and finds himself assaulted, left half dead and finally enslaved.

Little did those involved know they were taking part in God's plan of salvation. Unwittingly, Joseph finds himself playing out a pattern that is repeated throughout the Scriptures. The godly servant goes through abuse but eventually becomes the rescuer of the very people who abuse him.

We see that pattern in the suffering servant of Isaiah who bears the sorrows of those who despised him. And we see it fulfilled in the life of Jesus, who prays for those who nailed him to the cross and dies for sinful men and women that they might be set free for ever.

It's a pattern that can still be seen today. The most significant acts of Christian ministry are invariably those we don't even know we're doing. A casual conversation, a small act of kindness or some simple words of forgiveness can have an impact that we will never understand because God uses us and our ordinary lives in ways we can't even imagine. Even unwittingly we play a part in his great plan to love a fallen world back to life.

Holy God,
you know the disorder of our sinful lives:
set straight our crooked hearts,
and bend our wills to love your goodness and your glory
in Jesus Christ our Lord.

COLLECT

Reflection by **Philip North** | 89

Wednesday 2 March
Ash Wednesday

Psalm **38**
Daniel 9.3-6, 17-19
I Timothy 6.6-19

Daniel 9.3-6, 17-19

'... sinned and done wrong, acted wickedly and rebelled' (v.5)

We live in a culture that values unconditional positivity. We are expected to affirm, to encourage and to build up the self-esteem of those around us. And yet today, in churches across the world, priests will sign their people with ash using words that do the precise opposite. 'Remember you are dust, and to dust you will return.'

It is a brutal reminder of the hard truth that most people spend their lives running away from. Without God, we are nothing. Mere accidents of evolution, taunted by consciousness, living short and brutish lives, destined for annihilation. Yet the moment we accept our dependence upon him, God forgives us and changes us.

In chapter 9, Daniel accepts his own dependence on the Lord and turns to him in the deepest possible contrition. As he ponders the ruins of exilic Jerusalem, he speaks on behalf of a repentant nation, punished for their sin, for he knows that restoration can only come though the action of God.

In Lent, Daniel's contrite prayer becomes our own. It is the season to name and deal with sin, to confess our own apartness from God, our wilful rebellion and greed, our arrogant pride. For it is only through the gracious action of God who sent his Son to die for us that our lives make any sense. Without him, we are as much dust as the ruins of Jerusalem. Yet through our contrition, our lives are remade. For those who acknowledge their need, the New Jerusalem awaits.

COLLECT

Almighty and everlasting God,
you hate nothing that you have made
and forgive the sins of all those who are penitent:
create and make in us new and contrite hearts
that we, worthily lamenting our sins
and acknowledging our wretchedness,
may receive from you, the God of all mercy,
perfect remission and forgiveness;
through Jesus Christ your Son our Lord,
who is alive and reigns with you,
in the unity of the Holy Spirit,
one God, now and for ever.

Reflection by **Philip North**

Thursday 3 March

Genesis 39

'Joseph's master took him and put him into the prison' (v.20)

Truth is costly. It entails sacrifice and pain and so can always be found walking hand in hand with suffering. That is what Joseph learns in his dealings with the Potiphar family.

It would have been so much easier if Joseph had just slept with Potiphar's wife. A well-concealed and doubtless juicy affair would have increased his popularity and given him power over the whole household. But Joseph chooses the path of truth and as a result finds himself in gaol.

What is striking in this narrative is that Joseph, who later wears his emotions very much on his sleeve, is so lacking in self-pity. He seems to accept the trials and tribulations of life with the carefree insouciance of a character in an Evelyn Waugh novel. That's because he trusts deeply in God and so knows that if he speaks and lives the truth, he will be vindicated. That vindication may take time, but it will come.

Dishonesty is a highly attractive temptation for all of us because it provides quick fix solutions to difficult problems. That is why so many people drift into deceitful behaviour without even properly thinking it through.

By contrast, truth is a long-term strategy that will often entail short-term pain and sacrifice. But God is truth, and he will always vindicate the one who bears the cost of truth. That vindication may be slow. But it will come.

Holy God,
our lives are laid open before you:
rescue us from the chaos of sin
and through the death of your Son
bring us healing and make us whole
in Jesus Christ our Lord.

COLLECT

Reflection by **Philip North**

Friday 4 March

Psalms **3**, 7 *or* **88** (95)
Genesis 40
Galatians 3.1-14

Genesis 40

'Do not interpretations belong to God?' (v.8)

How can we tell what the future holds? In ancient Egypt, a chief method was through the interpretation of dreams. The butler and the baker, both imprisoned by Pharaoh, would have been desperate to know their future as revealed to them by their vivid dreams of grapes and baskets, but they were denied access to the skilled magicians and wise men who could have performed the task.

They would not have expected to find a solution in a fellow prisoner, let alone a Hebrew, but Joseph cheekily comes to their rescue. He may not have any training, but, he asks, 'Do not interpretations belong to God?'

Behind that simple question there lies the most massive theological claim. If God can interpret dreams, then the future must lie in God's hands. Joseph is claiming the sovereignty of the God of the Hebrews over all time and eternity.

Today, as Christians, we have no need for diviners or dream interpreters to tell the future. That future is revealed to us by the dying and rising of Jesus; it is set forth in the Scriptures and in the creeds and teachings of the Church. The future is Christ and the fullness of life in him. It is he who meets us in the prison cell of our mortality and sets us free. We can know for sure that all in the end will be glory.

COLLECT

> Almighty and everlasting God,
> you hate nothing that you have made
> and forgive the sins of all those who are penitent:
> create and make in us new and contrite hearts
> that we, worthily lamenting our sins
> and acknowledging our wretchedness,
> may receive from you, the God of all mercy,
> perfect remission and forgiveness;
> through Jesus Christ your Son our Lord,
> who is alive and reigns with you,
> in the unity of the Holy Spirit,
> one God, now and for ever.

Reflection by **Philip North**

Psalm **71** *or* 96, **97**, 100
Genesis 41.1-24
Galatians 3.15-22

Saturday 5 March

Genesis 41.1-24

'It is not I; God will give Pharaoh a favourable answer.' (v.16)

Joseph is taken before Pharaoh, and in just a few moments, the most formidable structures of power are utterly subverted.

This is a remarkable scene. For years Joseph has been languishing away in a filthy prison cell, forgotten by everyone but never losing his trust in God. Then all of a sudden, he shaves, gets a haircut, changes his clothes and finds himself before Pharaoh who shares with him the deepest secrets of his heart. Only Joseph can interpret the traumatic dream. The most powerful man on the planet needs the jailbird.

How can this be? Because Joseph speaks in the name of the God whose power utterly subverts all the structures and institutions conceived through the human mind. As St Paul would later write: 'Has not God made foolish the wisdom of the world?' (1 Corinthians 1.20)

We live in a world in which the colossal global strongholds of political power, military might and corporate dominance seem all pervasive – a world in which the gentle teaching of a roving preacher who lived 2,000 years ago in Galilee can so swiftly be drowned out or perceived as irrelevant.

But just as mighty Pharaoh needed the jailbird, so even the powers of the twenty-first century need with all their hearts the man nailed to the cross. For his wisdom makes foolish the wisdom of the world, and in him alone is life.

Holy God,
our lives are laid open before you:
rescue us from the chaos of sin
and through the death of your Son
bring us healing and make us whole
in Jesus Christ our Lord.

COLLECT

Reflection by **Philip North**

Monday 7 March

Genesis 41.25-45

'See, I have set you over all the land of Egypt' (v.41)

The passage ends with Joseph elevated to a position of power with seemingly every human need provided for. Many would see that as a dream come true, yet the passage began with a very different sort of dream.

In the interpretation of Pharaoh's strange dream, Joseph has God-given insight into some important aspects of the future and is able to offer wisdom about preparing well for the years ahead. Yet this is far from altruistic. There is a strong sense of Pharaoh's desire to understand in order to be in control of the future, and Joseph is to be a partner in that. That theme of control has never been far from the surface throughout the Genesis narrative of Jacob and sons.

Lent is a time of preparation and there is a challenge for us in how we look beyond the immediate surface of the present to seek God's wisdom about how to live it well for the good of the future. However, despite endless forecasting and interpretation of data, we cannot predict or control all that lies ahead, but we can prayerfully pay attention to how what we do and are in the present will contribute to the shaping of the future and a vision of wellbeing for all people.

Our actions, choices and decisions today will have implications for tomorrow and beyond.

COLLECT

Almighty God,
whose Son Jesus Christ fasted forty days in the wilderness,
and was tempted as we are, yet without sin:
give us grace to discipline ourselves in obedience to your Spirit;
and, as you know our weakness,
so may we know your power to save;
through Jesus Christ your Son our Lord,
who is alive and reigns with you,
in the unity of the Holy Spirit,
one God, now and for ever.

| *Reflection by* **Rachel Treweek**

Psalm **44** *or* **106*** (*or* 103)
Genesis 41.46 – 42.5
Galatians 4.8-20

Tuesday 8 March

Genesis 41.46 – 42.5

'The second he named Ephraim, "For God has made me fruitful in the land of my misfortunes."' (41.52)

This next episode brings into sharp relief the truth that there are many different layers of narrative at any particular point in time. This passage tells something of the big story of what is going on in the world regarding famine and Egypt's response; then against this panoramic backdrop, there is the detail of individual lives set within relationship in different locations. Names are both prominent and important, and all of it has something to say about identity. Interestingly, the names of Joseph's children reflect the threads of his own story. His seeming happiness in the present cannot be separated from the pain of the past. The story is not over yet.

In all of this we are reminded of the connectedness of our own story regarding people, place and time. There is mess and brokenness as well as beauty and yet somehow it is mysteriously held in the overarching story of God's purposes.

We each have a name and a unique identity with a story, past and present, lived out in specific places, and yet we are part of a bigger story that spans not only the world but time itself. God's creative work continues in our present within both the loveliness and the ugliness, rooted in what God has done through Christ in the past and the promise of what is to come. The story is not yet finished.

Heavenly Father,
your Son battled with the powers of darkness,
and grew closer to you in the desert:
help us to use these days to grow in wisdom and prayer
that we may witness to your saving love
in Jesus Christ our Lord.

COLLECT

Reflection by **Rachel Treweek** | 95

Wednesday 9 March

Psalms **6**, 17 *or* 110, **111**, 112
Genesis 42.6-17
Galatians 4.21 – 5.1

Genesis 42.6-17

'Joseph also remembered...' (v.9)

As we engage with the next scene in the dramatic saga, we have narrative and speech, but it is devoid of any reference to emotions. Yet behind all these words there is much going on within people's hearts. The one tiny hint of this is in those words 'Joseph also remembered...' Many years previously, Joseph's dreams had revealed a time when his brothers would bow down to him; his interpretation had ignited strong anger and jealousy within his siblings, provoking them to ruthless action to dispose of him.

Now, as Joseph recognizes his brothers, his response to the human visceral reaction is not one of fond reunion but rather something more akin to spiteful revenge. Once he had suffered at their exercise of power and control, and now it is their turn. There is irony in the use of the word 'remembering' because what Joseph recalls is a *dis*membering and an intentional tearing of familial bonds.

While there is the potential for a true re-membering, Joseph is perhaps understandably not yet in a place to live reconciliation, but these are dangerous moments as Joseph chooses to opt for manipulation and a power game.

How might you more deeply recognize the powerful emotions within you sparked by particular events or actions and pay careful attention to the choices you make in the light of them? Can you choose a re-membering rather than something potentially dangerous and destructive?

COLLECT

Almighty God,
whose Son Jesus Christ fasted forty days in the wilderness,
and was tempted as we are, yet without sin:
give us grace to discipline ourselves in obedience to your Spirit;
and, as you know our weakness,
so may we know your power to save;
through Jesus Christ your Son our Lord,
who is alive and reigns with you,
in the unity of the Holy Spirit,
one God, now and for ever.

Reflection by **Rachel Treweek**

Thursday 10 March

Genesis 42.18-28

'That is why this anguish has come upon us' (v.21)

Seeing trauma and turbulence as divine punishment is never a life-giving place to begin; it often leads to blame and finger-pointing rather than opening up the question about how we might live the present well in the light of the past and looking forwards. This is an important question for us and not one we yet see being asked by Joseph and his brothers.

The past is dominating the present and Joseph is determined to continue his game of one-upmanship; at the same time, the brothers are not yet willing to openly name their abhorrent dark secret.

However, we do begin to see human vulnerability cracking open new possibilities. For the first time, Joseph hears something of his brothers' regret and anguish as they acknowledge hearing his. Until now, they have all failed to hear the cries of each other's hearts and look at things through each other's eyes.

Perhaps Joseph's weeping is not only because the remembering is surfacing but also because he now sees the human brokenness in his brothers and can reframe what he once saw as only hard-hearted cruelty.

We are not asked to ignore people's abhorrent past actions, but it is important that we don't fail to see our own brokenness too. Repentance frees us to love not only love ourselves more deeply but also our neighbour. It is all rooted in first allowing God to love us.

COLLECT

Heavenly Father,
your Son battled with the powers of darkness,
and grew closer to you in the desert:
help us to use these days to grow in wisdom and prayer
that we may witness to your saving love
in Jesus Christ our Lord.

Reflection by **Rachel Treweek** | 97

Friday 11 March

Psalm **22** *or* **139**
Genesis 42.29-end
Galatians 5.16-end

Genesis 42.29-end

'... they told him all that had happened to them' (v.29)

Over recent years, there has been much talk of an erosion of trust in many spheres of life from the national to the local. In times of anxiety and fear especially, people need people they can trust – relationships in which there is commitment to wellbeing and honest communication. In this ancient family saga, no one is handling anxiety well; honesty and trust are lacking.

Throughout chapter 42 of Genesis, the brothers have repeatedly described themselves as 'honest men', yet we, like Joseph, know this is not true. So today when we read that the brothers told their father '*all* that had happened' we know that this has not been their modus operandi in the past. There is also a hint in verse 36 that Jacob knows this, that he has never really trusted them ever since the day they returned without Joseph and presented him with a blood-stained robe implying Joseph had been killed by wild animals (Genesis 37). Perhaps even more darkly, Jacob cannot trust his sons because he knows how he dealt with his own brother Esau and deceived *his* father Isaac (Genesis 27).

It would be foolish to believe that all would suddenly be well if the brothers now truly told Jacob 'all' that had ever happened, but at least their decisions in a messy place would be lived in the light rather than trying to negotiate from the shadows. What might this mean for us today?

COLLECT

Almighty God,
whose Son Jesus Christ fasted forty days in the wilderness,
and was tempted as we are, yet without sin:
give us grace to discipline ourselves in obedience to your Spirit;
and, as you know our weakness,
so may we know your power to save;
through Jesus Christ your Son our Lord,
who is alive and reigns with you,
in the unity of the Holy Spirit,
one God, now and for ever.

| *Reflection by* **Rachel Treweek**

Psalms 59, **63** *or* 120, **121**, 122
Genesis 43.1-15
Galatians 6

Saturday 12 March

Genesis 43.1-15

'... may God Almighty grant you mercy' (v.14)

A viral pandemic, like a time of famine, highlights the limits of our control, and at times in our lives we can feel helpless in the situations we find ourselves in. Furthermore, in our desire to be in control, we can sometimes be tempted to act in ways that are manipulative, deceitful or selfish. We have seen it all in this family story.

Yet, if the lies and deception so prevalent in the episodes thus far have left a bad taste in our mouths, there is now a sweetness emerging not only literally in the gifts of honey and nuts, but also metaphorically in the truth-telling we are now witnessing and the good desire for people's wellbeing expressed by both Jacob and Judah.

In this place of truth and love, we see an embracing of the present that is to be lived to the best of Jacob's ability and yet with a letting go and an acceptance that he is not in control. Whether the outcome is to be joy or pain, God will not abandon him.

Whether we are facing today with a sense of dread or joyful expectancy, how might we live the reality of today to our utmost best, entrusting ourselves and those we are concerned about to God whose love is unchanging and who will not abandon us?

Heavenly Father,
your Son battled with the powers of darkness,
and grew closer to you in the desert:
help us to use these days to grow in wisdom and prayer
that we may witness to your saving love
in Jesus Christ our Lord.

COLLECT

Reflection by **Rachel Treweek** | 99

Monday 14 March
Psalms 26, **32** or 123, 124, 125, **126**
Genesis 43.16-end
Hebrews 1

Genesis 43.16-end

'When Joseph came home ...' (v.26)

In today's episode, there is much mention of the word 'house' – the place where Joseph dwells. This is where the brothers are invited to enter, and initially they do so with fear in their hearts. The steward reassures them, but they remain on edge as they await Joseph's return and the pending meal.

At this point the translation says that Joseph returned 'home' – a word that is subtly different from house and perhaps stands out because there is a question mark over whether Joseph is yet truly 'at home'. He is certainly not yet 'at home' with his family, and the pain of the separation from his brother Benjamin runs deep. Thankfully, the episode ends with anticipation that a home-coming is in sight. As the brothers eat from Joseph's table and are 'merry with him', there is a sense of being on the threshold of reconciliation, with the possibility of peace between them and within them.

The word 'homeless' is often used to describe someone who has no permanent building to inhabit, but it might be more accurate to use the word to describe a state of being. St Augustine of Hippo once wrote 'Thou hast made us for thyself O Lord, and our heart is restless until it finds its rest in thee.' Amid the activity of your life and the places you inhabit, how at home are you today?

COLLECT

Almighty God,
you show to those who are in error the light of your truth,
that they may return to the way of righteousness:
grant to all those who are admitted
    into the fellowship of Christ's religion,
that they may reject those things
    that are contrary to their profession,
and follow all such things as are agreeable to the same;
through our Lord Jesus Christ,
who is alive and reigns with you,
in the unity of the Holy Spirit,
one God, now and for ever.

Psalm **50** *or* **132**, 133
Genesis 44.1-17
Hebrews 2.1-9

Tuesday 15 March

Genesis 44.1-17

'What deed is this that you have done?' (v.15)

Being wrongfully accused is torturous where there is no one able to prove your innocence. Those who are accused are left utterly vulnerable and seemingly helpless. This is what we now see in this complex web of relationships among the brothers, and it is uncomfortable to watch.

We don't know whether Benjamin attempted to assure his brothers that he was innocent or whether the brothers' voicing of guilt is rooted in a genuine belief that Benjamin has somehow undermined them. Either way, there is something to be admired in the brothers' care for Benjamin, and it is important for Joseph to see this. Here are his brothers who are changed and who now wish to live in peace, although it is impossible for them to feel peaceful despite Joseph telling them to 'go up in peace.'

If, as Christ's followers, we wish to be people of peace, then we need to ask ourselves not only about how we speak up for those in our world today who are wrongfully accused and subjected to humiliation, but also how we support and care for those who are genuinely guilty of wrongdoing yet remain fellow human beings. It is an uncomfortable question; it raises numerous issues for us as individuals, communities and as society, but it is an appropriate question to ponder in Lent as we reflect on our own lives in a spirit of repentance and hope.

> Almighty God,
> by the prayer and discipline of Lent
> may we enter into the mystery of Christ's sufferings,
> and by following in his Way
> come to share in his glory;
> through Jesus Christ our Lord.

COLLECT

Reflection by **Rachel Treweek**

Wednesday 16 March

Genesis 44.18-end

'... please let your servant remain as a slave' (v.33)

Years earlier, in Genesis 37, it was Judah who proposed that they sell Joseph as a slave. There was no regard for the welfare of his brother or his father. Now it is Judah who boldly offers *himself* as a slave to ensure that his father and his brother Benjamin are honoured. Here is love, but we are unable to see Judah's heart and mind, and thus we cannot be sure of all that is driving him. Mingled with love there may also be guilt or pride or a fear of failure.

Our desire to grow in love of God, neighbour and self will rarely be free of the influence of our darker inner drivers, and so it is that the apostle Paul writing to the church in Philippi says: 'Do nothing from selfish ambition or conceit, but in humility regard others as better than yourselves. Let each of you look not to your own interests, but to the interests of others. Let the same mind be in you that was in Christ Jesus.' (Philippians 2.3-5)

Jesus Christ was motivated purely by love, and it was love alone that resulted in him emptying himself and taking the form of a slave (Philippians 2.7). For us, as followers of Christ, the days of Lent offer the opportunity to recognize our mixed motives more clearly and to open ourselves more fully to the unconditional love of God revealed in Christ.

COLLECT

Almighty God,
you show to those who are in error the light of your truth,
that they may return to the way of righteousness:
grant to all those who are admitted
    into the fellowship of Christ's religion,
that they may reject those things
    that are contrary to their profession,
and follow all such things as are agreeable to the same;
through our Lord Jesus Christ,
who is alive and reigns with you,
in the unity of the Holy Spirit,
one God, now and for ever.

Reflection by **Rachel Treweek**

Psalm **34** *or* **143**, 146
Genesis 45.1-15
Hebrews 3.1-6

Thursday 17 March

Genesis 45.1-15

'And he kissed all his brothers and wept upon them ...' (v.15)

In today's episode, there is revelation and resolution. Yet perhaps it is surprising that that the brothers respond with such grace and appear to show no resentment. After all, once again Joseph has acted with superiority and power not unlike those years before when he taunted them with his dreams, which of course have now come true. Joseph has put his brothers through the wringer, yet perhaps there is a sense of having been absolved from their own game-playing all those years ago when they sold Joseph into slavery and deceived their father. We can only speculate as to the content of their conversation when they finally talked with each other.

For both Joseph and the brothers, there must be a sense of relief that all has been brought into the light. It is that crossroads described in Psalm 85.10 and translated so poignantly in the Authorized Version: 'Mercy and truth are met together, righteousness and peace have kissed each other.'

Lent is a good time to examine ourselves and name those places in our lives where there is a need for revelation and resolution, those places where the hiding or the pretence needs to stop and the truth be named. Sometimes, it is about putting something down or letting something go. The relief that will follow will be accompanied by all sorts of thoughts and emotions, but the good news is that God's work of healing can unfold.

Almighty God,
by the prayer and discipline of Lent
may we enter into the mystery of Christ's sufferings,
and by following in his Way
come to share in his glory;
through Jesus Christ our Lord.

COLLECT

Reflection by **Rachel Treweek** | 103

Friday 18 March

Psalms 40, 41 *or* 142, 144
Genesis 45.16-end
Hebrews 3.7-end

Genesis 45.16-end

'He was stunned; he could not believe them' (v. 26)

All the fear, sadness and loss in the family's story is now met with abundance and joy. There is almost a sense of 'happy ever after', yet the source of the happiness is not in the giving of the multiplicity of goods but rather in love and restored relationship.

Many years previously, Jacob too had proffered a lavish gift of material goods to family, although this time in fear (Genesis 33). He had gone to meet his estranged brother Esau and hoped that the numerous herds and flocks would be a gift to appease his brother whom he had wronged. However, Esau wanted none of it. The desired gift was that of reconciliation, and when Esau embraced Jacob, it seemed too good to be true, and he exclaimed that it was as if he had seen the face of God. There are resonances of that time of grace as Jacob now hears that Joseph is alive, and the brothers discover forgiveness and new possibility.

In these days of Lent, as we stumble towards Good Friday with all our struggles and flaws, the abundant treasure of Easter Day is still present. God is making all things new, and yet it is only by opening ourselves to the undeserved gift of God's overwhelming and abundant love that we will discover the gift of restoration and the 'happy ever after' that will one day be made complete.

COLLECT

Almighty God,
you show to those who are in error the light of your truth,
that they may return to the way of righteousness:
grant to all those who are admitted
    into the fellowship of Christ's religion,
that they may reject those things
    that are contrary to their profession,
and follow all such things as are agreeable to the same;
through our Lord Jesus Christ,
who is alive and reigns with you,
in the unity of the Holy Spirit,
one God, now and for ever.

| *Reflection by* **Rachel Treweek**

Psalms 25, 147.1-12
Isaiah 11.1-10
Matthew 13.54-end

Saturday 19 March
Joseph of Nazareth

Matthew 13.54-end

'Is not this the carpenter's son?' (v.55)

Too often, we make assumptions about people based on what we know or have been told. Here, the people are blinded by their assumptions about Jesus, not least that he is the son of Joseph the carpenter.

We know very little about *this* Joseph, but we do know that he acted radically in not abandoning Mary. Any man betrothed to a woman who was found to be pregnant would usually have ensured she was publicly disgraced and probably stoned. What life had been like for Joseph and Mary as their young family grew up surrounded by rumour, we can only begin to imagine.

Yet it is not only Jesus' family who were potentially diminished by their community's assumptions; it was also the people themselves. They could have received so much blessing from opening their eyes and ears to the good news of Jesus Christ among them and allowed their astonishment to lead them to new discovery about God and themselves. Instead, their small-mindedness prevented them from tasting life in all its fullness.

Today is a good day to be aware of assumptions we may have of particular individuals around us that may prevent us from encountering God at work in them and through them. It may also be a day to challenge some of the assumptions we have about ourselves, a day to be expectant about what Christ can do in us and through us by the power of the Holy Spirit.

God our Father,
who from the family of your servant David
raised up Joseph the carpenter
to be the guardian of your incarnate Son
and husband of the Blessed Virgin Mary:
give us grace to follow him
in faithful obedience to your commands;
through Jesus Christ your Son our Lord,
who is alive and reigns with you,
in the unity of the Holy Spirit,
one God, now and for ever.

COLLECT

Reflection by **Rachel Treweek**

Monday 21 March

Genesis 47.1-27

'... few and hard have been the years of my life' (v.9)

Today's reading foreshadows the history of redemption. It first has Jacob's family migrating to Egypt and coming under Pharaoh's protection. It then has Joseph enslaving the entire population of Egypt as famine engulfs the land. So Israel goes down into Egypt and yet, in the person of Joseph, prevails over the Egyptians. But that victory is here only prefigured. (It may also make us morally squeamish.) The true victory will come with Moses and the Exodus.

At the heart of faith is a story of slavery and freedom. Human experience is a struggle for survival, and nature is not benign, as the famine in Egypt demonstrates. We are all limited by forces beyond ourselves and have to seek to make the best of our few years on earth. However good our intentions may be, our actions have unforeseen consequences. There were good reasons for Jacob's family to migrate to Goshen, but we already know they will end up enslaved and oppressed.

We should consider today how far we have participated in the oppression of others through ignorance, weakness and our own deliberate fault. We should also reflect on any oppressions we have internalized, to our own and others' harm.

What talents and skills do we bring to the wellbeing of those around us and to their flourishing and freedom?

COLLECT

Almighty God,
whose most dear Son went not up to joy
    but first he suffered pain,
and entered not into glory before he was crucified:
mercifully grant that we, walking in the way of the cross,
may find it none other than the way of life and peace;
through Jesus Christ your Son our Lord,
who is alive and reigns with you,
in the unity of the Holy Spirit,
one God, now and for ever.

| *Reflection by* **Angela Tilby**

Psalms 6, **9** *or* **5**, 6 (8)
Genesis 47.28 – end of 48
Hebrews 5.11 – 6.12

Tuesday 22 March

Genesis 47.28 – end of 48

'God Almighty appeared to me … in the land of Canaan' (48.3)

The story of Jacob's blessing of Joseph's sons has some confusing features, but we can discern a repeat of the pattern that has already emerged in earlier stories about Jacob. Jacob adopts Joseph's two sons, giving them a place within the tribes of Israel. But then, just as Jacob, the younger son, was preferred over the older son, Esau, so Joseph's younger son, Ephraim, is preferred over Manasseh.

Scripture is full of these jarring moments, and they point to the activities of a God who constantly points beyond human preference and tradition in enacting salvation. God will not be confined to human rules and traditions, no matter how time-honoured and respected they are.

Today's reading also has Jacob pleading to be buried in Bethlehem, in the land of Canaan where his beloved wife Rachel died. Before he makes this request, he tells Joseph of his encounter with God at Haran (Genesis 28.10-32) in the vision of the heavenly staircase and the angels. God does not forget us in old age, as we draw near to death. It is often here that the meaning of our lives is revealed to us and passed on to the next generation.

In a society that often seems to find death unacceptable, how do we prepare for a good death?

Eternal God,
give us insight
to discern your will for us,
to give up what harms us,
and to seek the perfection we are promised
in Jesus Christ our Lord.

COLLECT

Wednesday 23 March

Psalm **38** or **119.1-32**
Genesis 49.1-32
Hebrews 6.13-end

Genesis 49.1-32

'The sceptre shall not depart from Judah ...' (v.10)

Jacob's dying wish is to preserve continuity, and so preserve the promise of God to his descendants. Jacob's last words are a series of predictions about the character and fate of the twelve tribes. As one who has shown in his lifetime a blend of faithfulness and deceit, Jacob has some penetrating insights into the characters of his progeny. They will not all enjoy a happy and prosperous future. As with any family, some members will bring glory to the family name while others bring shame.

The Bible does not idealize the chosen people. The twelve tribes are not exceptional; their legacy is as full of human violence and error as it is of obedience and blessing. The tribe of Judah will carry on the faith of Israel into the future. This is a hint of the Messiah's future reign.

During Lent, it is worth reflecting on our own family history and on what we have inherited for good or ill. Is there a patriarchal or matriarchal figure who looms large in family history? And has their effect been benign or destructive?

Jacob's predictions are his blessings. Whether for good or ill, he cares for his sons individually. Our family and tribal identity may be important, but God knows us intimately, by name.

COLLECT

Almighty God,
whose most dear Son went not up to joy
    but first he suffered pain,
and entered not into glory before he was crucified:
mercifully grant that we, walking in the way of the cross,
may find it none other than the way of life and peace;
through Jesus Christ your Son our Lord,
who is alive and reigns with you,
in the unity of the Holy Spirit,
one God, now and for ever.

| *Reflection by* **Angela Tilby**

Psalms **56**, 57 *or* 14, **15**, 16
Genesis 49.33 – end of 50
Hebrews 7.1-10

Thursday 24 March

Genesis 49.33 – end of 50

*'... though you intended to do harm to me, God intended it
for good' (v.20)*

After a significant death there are often complicated family
emotions to be played out. The death of Jacob is no exception. In
spite of the years they have been settled in the land of Goshen,
Joseph's brothers are still plagued with guilt going back to their
original plot to kill him, and then, when this was foiled, their casual
selling of him into slavery (chapter 37). Guilt is not easily admitted,
and the brothers make up a story suggesting Jacob has begged him
to forgive them. When Joseph weeps, it is not clear whether he is
moved by his father's supposed plea or by his brothers' continued
deceit.

In the end it doesn't matter. When there is a heart to forgive, simple
contrition is enough. A clinical reckoning of wrongs is beside the
point as the currency of forgiveness is new life, not point scoring.
Joseph's willingness to forgive his brothers is enough, and he readily
provides for their continuity and wellbeing.

Lent is a season of repentance and forgiveness. Are there ancient
family wrongs in our lives waiting to be forgiven? What steps can
we take to acknowledge them and put them right? The opportunity
will not be there for ever. But if we take the time at least to
acknowledge what is wrong, we may find liberation and blessing.

Eternal God,
give us insight
to discern your will for us,
to give up what harms us,
and to seek the perfection we are promised
in Jesus Christ our Lord.

COLLECT

Reflection by **Angela Tilby**   109

Friday 25 March

Annunciation of Our Lord
to the Blessed Virgin Mary

Psalms 111, 113
1 Samuel 2.1-10
Romans 5.12-end

1 Samuel 2.1-10

'The Lord ... brings low, he also exalts' (v.7)

Today's reading is chosen for the Feast of the Annunciation. Hannah, the once barren wife of Elkanah, has prayed for a child and her prayer has been answered. Her little son's name, Samuel, means 'asked of the Lord'. Her song of triumph prefigures Mary's Magnificat (Luke 1.46-55), introducing phrases that are almost identical to that of Mary's song.

There are major differences, however. Hannah had pleaded with God for a child; Mary was not expecting the angel's call and was troubled by it. Hannah's response was unambiguous joy; Mary, 'with child from the Holy Spirit', faced the possibility of shame and exclusion. But in spite of these differences, the Song of Hannah and the Song of Mary express a similar response of sheer delight in God's readiness to hear the cry of the poor and humble.

Prayer begins in a recognition of our need of God. We come to God not in the strength of our achievements, but in our littleness and insignificance. However important our daily work, however necessary we are to those around us, there is a part of us that is empty, needy, small in every sense. That is where God's Spirit prays in us and where God comes to make his home in us, and where our lives become truly fruitful. Rejoice in God your Saviour!

COLLECT

We beseech you, O Lord,
pour your grace into our hearts,
that as we have known the incarnation of your Son Jesus Christ
    by the message of an angel,
so by his cross and passion
we may be brought to the glory of his resurrection;
through Jesus Christ your Son our Lord,
who is alive and reigns with you,
in the unity of the Holy Spirit,
one God, now and for ever.

| *Reflection by* **Angela Tilby**

Psalm **31** *or* 20, 21, **23**
Exodus 1.22 – 2.10
Hebrews 8

Saturday 26 March

Exodus 1.22 – 2.10

'I drew him out of the water' (v.10)

It is appropriate to read from the book of Exodus in the weeks before Easter. In the cycle of the Christian year, we are being brought to encounter the dark side of our nature, our captivity to habits and limitations we have imposed on ourselves and which others have imposed on us.

So we read of the Hebrew people in captivity in Egypt. Any newborn male offspring is under sentence of death. The preservation of the baby Moses is orchestrated by women: his mother and sister, the daughter of Pharaoh and her attendants. There is nothing obviously miraculous about the protection given to Moses. It comes about as a result of cunning, watchfulness, kindness and care.

Moses stands here for the future of God's people and for hope. We know that Moses will grow up to become Israel's saviour and deliverer. But at this stage he is helpless. His future depends on the faithfulness of those who simply will not let him die, who in the midst of deep oppression and violence, choose life.

This fundamental choice of life is significant for all of us. What today would we guard at all costs, refuse to let go of, protect and preserve against all adversaries? Our answer may tell us something about where our true vocation lies and what we should concentrate on in our work and leisure this weekend.

Eternal God,
give us insight
to discern your will for us,
to give up what harms us,
and to seek the perfection we are promised
in Jesus Christ our Lord.

COLLECT

Reflection by **Angela Tilby**

Monday 28 March

Psalms 70, **77** or 27, **30**
Exodus 2.11-22
Hebrews 9.1-14

Exodus 2.11-22

'I have been an alien residing in a foreign land' (v. 22)

It is not clear from today's reading how Moses came to understand that he was the child of a slave race and not an Egyptian prince. It can be assumed that his mother must have told him, but he was still brought up as the son of Pharaoh's daughter.

In the New Testament, Moses' identification with his suffering people is seen as an archetype of what it means to suffer for Christ (Hebrews 11.23-26). Yet this was not a choice so much as a revelation. It is the casual beating up of a Hebrew slave by an Egyptian overseer that brings Moses, violently, to an awareness of his true identity. By killing the Egyptian, he discovered who he was. Yet coming to terms with this was not easy. Even after he had fled from Egypt, the daughters of the priest of Midian made the assumption that he was an Egyptian.

This passage is a reminder that Christian vocation often begins in a murky place, and it is sometimes brought into focus through threat and disaster. The birth of Moses' son suggests that it took time for him to recognize that he had a task ahead. He has been alien in two senses, both in Egypt as a Hebrew and from Egypt during his time in Midian. The wake-up call is at hand.

COLLECT

Merciful Lord,
absolve your people from their offences,
that through your bountiful goodness
we may all be delivered from the chains of those sins
which by our frailty we have committed;
grant this, heavenly Father,
for Jesus Christ's sake, our blessed Lord and Saviour,
who is alive and reigns with you,
in the unity of the Holy Spirit,
one God, now and for ever.

Reflection by **Angela Tilby**

Tuesday 29 March

Exodus 2.23 – 3.20

'And he said, "Here I am."' (3.4)

This is one of the most extraordinary and powerful passages of Scripture. God's disclosure to Moses of his true name and his saving intention is fundamental to both Jewish and Christian faith. Historically, this is often considered to be the original moment of divine revelation, pre-dating the patriarchal stories that have come down to us more in the form of saga or myth than history.

The core of it is that God is mystery. No one knows precisely what the Hebrew consonants of his name mean, and in Jewish tradition, the name must never be vocalized. God is ultimately free and sovereign. We cannot control or contain God. Yet this mysterious 'I am' chooses to liberate his people and to make Moses the agent of his deliverance.

Our Christian identity is bound up with our personal relationship with God. The God who is mystery, whose name cannot be spoken, addresses us by name, knowing us far more deeply than we can ever know ourselves and seeing potential in us that is far different from what we might imagine. Moses is not everyone's idea of a hero. He is full of doubt and questioning, fully aware of his past, exiled even from his place of exile. He is simply not the stuff leaders are made of. And yet ...

What resonances are there here with your own experience of Christian call and obedience?

Merciful Lord,
you know our struggle to serve you:
when sin spoils our lives
and overshadows our hearts,
come to our aid
and turn us back to you again;
through Jesus Christ our Lord.

COLLECT

Reflection by **Angela Tilby**

Wednesday 30 March

Exodus 4.1-23

'I will be with your mouth and teach you what you are to speak'
(v.12)

Moses needs to be prepared for the task ahead. He has to be trained for the job, and God is presented here as his 'personal trainer' in a series of exercises that are both physically and mentally demanding.

What the training reveals is Moses' insecurity. The miracles of the staff and of the sudden leprosy suggest Moses has to understand both his fear and his inner violence. His stammer makes him unfit in his own eyes to be God's messenger to Pharaoh. God engages with Moses angrily, and yet the anger gives way to care and a readiness to compromise. Having Aaron as a mouthpiece will not be an unmixed blessing to Moses (think ahead to the incident of the Golden Calf in chapter 32!), but for now God is prepared for Moses to have a representative to speak his words.

God's training comes with a warning: Pharaoh will not listen to Moses' request to let the people go. The story that follows is one of persistence and determination. Moses has to learn as he goes along. He does not have natural gifts of confidence or charisma. Yet as he takes the first step of obedience in leaving Midian, he is learning to trust his divine trainer.

COLLECT

Merciful Lord,
absolve your people from their offences,
that through your bountiful goodness
we may all be delivered from the chains of those sins
which by our frailty we have committed;
grant this, heavenly Father,
for Jesus Christ's sake, our blessed Lord and Saviour,
who is alive and reigns with you,
in the unity of the Holy Spirit,
one God, now and for ever.

| *Reflection by* **Angela Tilby**

Psalms 53, **86** *or* **37***
Exodus 4.27 – 6.1
Hebrews 10.19-25

Thursday 31 March

Exodus 4.27 – 6.1

'... by a mighty hand he will let them go' (6.1)

So, at the time of year when we are trudging through Lent, we begin to read the saga of Israel's deliverance from salvery, a foreshadowing of our deliverance from sin and death at Easter. The struggle for freedom is a long one. Pharaoh justifies his oppression by insisting that he 'does not know the Lord' and therefore has no responsibility towards his people.

We recognize here the strategy of present-day tyrants who stir up resentment against hard-pressed minorities. Again, like demagogues of our own time, Pharaoh secretly fears the people he is oppressing and calculates that they will be more effectively subdued if their task is made impossible. This sparks further protest, which, in turn, deepens the oppression. Inevitably, the people turn on Moses and Aaron who have raised their hopes in vain. Never a natural leader, Moses has little resilience when he meets opposition, and he turns to God in complaint. God's response is to reassert his promise: Pharaoh will let the people go.

The Exodus story has inspired protest movements in our own time. It gives a model of how oppressed people come to understand their own oppression and challenge it. This requires both courage and faith. The oppressor is never as strong as he appears.

What are the obstacles that we face that seem immovable, the forces that restrict our freedom in Christ?

Merciful Lord,
you know our struggle to serve you:
when sin spoils our lives
and overshadows our hearts,
come to our aid
and turn us back to you again;
through Jesus Christ our Lord.

COLLECT

Reflection by **Angela Tilby** | 115

Friday 1 April

Psalms **102** *or* **31**
Exodus 6.2-13
Hebrews 10.26-end

Exodus 6.2-13

'I will take you as my people, and I will be your God' (v.7)

This chapter begins a new phase in God's relationship with his captive people as God promises to draw them into a personal covenant with himself and give them the land promised to the patriarchs. This is God's sovereign choice and will eventually be enacted at Sinai after the escape from Egypt.

It is poignantly sad that this sign of favour is not received by the people. They are simply too broken to listen. When God instructs Moses to approach Pharaoh again with the demand to let his people go, Moses is reluctant and even seems to blame himself for the people's indifference to God's promise.

When life is strained by suffering or injustice it becomes impossible to hear news of hope. It is almost easier to plod on in despair than to be open to what might turn out to be another disappointment.

The Christian life does not guarantee that we shall not at times be overwhelmed. What it does guarantee is that God does not reject us or forget us. Even as the people are languishing in misery, Moses and Aaron are being trained for their next confrontation with Pharaoh. The powers of darkness are sometimes overwhelming, but even they will eventually yield to the truth and mercy of God.

COLLECT

Merciful Lord,
absolve your people from their offences,
that through your bountiful goodness
we may all be delivered from the chains of those sins
which by our frailty we have committed;
grant this, heavenly Father,
for Jesus Christ's sake, our blessed Lord and Saviour,
who is alive and reigns with you,
in the unity of the Holy Spirit,
one God, now and for ever.

Reflection by **Angela Tilby**

Psalm **32** *or* 41, **42**, 43
Exodus 7.8-end
Hebrews 11.1-16

Exodus 7.8-end

'By this you shall know that I am the Lord' (v.17)

The long process of wearing down Pharaoh's resistance begins. God demonstrates through Moses and Aaron that his divine powers over life and death are greater than anything Pharaoh can imitate, although he and his magicians will try their best. Moses' turning of the river water to blood was a strike at the heart of Pharaoh's power and prosperity, for the fertility of the land depended entirely on the great River Nile.

Pharaoh's indifference even to his own people's welfare is revealed by the imitative tricks of his own sorcerors. He wants to demonstrate his strength and simply doesn't care that his people are left scrabbling for water.

What is being shown is the fragility of those who claim to be all-powerful. Narcissistic egoism eventually undermines itself. When we find ourselves up against authority that is all about ego, we need to remember that the appearance of strength often masks inner weakness. If you know your weakness and depend on God, you will ultimately prevail.

How does this affect your prayer today, especially for those who wield power? How would you pray for those who are mistreated by irresponsible leaders? And how might you demonstrate the power made perfect in our human weakness for the sake of those who are unjustly oppressed?

Merciful Lord,
you know our struggle to serve you:
when sin spoils our lives
and overshadows our hearts,
come to our aid
and turn us back to you again;
through Jesus Christ our Lord.

COLLECT

Reflection by **Angela Tilby**   117

Monday 4 April

Psalms **73**, 121 *or* **44**
Exodus 8.1-19
Hebrews 11.17-31

Exodus 8.1-19

'If you refuse to let them go, I will plague your whole country with frogs' (v.2)

This is glorious knockabout stuff. There's a goody (Moses) and a baddy (Pharaoh), and in the struggle to see who wins, the goody has the advantage of having incredible magic powers, whereas the baddy has the upper hand because he's the boss. The irony, of course, is that we know who is going to win in the end – and it's not the boss.

So, how can we imaginatively enter this story? Perhaps in the way it was originally intended, as a tall story, to be told in a darkened room late at night with firelight flickering on the walls – as a 'Once upon a time' story, a fairy tale.

Or, maybe we can enter it, as might also have been intended, as a saga. Sagas need to be told where lots of people gather to listen to a storyteller who, with sweeping gestures and a thunderous voice, enraptures us with the rhythm of the narrative. We are taken out of the here-and-now and transported to a world of danger and delight.

But suppose that a truth is lurking in the story-saga and in the fairy tale: a truth about God. Could it be that at the heart of all great stories lies the Original Story? The Word behind and within the words – words that, like the most haunting music, lift us into a new place and help us to see, even if only for a moment, the power and majesty and infinite possibility of God.

COLLECT

Most merciful God,
who by the death and resurrection of your Son Jesus Christ
delivered and saved the world:
grant that by faith in him who suffered on the cross
we may triumph in the power of his victory;
through Jesus Christ your Son our Lord,
who is alive and reigns with you,
in the unity of the Holy Spirit,
one God, now and for ever.

| *Reflection by* **Christopher Herbert**

Psalms **35**, 123 *or* **48**, 52
Exodus 8.20-end
Hebrews 11.32 – 12.2

Tuesday 5 April

Exodus 8.20-end

'Then the Lord said to Moses, "Rise early in the morning and present yourself before Pharaoh"' (v.20)

Political subtlety now enters the story. Moses waylays Pharaoh as he is going down to the river. In the world of the media, ambushing your victim to get an interview is known as 'door-stepping'; anyone who has been on the receiving end of it will know how irritating and threatening it can be. Moses is being ruthlessly crafty.

But a night passes – filled with the tormenting buzzing of flies. Pharaoh thinks things through and knows that he must get the upper hand again. So, he summons Moses and Aaron and offers them a deal: to go into the wilderness to make a sacrifice, on condition that they must return.

Politically, it's risky. What if Moses and Aaron and their followers don't come back? Pharaoh weighs it up and decides the risk is worth taking. Fortunately, Moses, Aaron and their people keep their promise and return. Pharaoh is back on top, except, of course, as we know, he isn't.

This is a story that subtly twists and turns. No doubt the actions of Moses, as presented by the author, are designed to be emulated. It calls to mind Jesus' injunction about being wise as serpents and innocent as doves.

So, now recall any negotiations you have ever been involved in. Would you class yourself as astute, like the serpent, or innocent, like the dove? But perhaps our task is not to be either like the serpent or like the dove, rather to be both.

COLLECT

Gracious Father,
you gave up your Son
out of love for the world:
lead us to ponder the mysteries of his passion,
that we may know eternal peace
through the shedding of our Saviour's blood,
Jesus Christ our Lord.

Reflection by **Christopher Herbert** | 119

Wednesday 6 April

Psalms **55**, 124 *or* **119.57-80**
Exodus 9.1-12
Hebrews 12.3-13

Exodus 9.1-12

'Then the Lord said ... "Take handfuls of soot from the kiln"' (v.8)

Here comes divine retribution: a pandemic caused by something as simple as soot from a chimney...

If this were a fairy story, the morality would not matter, because justice and goodness would win in the end. But if we see the story from the point of view of the Egyptians, it becomes horrific and completely unjust. This god, the god of Moses, is apparently all-powerful but is also entirely amoral. Pharaoh is being obdurate and is made so because the Lord (note this) has created him that way. And, because Pharaoh won't give in, everyone gets it in the neck, literally with a plague of boils. This painful, inflammatory skin condition miraculously does not affect Moses and his people but invades everyone in the host community.

It is not the fantastical content of the story that is bothersome – one can cope with that; it's the implied theology that is so impossible. Let's get this straight. Our moral outrage consists of two things: first, the gross injustice of the entire population of Egypt suffering, and second, the Lord himself deliberately causing Pharaoh to be obtuse by 'hardening his heart'. In our terms, therefore, it is the Lord who is morally culpable.

No amount of casuistry will prevent us seeing this. This leaves us in a deep quandary. If we cannot tolerate such unjust behaviour, even in a story, what can we do about it, apart from just noting the fact? The answer lies in Christ, in whom the true justice at the heart of God was revealed.

COLLECT

Most merciful God,
who by the death and resurrection of your Son Jesus Christ
delivered and saved the world:
grant that by faith in him who suffered on the cross
we may triumph in the power of his victory;
through Jesus Christ your Son our Lord,
who is alive and reigns with you,
in the unity of the Holy Spirit,
one God, now and for ever.

| *Reflection by* **Christopher Herbert**

Psalms **40**, 125 *or* 56, **57** (63*)
Exodus 9.13-end
Hebrews 12.14-end

Thursday 7 April

Exodus 9.13-end

*'Those officials of Pharaoh who feared the word of the Lord
hurried their slaves and livestock off to a secure place' (v.20)*

And now there is dissension in the Egyptian court. Some believe very readily in the threats being made by Moses; others take no notice. There's no longer a common front, and with division comes the faint possibility, from Moses' point of view, of success. But it is not just the success of leading his people out of slavery, it is a theological victory that is almost within sight.

You will have noticed that when Moses addresses Pharaoh, he refers to his message of liberation as one he has been given by the 'God of the Hebrews'. In a country with many gods – including Amun, the king of the gods, and Isis, the protector goddess – the God of the Hebrews would have been regarded as a little, local, tribal deity. Nothing to worry about. However, the message from Moses is that the God of the Hebrews is like no other: '... there is no one like me in all the earth'.

This is a titanic struggle. It is not just about the freedom of the Hebrew slaves but is also about the very nature of the Divine. Preposterous as it must have sounded, the argument is that what others might regard as a tiny, unimportant god, is actually the God above all gods, the Creator of the Universe, the one who has chosen a slave-people to be the carriers of his Name for evermore.

It is worth considering, therefore, whether our own concept of God is too small.

Gracious Father,
you gave up your Son
out of love for the world:
lead us to ponder the mysteries of his passion,
that we may know eternal peace
through the shedding of our Saviour's blood,
Jesus Christ our Lord.

COLLECT

Reflection by **Christopher Herbert**

Friday 8 April

Psalms **22**, 126 *or* **51**, 54
Exodus 10
Hebrews 13.1-16

Exodus 10

'... a darkness that can be felt' (v.21)

Sometimes, in sagas that have been written by many authors, as the plague stories appear to have been, there is a flash of poetry. So it is in today's reading with the phrase 'a darkness that can be felt'. It is difficult in our overlit, urbanized world to experience real darkness, but if you have been caving, you will know that when you turn off your helmet-light deep underground, the darkness is total. Even so, disorientating though the experience is, it is not a darkness that can be 'felt'. The darkness of a cave is thinner than that.

But a darkness that can be felt is a different matter. It is the darkness of nightmares. The darkness that has an inchoate shape. The darkness in the depths of our being. It was perhaps a darkness of soul containing intense uncertainty that was beginning to trouble Pharaoh. He starts to shout and threaten.

The long drama of the plagues is obviously moving to a climax. The two adversaries have been battling with each other for some time, and only with an assertion of naked power can Pharaoh retain control.

For those of us who try to follow Christ, there are also moments of deep darkness – an emptiness, a barrenness of soul, an absence that is like a presence. Unable to feel our way forward, we are reduced to doing nothing. Kneeling in a darkness so dense it can be felt, all we can do is to await the light of grace.

COLLECT

Most merciful God,
who by the death and resurrection of your Son Jesus Christ
delivered and saved the world:
grant that by faith in him who suffered on the cross
we may triumph in the power of his victory;
through Jesus Christ your Son our Lord,
who is alive and reigns with you,
in the unity of the Holy Spirit,
one God, now and for ever.

| *Reflection by* **Christopher Herbert**

Psalms **23**, 127 *or* **68**
Exodus 11
Hebrews 13.17-end

Saturday 9 April

Exodus 11

'... so that you may know that the Lord makes a distinction between Egypt and Israel' (v.7)

It is a question about choice. If you believe that God chose the people of Israel and established a special and everlasting covenant with them, then this story fits into that overarching narrative. But remember that this is a story. It is not history. It is not journalistic reportage. It is a story written down many centuries after the events it purports to describe.

So why was it written when it was written? Some scholars argue that the stories of Moses represent an ancient oral tradition; they point out that the name 'Moses' is very like other Egyptian names. Others argue that the various author-editors of the book of Exodus adapted those oral traditions and, in the eighth century BC, or maybe even later, wove them into a coherent narrative about Israel's early origins. Perhaps they did this at a time when Israel felt it was under external military threat, a time when God's special relationship with a legendary hero might have had a morale-boosting contemporary relevance. We cannot be sure.

What is abundantly clear is that it is a story both about the almighty power of the Divine and also about the choice of a special people. Nothing and no one, not even a Pharaoh, can get in the way of that special covenantal relationship.

So, suppose that, through Jesus, God has extended that original covenant. Does God continue to call and challenge people? Can we stand in the way of that call? How shall we respond?

Gracious Father,
you gave up your Son
out of love for the world:
lead us to ponder the mysteries of his passion,
that we may know eternal peace
through the shedding of our Saviour's blood,
Jesus Christ our Lord.

COLLECT

Reflection by **Christopher Herbert**   123

Monday 11 April
Monday of Holy Week

Psalm 41
Lamentations 1.1-12*a*
Luke 22.1-23

Lamentations 1.1-12*a*

'Look and see if there is any sorrow like my sorrow' (v.12)

The picture that today's reading presents is not just about abandoned streets and closed shops. There is more going on than a lockdown. Jerusalem after its people have been deported by the Babylonians is left violated, humiliated: the shocking image is of a woman who has been raped by enemy soldiers, left in torn clothes, sobbing with pain and terror.

The harrowing poems that make up the book of Lamentations convey the sense of disbelieving horror that must have overwhelmed those who witnessed the city's capture and the brutal expulsion of its people. It highlights the question: 'Is God to be trusted?'

The Holy Week journey begins uncompromisingly with the moment when the answer seems to be 'No'. It prompts us to think not just about human suffering in general, but about that very specific kind of suffering that has to do with betrayal and desertion. 'Look and see', insists the poet: don't look away, don't make light of this cry from the depths.

But we need to remember: *this is the Word of the Lord*. The anguished crying of those who are betrayed and believe they are forgotten, unseen and unheard, becomes God's call to us – so that the terrible betrayal and abuse of human beings is not God's betrayal of us but ours of God. Refusing to 'look and see', to acknowledge the pain of those doubly betrayed by being hurt *and* being silenced, is turning from God. Hard as it is, looking honestly at this is a turning to him; a conversion.

COLLECT

Almighty and everlasting God,
who in your tender love towards the human race
    sent your Son our Saviour Jesus Christ
to take upon him our flesh
and to suffer death upon the cross:
grant that we may follow the example of his patience and humility,
and also be made partakers of his resurrection;
through Jesus Christ your Son our Lord,
who is alive and reigns with you,
in the unity of the Holy Spirit,
one God, now and for ever.

| *Reflection by* **Rowan Williams**

Psalm 27
Lamentations 3.1-18
Luke 22. [24-38] 39-53

Tuesday 12 April
Tuesday of Holy Week

Lamentations 3.1-18

'... he has made me dwell in darkness' (v.6, RSV)

It feels sometimes as though God is the real enemy. He has lured us into trusting in him, and now our confidence is shown to be empty. The poet's mind and heart are described as if they were a city under siege, a soldier under fire. He is exposed to the derision of those who never took the risk of faith in the first place.

As the chapter unfolds, the poet's voice shifts bit by bit. He has been silenced – not by human indifference and cruelty, like the tragic voice we heard in the first chapter, but by the sheer impossibility of making anything melodious and eloquent out of the world as it really is.

Patience: don't think you have a formula that will make it all easier. Sit with the reality of this pain and chaos beyond your control. Don't tidy it up to suit yourself.

Perhaps all you're left with is hope. And perhaps the readiness to stay and not turn away or tidy up hints at how we could think of God himself. It is not at all that he has set out to inflict pain; but in a world where pain happens, he is never pushed out or immobilised.

To come anywhere near grasping this, we have to let go of any confidence that we can make satisfying sense of things by our own effort and ingenuity. We must share the loss and disorientation of the most vulnerable – the cities under siege, the soldiers under fire. Silence; but a knowledge – *in* the silence – of something not defeated.

COLLECT

> True and humble king,
> hailed by the crowd as Messiah:
> grant us the faith to know you and love you,
> that we may be found beside you
> on the way of the cross,
> which is the path of glory.

Reflection by **Rowan Williams** | 125

Wednesday 13 April
Wednesday of Holy Week

Psalm 102 [or 102.1-18]
Wisdom 1.16 – 2.1; 2.12-22
or Jeremiah 11.18-20
Luke 22.54-end

Jeremiah 11.18-20

'... that his name will no longer be remembered!' (v.19)

The prophet's enemies want to make sure that he is not *remembered*. The fact that he spoke of judgement and hope, that he named the wounds and the violence and the urgent summons of God in the midst of it all – this must be forgotten. There is not really that much wrong with the world – or if there is, it is someone else's problem, someone else's business. And the crying of the violated and abused is at worst a matter of sad 'noises off', not the word of the Lord.

The prophet walks into the trap. He has no strategy or defence but the truth of what he sees and hears, what has been shown him. He is not there to advance a theory, but to witness to the God whose silent working in the heart of things never disappears. So the prophet's guileless simplicity of response puts him at mortal risk.

Yet it is only his simple wholeness of seeing and hearing that makes him a true prophet. If he wraps it up with his own agenda and his own security, he stops showing the truth in its nakedness. His witness would come and go like that of others.

But it's because he is exposed to God, fearlessly open to God, that what he says and what he shows can't be forgotten, whether he lives or dies. He has bound himself to the truth; and the living truth binds itself to him, and makes his memory live and his words keep on piercing the heart.

COLLECT

Almighty and everlasting God,
who in your tender love towards the human race
    sent your Son our Saviour Jesus Christ
to take upon him our flesh
and to suffer death upon the cross:
grant that we may follow the example of his patience and humility,
and also be made partakers of his resurrection;
through Jesus Christ your Son our Lord,
who is alive and reigns with you,
in the unity of the Holy Spirit,
one God, now and for ever.

Reflection by **Rowan Williams**

Psalms 42, 43
Leviticus 16.2-24
Luke 23.1-25

Thursday 14 April
Maundy Thursday

Leviticus 16.2-24

'He shall ... send him away into the wilderness' (v.21, RSV)

The strange and haunting ritual described seems at first sight to suggest that for things to be healed and renewed, the past has to be sent away. The scapegoat carries the people's sins out of sight, into the remote desert.

But this does not mean that the past is just obliterated. This is a ritual of *healing*. Before the goat is sent away, the priest has recited over its head the record of failure and injury and rebellion. We're not told to forget, but to remember in a way that makes us able to be free. Our sins and our wounds are named, not ignored, as we saw yesterday with the words of the prophet; and then they are set in the context where they can be healed.

In Hebrew Scripture, the desert is the place where God's people can begin again, where the familiar protections are taken away so that God's call can be heard. So the scapegoat takes into that empty and comfortless place all the memories of hurts given and received, of anger, fear, rejection. In the harsh light of the desert, these things are stripped bare to the life and love of God. In this light we can see the true weight and cost of saying no to God and each other. And we remember the God whose purpose is atonement, making us 'at one' both with the divine life and with the life of the world we share.

'Do this in remembrance.' Be at one, in service and communion.

True and humble king,
hailed by the crowd as Messiah:
grant us the faith to know you and love you,
that we may be found beside you
on the way of the cross,
which is the path of glory.

COLLECT

Reflection by **Rowan Williams** | 127

Friday 15 April
Good Friday

Psalm 69
Genesis 22.1-18
John 19.38-end
or Hebrews 10.1-10

Genesis 22.1-18

'I will indeed bless you' (v.17)

All through the week's readings, we have been reminded of how deep the suspicion is that God is our enemy: how could we not suspect it, in a world as brutal as this? Today's story brings this right into the spotlight. The God Abraham has trusted suddenly demands a death, the death of what Abraham holds most precious, what speaks to him most directly of God's faithfulness.

So what does God want? Life or death?

All through the week's readings we have also been reminded of how we rediscover God's presence and freedom just when everything else falls away. Here too, it is as Abraham faces this most dreadful of deaths that suddenly what bursts upon him is the God who does not want death but life.

It's as though Abraham has to feel the unbearable *gravity* and preciousness of a human life, as he imagines the nightmare of being responsible for the death of the person he most loves, before he can see fully what human life means to *God* – how, in God's eyes, every human life is the life of a child loved without limit, for whom no risk, no cost, is too great.

So precious are human selves to God that God does not crush human freedom even at its most deluded and violent, and yet at one and the same time draws back the veil from his face to show the love that will not let go – of Abraham or Isaac or you and me. His will, his *passion*, is life for the world.

COLLECT

Almighty Father,
look with mercy on this your family
for which our Lord Jesus Christ was content to be betrayed
    and given up into the hands of sinners
    and to suffer death upon the cross;
who is alive and glorified with you and the Holy Spirit,
one God, now and for ever.

Reflection by **Rowan Williams**

Psalm 142
Hosea 6.1-6
John 2.18-22

Saturday 16 April
Easter Eve

Hosea 6.1-6

'I desire steadfast love' (v.6)

We have been 'hewn', cut deeply, like stones from a quarry, by the words of the prophets. We have been invited to look at the violence and horror of the human world without any attempt to soften it – and to put into words the terrible suspicion that God is hostile or absent. We have been shown the full cost of human cruelty and rejection. We have been pushed to see more clearly the truth of human pain and human sin. It cuts deep.

At the heart of it all is, again and again, a revelation of something more than we can really imagine: the deeper truth that God cannot and will not be torn away from his creation. The future that God promises can't be imagined or controlled, but it is as sure as the expectation of the spring rains.

Within and beneath everything in creation is God's passion for life and joy. Nothing can separate us from this. And nothing can tear God away from the One who is the greatest of the prophets, the Son that God loves, the Word who is eternally with God. In the humanity which he lives out on earth, he absorbs the world's violence and hatred without ever passing it on. He does not crush or deny our dangerous freedom. And so he remains in his Father's heart, anchored in eternal love and life.

Death itself cannot defeat this. And if we come to stand where he stands, living in his Spirit, death cannot defeat us. We shall live before him.

COLLECT

Grant, Lord,
that we who are baptized into the death
of your Son our Saviour Jesus Christ
may continually put to death our evil desires
and be buried with him;
and that through the grave and gate of death
we may pass to our joyful resurrection;
through his merits,
who died and was buried and rose again for us,
your Son Jesus Christ our Lord.

Reflection by **Rowan Williams** | 129

Monday 18 April

Monday of Easter Week

Psalms 111, 117, 146
Exodus 12.1-14
1 Corinthians 15.1-11

1 Corinthians 15.1-11

'Now I should remind you, brothers and sisters, of the good news...' (v.1)

Paul helpfully condenses the gospel into a few short verses here for us in what is the earliest summary of the post-resurrection accounts of Jesus. He reminds the Corinthian church of the central message of their faith which he has already proclaimed to them: that Jesus died for our sins, was buried and rose from the dead. Many saw him in the flesh including Cephas, James, the apostles and many more. And of course, Paul encountered the resurrected Christ for himself as well.

Paul rests the authority of this gospel message on three supports – the evidence of Scripture, the testimony of others and individual experience. All of these are of equal significance to Paul – 'Whether then it was I or they...' he says. In affirming the gospel message in this way, Paul also outlines the Christian life. This is a life that is rooted in the Scriptures, bolstered by community and enriched by the individual encounter with the living God.

In Eastertide, we have an opportunity to encounter both the living God and this Christian life, in a new way. Do you value these three elements – the Scriptures, Christian community, individual encounter with God – in the same way? Perhaps now is a good time to seek out a balance in these three things, picking up your Bible, committing to Church, seeking out God for yourself. These things renew our faith.

COLLECT

Lord of all life and power,
who through the mighty resurrection of your Son
overcame the old order of sin and death
to make all things new in him:
grant that we, being dead to sin
and alive to you in Jesus Christ,
may reign with him in glory;
to whom with you and the Holy Spirit
be praise and honour, glory and might,
now and in all eternity.

| *Reflection by* **Karen O'Donnell**

Psalms 112, 147.1-12
Exodus 12.14-36
1 Corinthians 15.12-19

Tuesday 19 April
Tuesday of Easter Week

1 Corinthians 15.12-19

'If for this life only we have hoped in Christ, we are of all people most to be pitied' (v.19)

Some people in the Corinthian church have been saying that there is no resurrection of the dead. Writing around 15 years after the death and resurrection of Christ, but only two or three years after the establishment of the church in Corinth, perhaps they had seen their first believers die, be buried and remain dead, much to their disappointment.

Paul reminds us that believing in the resurrection of the dead, and Jesus' own resurrection specifically, is of central importance to our faith. It is not an optional extra to be ditched when it seems too difficult to continue believing in it. If Jesus is not resurrected then our faith is pointless and we are to be pitied if we only have faith and hope in Christ during this life.

It is, of course, relatively easy to have confidence in Christ when things are all going well. But when life takes a trickier turn, we might have to reconsider what it means to believe in a resurrected Saviour and to have hope in Jesus. In the darkness of despair, it might be all we can do to light a small candle and remember that God is the living flame. Hope in Christ for eternal life might only be the dim assurance that, while we may carry the scars on our resurrected body, we won't carry the sadness. In this Eastertide, how might you renew your hope in the resurrected Christ each day?

COLLECT

God of glory,
by the raising of your Son
you have broken the chains of death and hell:
fill your Church with faith and hope;
for a new day has dawned
and the way to life stands open
in our Saviour Jesus Christ.

Reflection by **Karen O'Donnell** | 131

Wednesday 20 April

Wednesday of Easter Week

1 Corinthians 15.20-28

'... for as all die in Adam, so all will be made alive in Christ' (v.22)

Hope is the beating heart of our faith. Hope for a change in circumstances. Hope for a change of heart. Hope for understanding, reconciliation, peace. Hope for a brighter tomorrow. Hope for a better future. Hope is what gets us up in the morning and keeps us going.

In this passage, we find two things to have hope in. The first that 'all will be made alive in Christ'. This verse is one of a number in the Bible that point towards the idea of universal salvation – that ultimately all people will be reconciled to God.

The second thing that brings us hope is the destruction of death. Death is the last enemy to be destroyed and subjected to the reign of God. This destruction of death releases life; in this case Paul is writing about the bodily resurrection of the dead. But we might also consider this hope in the future destruction of death as a hope that brings life, comfort and even joy in the here and now.

That death will be destroyed, and that all will one day be made alive in Christ – all human lives, however fleeting – offers comfort to all who grieve – not least those who have lost children to miscarriage, stillbirth and neo-natal death. The reign of God brings life – in that we can have hope.

COLLECT

Lord of all life and power,
who through the mighty resurrection of your Son
overcame the old order of sin and death
to make all things new in him:
grant that we, being dead to sin
and alive to you in Jesus Christ,
may reign with him in glory;
to whom with you and the Holy Spirit
be praise and honour, glory and might,
now and in all eternity.

| *Reflection by* **Karen O'Donnell**

Psalms 114, 148
Exodus 13.1-16
1 Corinthians 15.29-34

Thursday 21 April
Thursday of Easter Week

1 Corinthians 15.29-34

'... why are we putting ourselves in danger every hour?' (v.30)

What's the point to life? Why should we bother trying to accomplish anything? It's all pointless. We just die in the end. So we might as well just enjoy ourselves – eat, drink, and be merry. Lose ourselves in hedonism. Death is just the full stop at the end of the life sentence. For Paul, this is the implication if there is no resurrection. If there is no resurrection, then there is no point to our lives, and there is surely no point to Paul risking his life every day in service of the gospel.

It is easy to forget the realities of the resurrection and eternal life so that they become lines in a prayer or lyrics of song. But the implication of the resurrection is that our lives do have a point and that death is not the end of them. For Paul, this is a spur to his ministry. Paul often compares the Christian life to running a race. The reality of the resurrection brings new life to his legs for this race.

What might it mean for the implications of the resurrection and eternal life to be made real and fresh to you today? All runners have slow days, slow months, or even slow seasons. But remembering that our lives have a point, our ministries – whatever form they take – have a purpose, can spur us on to continue running towards the finish line.

God of glory,
by the raising of your Son
you have broken the chains of death and hell:
fill your Church with faith and hope;
for a new day has dawned
and the way to life stands open
in our Saviour Jesus Christ.

COLLECT

Reflection by **Karen O'Donnell** | 133

Friday 22 April

Friday of Easter Week

Psalms 115, 149
Exodus 13.17 – 14.14
1 Corinthians 15.35-50

1 Corinthians 15.35-50

'How are the dead raised? With what kind of body ...?' (v.35)

Popular culture has a fascination with the undead dead. Zombies (under the guise of a number of creative names) proliferate in films, TV and popular fiction. Beginning with the films of George Romero in the sixties, the zombie has since come to stand for unreasoning, destructive conformity. They are often the cause or symptom of complete societal breakdown. Such that when the real world is facing turbulence – economic crises, climate crises, health crises – our imaginations conjure up the zombie.

The resurrected body is not a zombie. It is not unthinking flesh, a decaying corpse with insatiable appetite. Nor is it pure spirit, finally freed from the prison of the body. The resurrected body is a body freed from the corrupting powers of sin and death, one that is glorious and full of strength and power. We know from the Gospel accounts of the resurrected Jesus that resurrected bodies will bear the marks and scars of their former life, remembering who they were and the experiences that made them.

The resurrected body is not an erasure of the earthly body but a deepening and intensification of it. The soul is a fundamental part of this body and not separate from it. Spiritual formation is then a bodily activity as well as a contemplative one. In the face of a culture that is obsessed with bodily conformity, nourishing and loving one's body as it is, not as it measures up against some ideal, is a radical act of spiritual resistance.

COLLECT

Lord of all life and power,
who through the mighty resurrection of your Son
overcame the old order of sin and death
to make all things new in him:
grant that we, being dead to sin
and alive to you in Jesus Christ,
may reign with him in glory;
to whom with you and the Holy Spirit
be praise and honour, glory and might,
now and in all eternity.

Reflection by **Karen O'Donnell**

Psalms 116, 150
Exodus 14.15-end
1 Corinthians 15.51-end

Saturday 23 April
Saturday of Easter Week

1 Corinthians 15.51-end
'Where, O death, is your victory?' (v.55)

Paul draws this chapter on the resurrection to a close with a climactic vision of the future. The trumpet will sound, the dead will be raised, and we will be changed. This climax is evidence of the final victory over death that has been established by God.

Death has preoccupied the mind of many great thinkers throughout time. The philosopher Socrates said that the true philosopher is always preparing for death and dying. Psychoanalyst Sigmund Freud often referred to 'the painful riddle of death', arguing that if life is to be endured, one must first come to terms with the fact of one's death, the end of life. Death preoccupies the mind of Paul as well; however, it is not the overriding power of death that he dwells on, rather the defeat of death. The perishable becomes imperishable, the mortal becomes immortal, and death loses its victory.

It is not, then, the end of life that one must come to terms with but rather the eternal life. The riddle of death, for the Christian, is that death is not the end but a transition from mortal to immortal, from perishable to imperishable. The final application of this reimagining of death is that because we are assured of our eternal destiny, our lives and the work we do within them have a point, a meaning, a purpose. We do not labour in vain.

God of glory,
by the raising of your Son
you have broken the chains of death and hell:
fill your Church with faith and hope;
for a new day has dawned
and the way to life stands open
in our Saviour Jesus Christ.

COLLECT

Reflection by **Karen O'Donnell** | 135

Monday 25 April

Mark the Evangelist

Psalms 37.23-end, 148
Isaiah 62.6-10
or Ecclesiasticus 51.13-end
Acts 12.25 – 13.13

Acts 12.25 – 13.13

'While they were worshipping the Lord and fasting …' (13.2)

Paul's first missionary journey saw him set out with Barnabas and John on a journey to Cyprus. The initiating factor in this story is the word of the Holy Spirit that comes to the group whilst they are worshipping. In other words, their active engagement in the spiritual disciplines of prayer and fasting revealed something of God's will for their lives.

The Christian tradition is filled with such accounts. Those who seek after God through spiritual disciplines tend to find God in some way or another. Consider, for example, the desert fathers and mothers or the mystics such as Hadewijch, a member of the medieval order of laywomen, the Beguines. For her, fasting was a central part of her devotion and played a key role in her mystical encounters with God. Her spiritual disciplines were part of how she came to encounter God.

Spiritual disciplines can be tough. They are, after all, a discipline! They are a habit to weave into each day, but they must never become rote or they lose meaning and significance. In worshipping God together and in fasting, this small group of Christians discerned something of the will of God. But they did it together in community. Think about whether there are opportunities to share your spiritual practices with others, encouraging them and being encouraged, in order that you might encounter God.

COLLECT

Almighty God,
who enlightened your holy Church
through the inspired witness of your evangelist Saint Mark:
grant that we, being firmly grounded in the truth of the gospel,
may be faithful to its teaching both in word and deed;
through Jesus Christ your Son our Lord,
who is alive and reigns with you,
in the unity of the Holy Spirit,
one God, now and for ever.

*Reflection by **Karen O'Donnell***

Psalms 5, 146
Joshua 1.1-9
Ephesians 6.10-20

Tuesday 26 April
George, martyr,
patron of England

Ephesians 6.10-20
'Therefore take up the whole armour of God...' (v.13)

Today is the feast of St George, one of the most prominent soldier saints in Christian tradition. What better day to reflect on the significance of wearing the whole armour of God, which gives you the strength of the Lord.

The detail of each piece of armour tells us something about ourselves. We need a belt of truth because truth holds us together; it prevents us from being pulled apart. We need a breastplate of righteousness to cover our heart because our emotions can lead us away from what is good and upright. Feet that are fitted with the shoes of the gospel of peace are feet that take peace with them wherever they go. Faith is a shield that must be wielded. It is active not passive – a shield cannot hang by your side limply, but must be raised up to protect from the blows in a fight. The helmet of salvation covers the head to help us to resist doubting that we are saved. Finally, the sword of the Spirit which is the word of God brings us into partnership with God. We are not alone in this battle.

The specificity of these pieces of armour has always struck me as a powerful example of the kindness of God. Knowing our weaknesses, knowing where we would struggle and fall, knowing the battles we would face, God provided exactly the right armour to protect us. The key to both putting on the armour and to winning the battle is prayer in the Spirit.

God of hosts,
who so kindled the flame of love
in the heart of your servant George
that he bore witness to the risen Lord
by his life and by his death:
give us the same faith and power of love
that we who rejoice in his triumphs
may come to share with him the fullness of the resurrection;
through Jesus Christ your Son our Lord,
who is alive and reigns with you,
in the unity of the Holy Spirit,
one God, now and for ever.

COLLECT

Reflection by **Karen O'Donnell**   137

Wednesday 27 April

Psalms 16, **30** *or* 119.1-32
Exodus 16.11-end
Colossians 2.1-15

Colossians 2.1-15

'... continue to live your lives in him' (v.6)

The author of the letter to the church in Colossae mixes their metaphors a little here, using both an agricultural (be rooted) and an architectural (be built up) metaphor for what it means to live your life in Christ. But the intention seems clear. To live your life in Christ is to have your foundations firmly planted in Christ and to be built up by Christ. 'Rooted' implies the beginnings of our faith, grounded in Christ, whilst the building up is a more active and continuing process. Scripture often compares believers to both plants (trees, branches, vines) and buildings (houses, temples). Both are rooted in and built up by God.

Often when we are 'in' something we take its characteristics. As a northerner living in the south of England, I have picked up a southern accent! In relationships – both romantic and familial – we can pick up the characteristics of those around us, certain features or habits. As those in Christ we take on the characteristics of Christ, sharing, through our baptism, in his death and resurrection, and knowing God. Being in Christ continually brings us to fullness in him so that nothing is lacking. We don't need to look elsewhere to find this fullness but rather be built up in Christ each day.

COLLECT

Almighty Father,
you have given your only Son to die for our sins
and to rise again for our justification:
grant us so to put away the leaven of malice and wickedness
that we may always serve you
in pureness of living and truth;
through the merits of your Son Jesus Christ our Lord,
who is alive and reigns with you,
in the unity of the Holy Spirit,
one God, now and for ever.

| *Reflection by* **Karen O'Donnell**

Psalms **28**, 29 *or* 14, **15**, 16
Exodus 17
Colossians 2.16 – 3.11

Thursday 28 April

Colossians 2.16 – 3.11

'... the whole body, nourished and held together' (2.19)

Each day we are bombarded with images of the body – the perfect body that is – and a wide variety of foods, diets, lotions, cosmetics, clothing and other products that will help you achieve that perfect body. No longer just an issue for girls and women, studies show that men are increasingly negatively impacted by the onslaught of such images and messages. Even spiritual seeking can reinforce these messages, especially in some types of yoga and alternative therapies. And as we read in verse 23, such messages can have the appearance of wisdom promoting self-imposed piety, humility and severe treatment of the body. But like a fashionable diet offering the promise of quick results, such messages are empty and dangerous.

We are not to succumb to such messaging and imagery but rather to set our minds on the things above. That is not to say that the body does not matter – indeed, it does. Being healthy, enjoying exercise, wearing makeup and nice clothes are all perfectly fine. But this does mean that when looking for an image of perfection to aim for, it is not to the media we turn but to Christ. It is to this likeness that we are to be conformed and in doing so, we eliminate the distinctions between us such that every life is hidden with Christ in God.

What opportunities might there be for you to be more Christ-like today?

Risen Christ,
for whom no door is locked, no entrance barred:
open the doors of our hearts,
that we may seek the good of others
and walk the joyful road of sacrifice and peace,
to the praise of God the Father.

COLLECT

Reflection by **Karen O'Donnell** | 139

Friday 29 April

Psalms 57, **61** *or* 17, **19**
Exodus 18.1-12
Colossians 3.12 – 4.1

Colossians 3.12 – 4.1

'Slaves, obey your earthly masters' (3.22)

2020 saw Black Lives Matter protests take place around the world in protest against the seemingly unending discrimination against people of colour by systems and institutions across the globe. With the toppling of statues connected to the slave trade and slave owning, questions were asked about the place of history within these conversations. The Bible is not immune from these conversations. Colossians 3.22 is one of a number of verses used, particularly in the US but in other parts of the world too, to justify slavery.

In commentaries on this text, writers often gloss over this verse arguing that owning slaves was culturally acceptable in the first century and slaves were members of the household, even drawing parallels between slavery, paid employment and respect for your boss. A more honest response might be to admit that the teachings of this verse are wrong and the way it has been weaponized to hurt so many people is reprehensible.

The passage begins by asking us to be compassionate, kind, humble and patient, particularly in our relationships with one another. These traits are best displayed not in tiptoeing our way around a morally relative explanation of the verse, but rather in humbly rejecting it and all it stands for and offering kindness and compassion to those who have been hurt by such teachings.

COLLECT

Almighty Father,
you have given your only Son to die for our sins
and to rise again for our justification:
grant us so to put away the leaven of malice and wickedness
that we may always serve you
in pureness of living and truth;
through the merits of your Son Jesus Christ our Lord,
who is alive and reigns with you,
in the unity of the Holy Spirit,
one God, now and for ever.

| *Reflection by* **Karen O'Donnell**

Psalms 63, **84** *or* 20, 21, **23**
Exodus 18.13-end
Colossians 4.2-end

Saturday 30 April

Colossians 4.2-end

'Let your speech always be gracious' (v.6)

I have a friend who is a genius at networking. She remembers lots of information about people really well and so when she introduces people, she always makes a point of telling them what they have in common with each other – an area they both work in, a similar interest, or even just a book they have both read. It's always such a great ice-breaker as it immediately gives you a reasonably interesting topic of conversation to begin with. She has a gift for bringing people together and enabling fruitful conversation.

In Paul's final greetings to the church in Colossae, he offers gracious words about a number of fellow Christians: people who have brought him comfort, people who have worked hard, people who have prayed hard, those who are faithful, those who will encourage the church. Paul has a similar gift for networking and is keen to remind his readers of the mutual endeavours of his companions. His final instruction, after exhorting them to pray, is that their speech might be gracious. This speech is seasoned with salt which adds both flavour and preservation, enabling the speech of Christians to be different to that of the non-believer and to preserve the good news of Jesus. In a world of fake news, spin, mistruths, half-lies and insults, let your speech always be gracious. Have something of a different flavour to say.

Risen Christ,
for whom no door is locked, no entrance barred:
open the doors of our hearts,
that we may seek the good of others
and walk the joyful road of sacrifice and peace,
to the praise of God the Father.

COLLECT

Monday 2 May
Philip and James, Apostles

Psalms 139, 146
Proverbs 4.10-18
James 1.1-12

James 1.1-12

'... consider it nothing but joy' (v.2)

The writer of this letter is called Jacob (James in English). He was traditionally identified with Jesus' brother who first appears in Mark 6.3, and who became a prominent leader in the early Church (Acts 15.13; Galatians 1.19). Many current scholars agree. There is an increasing consensus that his letter dates from as early as the AD 40s, making it perhaps the earliest book of the New Testament.

This should give us something of a chill. Whatever the precise relationship signified by 'brother', this is a letter from Jesus' inner family circle. Like Jesus, it is utterly Jewish. It dates from a time before his culture was wiped out by the Romans and while the memory of his earthly life was still fresh, containing many echoes of his words (e.g. James 5.12) and sharing his passionate concern for the poor.

Above all, it offers wise and practical counsel in the context of a situation of hardship and the threat of worse, now again familiar to many in our own time. It jumps straight in with a surprising statement: joy is not something to feel but to 'consider' (or 'regard'). As a cognitive therapist would say, the important thing is not what happens to us but what we make of it, and that begins with how we look at it. When times are hard we need reminding that we are no longer victims but active participants in a bigger story, one whose end is not simply survival but wholeness – and yes, joy – in Christ.

COLLECT

Almighty Father,
whom truly to know is eternal life:
teach us to know your Son Jesus Christ
as the way, the truth, and the life;
that we may follow the steps of your holy apostles
Philip and James,
and walk steadfastly in the way that leads to your glory;
through Jesus Christ your Son our Lord,
who is alive and reigns with you,
in the unity of the Holy Spirit,
one God, now and for ever.

| *Reflection by* **Joanna Collicutt**

Psalms **98**, 99, 100 *or* 32, **36**
Exodus 20.1-21
Luke 1.26-38

Tuesday 3 May

Luke 1.26-38

'Here am I, the servant of the Lord' (v. 38)

In classical Greek mythology, a young Phoenician girl called Semele is persuaded into a liaison with Zeus, the ruler of the Gods, and she becomes pregnant with his child, Dionysus. In revenge, Zeus' wife Hera tricks Semele into asking Zeus to reveal his divinity to her. He reluctantly does so and, as no mortal can look upon a god and live, Semele is consumed by fire (though Dionysus is miraculously saved).

This lurid story, surely known by Luke, throws into relief his own account of a young girl who will carry God's child. The obvious difference is that Mary is not destroyed by her encounter with the divine; the less obvious but equally important difference is that she is not lured into the pregnancy.

God accommodates to Mary's human limitations by way of an angelic mediator and messenger. Mary cannot look on God, but she can, albeit in fear and trembling, look on and converse with Gabriel. With exemplary clarity, Gabriel tells Mary exactly what the situation is. Then Mary does something extraordinary; she receives the message as an invitation rather than a command. She asks for further details; these are forthcoming; then she gives informed consent. What's more, she does this by an assertive act of self-identification. In words redolent of Isaiah, she refers to herself as the 'servant of the Lord', a true Israelite, totally committed to the mission of the son she is yet to bear. As Simeon will point out, she too is to be a suffering servant.

Almighty Father,
who in your great mercy gladdened the disciples
with the sight of the risen Lord:
give us such knowledge of his presence with us,
that we may be strengthened and sustained by his risen life
and serve you continually in righteousness and truth;
through Jesus Christ your Son our Lord,
who is alive and reigns with you,
in the unity of the Holy Spirit,
one God, now and for ever.

COLLECT

Reflection by **Joanna Collicutt**   143

Wednesday 4 May

Luke 1.39-56

'Mary set out and went with haste' (v.39)

In yesterday's reading, Mary received Gabriel's message actively and assertively, rather than by simple acquiescence, and was dignified in the process. This continues in today's reading, where the literal translation of v.39 is 'Having arisen, Mary eagerly went'; Mary has grown in stature and is intent on the goal of her journey. She is perhaps fleeing the prying eyes and gossiping tongues of her neighbours; she is certainly seeking companionship and wise counsel from an older mentor – her cousin Elizabeth.

Today's reading gives a rare biblical glimpse of a female-only space, a place of safety in which the two pregnant women may speak freely. It is also a priestly and prophetic place in which the vocation of each is mutually nurtured. Here the servant of the Lord greets a woman of priestly descent (1.5), who responds by interpreting the foetal movements in her own belly as a prophetic sign. Filled with the Spirit, Elizabeth pronounces a twofold blessing: on Mary as expectant mother and on Jesus as both Lord and fruit of her womb. She follows this with a beatitude delighting in Mary's trust in God's promise to her.

One way of understanding blessing is as seeing and drawing out the good in a situation, 'considering it nothing but joy' (James 1.2). Mary's situation is dire; many hardships probably await her – she is even in danger of being stoned as an adulteress. But in this blessed place of womanly solidarity, she is enabled to open her mouth in joyful praise.

COLLECT

Almighty Father,
who in your great mercy gladdened the disciples
    with the sight of the risen Lord:
give us such knowledge of his presence with us,
that we may be strengthened and sustained by his risen life
and serve you continually in righteousness and truth;
through Jesus Christ your Son our Lord,
who is alive and reigns with you,
in the unity of the Holy Spirit,
one God, now and for ever.

| *Reflection by* **Joanna Collicutt**

Psalm **136** *or* **37***
Exodus 25.1-22
Luke 1.57-end

Thursday 5 May

Luke 1.57-end

'But his mother said "No…"' (v.60)

In Luke's writings, there are three examples of something that looks a bit like 'mansplaining'. The most prominent of these is the disciples' dismissal of the witness of the women at the tomb as 'an idle tale' (24.11) but acceptance of Peter's word as authoritative (24.34). The second is the company's dismissal of Rhoda's encounter with Peter as a hallucination (Acts 12.15) until they hear him banging on the door.

Today's reading is the third example. Elizabeth speaks with the authority of the Angel of the Lord (1.13) when she dares to say 'No!' Yet her words are not received until confirmation is obtained from Zachariah. A gender-related issue is being played out here, but it is more than simple mansplaining. The problem is not with Elizabeth choosing her child's name but with the name itself; one that loosens his kinship ties with his father's line.

John literally means 'God is gracious', a reminder that he is a gift to an elderly couple who had all but given up hope of children. This will not be a young man who joins the family firm and preserves its name by having children of his own. He is from the very beginning 'other', his life set aside for a quite different vocation.

We begin to see that the resistance and denial evoked by the words of these women is to the 'otherness' of their messages; their gender simply provides a convenient excuse to disregard divine disclosure that exceeds the imaginative capacity of the hearer.

COLLECT

Risen Christ,
you filled your disciples with boldness and fresh hope:
strengthen us to proclaim your risen life
and fill us with your peace,
to the glory of God the Father.

Reflection by **Joanna Collicutt** | 145

Friday 6 May

Luke 2.1-20

'I am bringing you good news of great joy for all the people' (v.10)

The shepherds undergo an experience that exceeds their imaginative capacity but is so compelling that they cannot resist, deny or disregard it; instead, they are traumatized. Psychological trauma is, by definition, something that violently breaks down our defences and allows 'mighty dread to seize our troubled mind'. This is why the angel's first words are necessary: 'Don't be afraid – the facts are friendly.' But what are these friendly facts? The coming of the Messiah? A baby in a manger?

The clue is in the song of the angelic choir that forms the basis of what we now know as the 'Gloria'. It tells of peace and reconciliation between God and human beings (hence the placement of the Gloria after the confession and absolution in the Holy Communion service). As v.10 indicates, this peace includes 'all the people', a fitting message for shepherds who existed on the margins of respectable society.

This is not merely the weaker negative peace that comes from letting go past sins and offences; it is the complete harmony and wellbeing of *Shalôm* in which God is seen positively to delight in humankind. While v.14 is difficult to translate because the Greek is ambiguous and varies between manuscripts, the best reading is probably 'peace among human beings – they're pleasing to him'.

This is where the baby comes in; for it is in and through this fully human being, '...my Son, the Beloved' (3.22), that God says to each of us 'with you I am well pleased'.

COLLECT

Almighty Father,
who in your great mercy gladdened the disciples
    with the sight of the risen Lord:
give us such knowledge of his presence with us,
that we may be strengthened and sustained by his risen life
and serve you continually in righteousness and truth;
through Jesus Christ your Son our Lord,
who is alive and reigns with you,
in the unity of the Holy Spirit,
one God, now and for ever.

| *Reflection by* **Joanna Collicutt**

Psalms 108, **110**, 111 *or* 41, **42**, 43
Exodus 29.1-9
Luke 2.21-40

Saturday 7 May

Luke 2.21-40

*'... a light for revelation to the Gentiles and for glory
to your people Israel' (v. 32)*

The first two chapters of Luke's Gospel contain four of the earliest Christian hymns in existence, still sung regularly in corporate worship today: the Magnificat, Benedictus, Gloria, and now the Nunc Dimittis. This short song of Simeon's picks up the Gloria's message of peace where it left off.

The angels sang of a cosmic peace that extends to all humankind. Simeon's peace is more personal. It is not surprising that we sing or say his song as part of Evening and Night Prayer and at funerals; it speaks of the peace that allows us to let go of worries, concerns and even of life itself: 'The Lord almighty grant us a quiet night and a perfect end.'

This peace rests on the assurance that all is well with the world, something that Simeon senses as he holds the infant Jesus in his arms. Somehow, in this young family, God is acting 'according to your word' (the public words of Scripture and the private promise to Simeon). God thus shows himself to be consistent and trustworthy and also vindicates Simeon's faith in him.

Simeon's peace of mind comes from a life well lived, one in which the threads are finally being woven together into a meaningful and beautiful tapestry. Yet it doesn't stop there, for with prophetic vision he links his own small part in God's mission of peace with its broader scope: it is not just for 'your people Israel'; it is for the whole world.

Risen Christ,
you filled your disciples with boldness and fresh hope:
strengthen us to proclaim your risen life
and fill us with your peace,
to the glory of God the Father.

COLLECT

Monday 9 May

Psalm **103** *or* **44**
Exodus 32.1-14
Luke 2.41-end

Luke 2.41-end

'And Jesus increased in wisdom and in years' (v.52)

Luke's Gospel has two stories about a lost son: one concerns the 'prodigal'; the other is today's reading about the twelve-year-old Jesus. It is a coming-of-age story that is typical of patrilineal cultures: a boy who has throughout infancy and childhood been closely tied to his mother, intentionally loosens that bond and, as he steps into manhood, formally identifies with his father.

However, this one has a twist because it is not the father we might expect; the surprise is cleverly hammered home by Luke in the 'Your father/my Father' interchange between mother and son. Mary again plays an active and prominent part in this story; which of us who have been reunited with a wandering child and found ourselves torn between the desire to hug and harangue, will not identify with her?

Yet this is not Mary's story but that of her son. For an ancient culture that had little interest in childhood and no concept of adolescence, it is quite remarkable. While foregrounding Jesus' divine parentage, it at the same time asserts and communicates his full humanity: 'born of a woman' (Galatians 4.4), undergoing the normal and natural developmental phases of human young, cared for and disciplined by human parents, a continuing work in progress.

Part of this work, the task of adolescence, concerns establishing one's identity and calling. This is precisely what Jesus is doing as he searches the Scriptures and urgently questions the rabbis. As Mary and Joseph go about finding him, he is finding himself.

COLLECT

Almighty God,
whose Son Jesus Christ is the resurrection and the life:
raise us, who trust in him,
from the death of sin to the life of righteousness,
that we may seek those things which are above,
where he reigns with you
in the unity of the Holy Spirit,
one God, now and for ever.

| *Reflection by* **Joanna Collicutt**

Psalm **139** *or* **48**, 52
Exodus 32.15-34
Luke 3.1-14

Tuesday 10 May

Luke 3.1-14

'Bear fruits worthy of repentance' (v.8)

In all four Gospels, the beginning of Jesus' ministry is marked by John the Baptist, but each Gospel writer approaches him from a particular perspective. Matthew and Luke share word for word a section of John's preaching (vv.7-9 and Matthew 3.7-10), which must have been well remembered by their sources with its vivid imagery of snakes slithering out from under cover to escape fire. He was clearly worth a listen. John's point is that the tribe to which you belong (for which read school, club, religion and so on) is irrelevant if your heart does not turn Godwards, a process the New Testament calls *metanoia*. We can't see *metanoia* (here translated 'repentance'), but we can see the fruit it bears.

Luke is keen for his readers to understand the nature of this fruit and goes on to report more of John's teaching on this. He is writing for an urban audience, especially his patron Theophilus, whose culture was dominated by commerce rather than agriculture, and the examples he chooses concern honest business dealing and a 'fair shares for all' ethic.

This is a relatively modest standard amounting to basic human decency. People are not required either to denigrate or to give up their day jobs, but to do them well and honourably; not to give away all their possessions but to share their excess. There is a kindness here that begins where people are and takes them forward in small steps, but in so doing 'prepares the way of the Lord' in their hearts.

Risen Christ,
faithful shepherd of your Father's sheep:
teach us to hear your voice
and to follow your command,
that all your people may be gathered into one flock,
to the glory of God the Father.

COLLECT

Reflection by **Joanna Collicutt** | 149

Wednesday 11 May

Psalm **135** or **119.57-80**
Exodus 33
Luke 3.15-22

Luke 3.15-22

'You are my Son, the Beloved; with you I am well pleased' (v.22)

Matthew and Luke's accounts of John's words converge again (vv.16-17 and Matthew 3.11-12), but again Luke softens them by framing them as 'good news' (v.18). This may raise a smile given John's talk of 'unquenchable fire', but we should recall that he points to the coming of Christ and a day of reckoning that, as Mary has already proclaimed, is indeed to be good news for the poor and exploited. Jesus will shortly go on to present this day in exclusively positive terms as the 'year of the Lord's favour' (4.19) in the synagogue at Nazareth.

The adult Jesus now appears for the first time and comes for baptism. John has already asserted that this is no ordinary man, and then the heavens open and we are given the divine perspective on his identity. It is the definitive act of Father–Son affiliation, anticipated 18 years earlier in the incident in the temple, in which Jesus' status as Beloved Son is formally confirmed.

This is why what comes next (vv.23-38) is a patrilinear genealogy; the juxtaposition of the words from heaven with Jesus' earthly line show him to be Son of God by Mary and the Holy Spirit and Son of David according to the flesh (Romans 1.3). Furthermore, David's own lineage is traced back to Adam – 'everyman' – and through Adam to God. We are reminded that humankind was originally made in God's image, and that in Jesus this image is restored; we are, as in the beginning, well pleasing to God.

COLLECT

Almighty God,
whose Son Jesus Christ is the resurrection and the life:
raise us, who trust in him,
from the death of sin to the life of righteousness,
that we may seek those things which are above,
where he reigns with you
in the unity of the Holy Spirit,
one God, now and for ever.

| *Reflection by* **Joanna Collicutt**

Psalm **118** *or* 56, **57** (63*)
Exodus 34.1-10, 27-end
Luke 4.1-13

Thursday 12 May

Luke 4.1-13

'If you are the Son of God ...' (vv.3,9)

As Jesus comes out of the water, he receives definitive confirmation that he is God's Beloved Son, inherently pleasing to his Father, and is in communion with the Holy Spirit. This is a rare graphic disclosure of God's trinitarian nature and perhaps explains why Jesus' baptism has been a favourite subject of Christian art.

One might think that following this extraordinary mystical experience, which offered such depths of theological insight and personal assurance, Jesus would be well fitted to begin his mission. Instead, he is led by the Spirit into the physical and existential wilderness to be tormented by a voice that says, 'If you are God's son...' This period of testing is necessary. At a surface level, Jesus needs to be prepared for the rejection that he will receive (beginning in tomorrow's reading). At a deeper level, he needs to face the dark side of being special and beloved – narcissism. How easy it would have been to develop a sense of entitlement to necessities of life not readily available to others, or to power, dominion and wealth, no matter what their source.

Jesus uses the Scriptures he has known since his youth to do valiant battle with these temptations, which are all the while luring him towards the self-destruct button. We should learn from his example. But in the darkest move of all, the devil turns those same Scriptures to his own ends, something from which we should also learn; it is never as simple as saying 'The Bible teaches ...'

> Risen Christ,
> faithful shepherd of your Father's sheep:
> teach us to hear your voice
> and to follow your command,
> that all your people may be gathered into one flock,
> to the glory of God the Father.

COLLECT

Reflection by **Joanna Collicutt**   151

Friday 13 May

Luke 4.14-30

'Today this scripture has been fulfilled in your hearing' (v. 21)

Jesus emerges victorious from his wilderness battle 'filled with the power of the Spirit' (v.14), but this does not show itself in supernatural signs and wonders. Just as in the wilderness, its currency is Scripture. It is as if Jesus has graduated from a rigorous training course in biblical interpretation. He then deploys his knowledge and skill in the most natural place, a synagogue teaching ministry.

Like John before him, Jesus draws on the words of the prophet Isaiah, but he approaches them differently. First, instead of choosing a text that looks forward (Isaiah 40.3-5) he chooses one that speaks of the present time (Isaiah 61.1-2a). This is a shift from promise to fulfilment. Secondly, he receives this text as good news for those who are oppressed by poverty, sickness and injustice, consciously eschewing John's fire and brimstone preaching by leaving out Isaiah 61.2b, 'and the day of vengeance of our God'. Jesus' first rule for interpreting Scripture appears to be kindness.

Finally, and most importantly, Jesus understands Scripture to be about him. This is what he was exploring in the temple as an adolescent, while in the wilderness he was doing battle with the dangers of an 'it's all about me' mentality.

But Jesus' listeners cannot receive him as the fulfilment of Scripture here and now that he claims to be. They cannot see beyond his fleshly patrilineage back through Joseph and David to Adam everyman. Their imaginative capacity has been exceeded, so they expel him from their minds and their community.

COLLECT

Almighty God,
whose Son Jesus Christ is the resurrection and the life:
raise us, who trust in him,
from the death of sin to the life of righteousness,
that we may seek those things which are above,
where he reigns with you
in the unity of the Holy Spirit,
one God, now and for ever.

| *Reflection by* **Joanna Collicutt**

Psalms 16, 147.1-12
1 Samuel 2.27-35
Acts 2.37-end

Saturday 14 May

Matthias the Apostle

1 Samuel 2.27-35

'I will raise up for myself a faithful priest, who shall do according to what is in my heart and in my mind' (v.35)

This reading is set for the feast day of St Matthias, the disciple who took Judas' place among the Twelve (Acts 1. 26). It has some parallels with Matthias' story, but is more dramatic in tone and larger in scale.

Eli was a priest of the line of Aaron. His position and that of his male descendants appeared unassailable because God had promised that this family should be priests for ever (v.30 cf. Exodus 29.9). Earlier in this chapter, however, we are told that Eli's sons exploited their position, taking for their own consumption the sacrificial meat that had cost devout people dearly, and sexually abusing the female servers. We might draw some sad comparison with cases of clergy misconduct that have come to light in recent years.

Through a man of God, terrible judgement is pronounced on Eli and his sons; their behaviour has nullified God's original promise and a new spiritual leader will be raised up. This, of course, is Samuel, whose moral character is beyond reproach (1 Samuel 12.1-3). Samuel is an Ephraimite, not of the Aaronic priestly line, but this doesn't matter because he has God's heart and mind.

God cares about faith not tribe; the priestly privileges granted to Eli's family were a gift not a right; not to be taken for granted. The status of priest now passes sideways to Samuel, the prophet and judge, who is faithful to the One who desires 'steadfast love and not sacrifice, the knowledge of God rather than burnt offerings' (Hosea 6.6).

COLLECT

Almighty God,
who in the place of the traitor Judas
chose your faithful servant Matthias
to be of the number of the Twelve:
preserve your Church from false apostles
and, by the ministry of faithful pastors and teachers,
keep us steadfast in your truth;
through Jesus Christ your Son our Lord,
who is alive and reigns with you,
in the unity of the Holy Spirit,
one God, now and for ever.

Reflection by **Joanna Collicutt**   153

Monday 16 May

Psalm **145** *or* **71**
Numbers 9.15-end; 10.33-end
Luke 4.38-end

Luke 4.38-end

'I was sent for this purpose' (v.43)

We notice the power that emanates from Christ. His healing miracles stack up here in an impressive list: Simon Peter's mother-in-law, the sick with 'various diseases', and demoniacs. Christ is indeed the power of God at work in the world, and he brings healing. We should also notice that, as he heals, he rebuilds community. The woman with a high fever is not just cured, she then 'serves them'. The sick and the demoniacs, many of whom would have been forced to live on the edges of society, will be restored to relationship with family and friends. The demons know Christ and announce him. This startling healing is a miracle that overcomes division. It fosters recognition and relationships in which both we and God are named and known.

All our attention is focused on Capernaum and on the healing of a particular community. It is always *here* and *in these relationships* that we find the coming of God's kingdom. Then, however, attention shifts rapidly and decisively. There is more. Christ has a driving sense of purpose that will take him elsewhere, 'I must proclaim the good news of the kingdom'. Salvation is not restricted to one time and place. Reading Luke, we will be reminded over and again that we must follow Christ to the cross. Meeting Christ, in this moment, we are summoned into a faith that will ask and indeed offer so much more.

COLLECT

Almighty God,
who through your only-begotten Son Jesus Christ
have overcome death and opened to us the gate of everlasting life:
grant that, as by your grace going before us
    you put into our minds good desires,
so by your continual help
we may bring them to good effect;
through Jesus Christ our risen Lord,
who is alive and reigns with you,
in the unity of the Holy Spirit,
one God, now and for ever.

154 | *Reflection by* **David Hoyle**

Psalms **19**, 147.1-12 *or* **73**
Numbers 11.1-33
Luke 5.1-11

Tuesday 17 May

Luke 5.1-11

'I am a sinful man!' (v.8)

The 1980 *Alternative Service Book* had a theme for each Sunday of the year. On The Second Sunday after Epiphany it was 'Revelation: the First Disciples', and the reading came either from the beginning of St John (1.35-end) or St Mark (1.14-40). The emphasis did indeed fall on 'Revelation', and discipleship looked like a sudden commitment. In St Luke's hands, the call to Simon Peter reads very differently. We have already encountered Jesus as a teacher and a healer, by the time we come to the lake. We already know his power and his persuasiveness. He holds the attention of a crowd and he needs a boat to make the most of the acoustic at the shoreline.

Then, there is another demonstration of his power, a miraculous catch of fish. Simon was empty handed after a failed fishing trip, but he is also willing and biddable. He is rewarded in a way that reminds us that God's generosity is surprising and abundant (in a way that our own, carefully calibrated, gift-giving rarely matches). Simon should have been alarmed about the fact that the boat was close to sinking. What gives him pause, however, is a holiness that throws his sinfulness into sharp relief.

There is a double recognition at the heart of discipleship. The disciple knows Christ – perfectly human and perfectly divine, but the disciple also has self-knowledge. Here is the one who can rescue us from ourselves.

Risen Christ,
your wounds declare your love for the world
and the wonder of your risen life:
give us compassion and courage
to risk ourselves for those we serve,
to the glory of God the Father.

COLLECT

Wednesday 18 May

Luke 5.12-26

'Who is this ...?' (v.21)

The pace is relentless. Pressing human need surrounds Jesus. In curing the man with leprosy, we notice, again, that Jesus is determined to achieve a *complete* healing. After making an 'offering', this man will be permitted to resume his place in the worshipping community, something that had been denied him. The pressure on Jesus only grows, and we notice him turning aside, to pray. Luke has more to say about prayer than any other evangelist. The pace is possible because of the prayer.

Then the mood darkens. Luke gave us an early indication that Jesus was not always welcome, not always admired, even in his own home (see Luke 4.28-29). Now we enter real controversy and an argument about Jesus' power to heal and to forgive sins. The emphasis in this remarkable story about a man lowered through the roof is, surprisingly, not in the extravagance of the action and the cure. This is all about the pronouncement of forgiveness. Jesus lays bare, in an instant, the deep confusion of his critics who apparently believe it is easier to heal someone than to forgive sins. The crucial misunderstanding here is that the religious leaders do not recognize Jesus; 'Who is this?' they ask. It is the key question. It is so easy to debate our own processes and rules and fail to notice that the glory of God breaks around us.

COLLECT

Almighty God,
who through your only-begotten Son Jesus Christ
have overcome death and opened to us the gate of everlasting life:
grant that, as by your grace going before us
    you put into our minds good desires,
so by your continual help
we may bring them to good effect;
through Jesus Christ our risen Lord,
who is alive and reigns with you,
in the unity of the Holy Spirit,
one God, now and for ever.

| *Reflection by* **David Hoyle**

Thursday 19 May

Luke 5.27-end

'... he got up, left everything, and followed him' (v.28)

We have met a man with leprosy, a paralysed man and now a tax collector. Jesus is working at the boundaries of society, and he is radically inclusive. Levi (identified as 'Matthew' in Matthew 9.9) was another detested figure. On this occasion, Jesus' summons is swift, and Levi's response is sudden. In a beautifully crisp verse, Luke captures essential elements of discipleship: 'he... left everything, and followed him'. Levi abandons what he was, and what he had, in order to become what he might be.

Again, we are plunged into controversy. This time the issue is the company that Jesus keeps. A banquet is always a symbol of the joy that is to come; it is a glimpse of the great company of the redeemed. The implication is clear, and it is unwelcome to some: sinners can be welcomed into the kingdom. Interestingly, Mark's account of this event records only that Jesus calls sinners (Mark 2.17). Luke wants us to be sure that sinners are called to *repentance*.

Another argument follows. This time the issue is fasting, as the Pharisees note that Jesus and his followers 'eat and drink'. Jesus does not rule out a religious fast. He simply says that now is not the time. That is the point about garments and wineskins. Old and new are not compatible. Christ commands our undivided attention, and we are to look for nothing else. He is our only religion.

Risen Christ,
your wounds declare your love for the world
and the wonder of your risen life:
give us compassion and courage
to risk ourselves for those we serve,
to the glory of God the Father.

COLLECT

Reflection by **David Hoyle**

157

Friday 20 May

Luke 6.1-11

'The Son of Man is lord of the sabbath' (v.5)

St Luke invites us to answer the question that the Pharisees asked: 'Who is this?' We see Jesus performing acts of power and teaching. We also hear the attempt to build a case against him. That process now takes a more threatening turn. Sabbath observance is a serious business, rooted in the rest taken on the seventh day of the Creation and demanded in the Ten Commandments.

We are not told why the disciples took grain to eat, but can safely assume, from the justification Jesus offers, that they were hungry. In describing how the followers of David ate the bread of the Presence, Jesus is not, in fact, tackling the issue of *sabbath* observance. He is making the altogether more startling claim that in him we meet something more important even than David. Jesus declares himself 'Lord of the Sabbath'.

In the second story, Jesus again adopts a radical stance. While he would have known that there was some discussion about the possibility of saving life on the Sabbath, Jesus shifts the argument to the requirement simply to 'do good'. In both stories, Jesus side-steps an argument about religious practice in order to suggest that a new hope is set before us. We should think of that futile attempt to put new wine into old skins. We should be wide-eyed with the sheer *possibility* before us as we ask: 'Who is this?'

COLLECT

Almighty God,
who through your only-begotten Son Jesus Christ
have overcome death and opened to us the gate of everlasting life:
grant that, as by your grace going before us
    you put into our minds good desires,
so by your continual help
we may bring them to good effect;
through Jesus Christ our risen Lord,
who is alive and reigns with you,
in the unity of the Holy Spirit,
one God, now and for ever.

| *Reflection by* **David Hoyle**

Psalms **146**, 150 *or* **76**, 79
Numbers 14.26-end
Luke 6.12-26

Luke 6.12-26

'Blessed are you who are poor' (v.20)

The controversy stories end, and Jesus gathers his disciples into a common purpose. His followers are commissioned as apostles – they are to be *sent out*, as emissaries with a gospel.

That gospel answers the question 'Who is this?' and tells us what kind of humanity we must share with Christ.

Luke's 'Sermon on the Plain' is a sustained challenge to the great temptation we too often feel to take charge and take possession. 'Blessed are you who are poor ...' St Luke is ever insistent that wealth and possessions are a snare for us. The more deeply we are committed to enjoying good things now, the harder we will find it to commit to the goodness of a different kingdom. 'Blessed are you who are hungry now ...' We must have mastery of appetites that have us hankering for such *little* things (a new kitchen) when God invites us to accept greater gifts by far. 'Blessed are you who weep now ...' We saw in Peter that the proper response to meeting Christ is repentance. We should be sorry for our sins and weep over all that is disjointed and broken in a creation longing to be healed. 'Blessed are you when people hate you ...' We must be ready to face the consequences of longing for this world to be changed.

As the Dominican author Simon Tugwell explains in his book on the Beatitudes: 'We must learn the task of weakness, of non-achievement, of being able to cope with our own poverty and helplessness.'

Risen Christ,
your wounds declare your love for the world
and the wonder of your risen life:
give us compassion and courage
to risk ourselves for those we serve,
to the glory of God the Father.

COLLECT

Monday 23 May

Luke 6.27-38

Love your enemies, do good to those who hate you' (v.27)

There are four crisp commands: love, do good, bless and pray. This is not, though, our 'to do' list. The sin in Eden was possessiveness; Adam and Eve *took* something for themselves. Christ's great sermon is an invitation to learn to be dependent and to know how to be *given* things. We are not called to effort and to be doing good to one another. We are invited to share the life Christ has won for us. We should love because we have been loved; we should do good as a counterpoint to hatred; we should bless and pray because those gifts are given to us.

'Love your enemies ... bless those who curse you.' Not only must we turn away from our desire to possess and achieve, to be in charge of our destiny; we must actively turn to others. The life Christ describes is lived together in mercy and in love.

'Do not judge.' This is a different command – not to *do* something, but to *refrain from* doing something. We are to resist the temptation to criticize and find fault. The danger here is the temptation to be pompous. Who made us into judges? Finding fault, we assume that we know the facts and make the right judgements. We are taking the place of God. We will never receive what God will give us if we are forever seizing little victories of our own.

COLLECT

God our redeemer,
you have delivered us from the power of darkness
and brought us into the kingdom of your Son:
grant, that as by his death he has recalled us to life,
so by his continual presence in us he may raise us
    to eternal joy;
through Jesus Christ your Son our Lord,
who is alive and reigns with you,
in the unity of the Holy Spirit,
one God, now and for ever.

| *Reflection by* **David Hoyle**

Psalms 124, 125, **126**, 127 *or* 87, **89.1-18**
Numbers 16.36-end
Luke 6.39-end

Tuesday 24 May

Luke 6.39-end

'You hypocrite, first take the log out of your own eye' (v.42)

The parable about the speck of dust addresses the delight that we too often take in criticizing others. The word 'hypocrite' is interesting because it has roots in theatre. The hypocrite plays a role, and our criticism of others is indeed often a kind of performance. We might think that we see what is wrong with others with great clarity, but those conversations that begin 'The trouble with you is ...' assume that we are independent observers and not fellow citizens and sinners. It is not that we are forbidden to make any judgement; Christian faith requires us to think deeply about ethics. The task, though, is to be undertaken knowing that we are all under judgement and that what we really must not do is to *condemn* others.

What follows is a sustained summons into authenticity. There are moments when it can seem that it is our ability to profess or proclaim the faith that matters. In fact, the call to follow Christ is not to find words, but to become like him, to acquire character and virtue. The words will follow. It is a long and careful task, like building a house with deep foundations. We cannot help but notice that there is a lot of falling masonry in the Gospels. There is more than a hint here of the fall of the temple and of the need to build something better understood, better conceived.

Risen Christ,
by the lakeside you renewed your call to your disciples:
help your Church to obey your command
and draw the nations to the fire of your love,
to the glory of God the Father.

COLLECT

Wednesday 25 May

Psalms **132**, 133 *or* **119.105-128**
Numbers 17.1-11
Luke 7.1-10

Luke 7.1-10

'... not even in Israel have I found such faith' (v.9)

This story is also told in St Matthew's Gospel (Matthew 8.5-13), and there the emphasis falls on a healing miracle done for a gentile. We hear, indeed, that many will come from 'east and west', but the 'heirs of the kingdom' will find themselves in outer darkness. In Luke, the accent shifts. We are told that Jewish leaders commend the centurion for his good works. Here is someone 'worthy'.

Their commendation barely lands with Jesus, who is much more interested in the fact that this Roman soldier has 'faith'. Luke knows that faith matters and seems to have a particular sense of what it might mean. Later, he will describe the disciples asking that their faith might *increase* (Luke 17.5), and we will hear Jesus pray that Peter's faith will not 'fail' (Luke 22.32).

Faith might begin in listening to Christ and acknowledging him, but a critical characteristic is whether or not this faith can *persist*. In the parable of the sower, the seeds in the good soil refer to those who, 'when they hear the word, hold it fast in an honest and good heart, and bear fruit with patient endurance' (Luke 8.15). Those sinewy and unshowy virtues – resilience, patience and endurance – are an essential part of Christian character. The centurion (just like Peter after the miraculous catch of fish) knows himself unworthy, but he has a hope and trust that will never fail.

COLLECT

God our redeemer,
you have delivered us from the power of darkness
and brought us into the kingdom of your Son:
grant, that as by his death he has recalled us to life,
so by his continual presence in us he may raise us
    to eternal joy;
through Jesus Christ your Son our Lord,
who is alive and reigns with you,
in the unity of the Holy Spirit,
one God, now and for ever.

Thursday 26 May
Ascension Day

Hebrews 7. [11-25] 26-end
'... a Son who has been made perfect for ever' (v.28)

In the dense range of reference to Melchizedek in the Epistle to the Hebrews, some of us suspect we might be missing something. If we turn to commentaries, we learn that we were right to wonder. Jewish and Christian writers were fascinated by Melchizedek and speculated about him with enthusiasm. The writer of Hebrews will have known at least some of what was said about the significance of King Melchizedek of Salem who 'was priest of God Most High' (Genesis 14.18). There is, however, only *one* crucial idea in all this rich narrative. Hebrews urges on us the idea that 'You are a priest for ever, according to the order of Melchizedek' (also Psalm 110.4).

Hebrews wants us to know that the Levitical priesthood, that sustained the channels of grace, had been superseded. The sacrifices that they offered have been replaced with something else. Importantly, in Christ, we encounter a priesthood that lasts *for ever*. It was a principle of Jewish scholarship that what is not mentioned in Scripture did not exist and therefore Melchizedek was 'without father, without mother, without genealogy, having neither beginning of days nor end of life' (Hebrews 7.3).

At Ascension, disciples need reminding not to get stuck gazing into heaven (Acts 1.11). As though Ascension is all about Jesus going away! On this day, his life – and therefore our human lives – are carried into the heart of God. That movement is permanent and enduring. It lasts *for ever*.

> Grant, we pray, almighty God,
> that as we believe your only-begotten Son
> our Lord Jesus Christ
> to have ascended into the heavens,
> so we in heart and mind may also ascend
> and with him continually dwell;
> who is alive and reigns with you,
> in the unity of the Holy Spirit,
> one God, now and for ever.

COLLECT

Reflection by **David Hoyle**   163

Friday 27 May

Psalms 20, **81** *or* **88** (95)
Exodus 35.30 – 36.1
Galatians 5.13-end

Exodus 35.30 – 36.1

'He has filled them with skill to do every kind of work' (35.35)

We meet Bezalel and Oholiab twice in Exodus, because (in chapters 25 to 31) we hear God give Moses (during his forty days on Sinai) the instructions he repeats here. The story of how the sanctuary is equipped may not seem very interesting to us. Years ago, excited commentators found deep meanings here. Some suggested this was a symbol of the whole universe. Others thought this is a description of Christ and Christian faith – gold as preaching, silver as patience and so on. A few noticed how very diverted we can become when we think about religious buildings and decoration. Hermann Witsius, a seventeenth-century Dutch theologian, observed drily: 'God created the whole world in six days, but he used forty to instruct Moses about the tabernacle.'

What we *should* notice is that Exodus insists that the sanctuary was a staggering free-will offering made by all the people and then created through the skill and 'divine spirit' of two great artists. We have a miracle before us. It is the miracle of God's abiding presence. It is a miracle that asks for and summons up a joyful and generous response. It is a miracle that unleashes creative genius.

At the Ascension, Jesus lifts our human life into the life of God. There is an abiding, sure union. In *Being Human* (SPCK 2018), Rowan Williams imagines Jesus declaring: 'This is the humanity I have brought home.' That really is exciting, and we rightly respond in joy, generosity and great art.

COLLECT

Grant, we pray, almighty God,
that as we believe your only-begotten Son
    our Lord Jesus Christ
to have ascended into the heavens,
so we in heart and mind may also ascend
and with him continually dwell;
who is alive and reigns with you,
in the unity of the Holy Spirit,
one God, now and for ever.

| *Reflection by* **David Hoyle**

Psalms 21, **47** or 96, **97**, 100
Numbers 11.16-17, 24-29
I Corinthians 2

Saturday 28 May

Numbers 11.16-17, 24-29

'Are you jealous for my sake?' (v.29)

Earlier in this chapter, the people complain and long for the food of Egypt, 'the cucumbers, the melons ...'. They are, quite literally, challenging the sense of direction. This crisis of leadership prompts anger. The Lord destroys parts of the camp. Moses protests, 'Why have I not found favour in your sight, that you lay the burden of all this people on me?'. Even under stress, Moses displays courage and clarity. He names the difficulty.

The Lord comes 'down' and equips seventy elders to share the burden. Note that it is more of the *same* leadership. The same spirit that was in Moses is given to the elders. So, there is unity of purpose and voice; these leaders only speak when that spirit is with them. In the camp, however, the prophetic spirit in Eldad and Medad is different and disruptive. Yet Moses will not have it silenced. Rather, he rejoices that the presence and power of the Lord breaks out in rich diversity and in difference.

Leadership needs to offer a hope that can be shared, but it must never erase difference. The book of Numbers celebrates the miracle of God's presence, which is evident in the most unlikely places and most unlikely actions. That power and presence of God will always be surprising, always disturbing. It will always be rich and various and we must celebrate difference. The Jesuit priest and poet Gerard Manley Hopkins was right, 'Glory be to God for dappled things'.*

* 'Pied Beauty', *Gerard Manley Hopkins: Poems and Prose* (Penguin Classics, 1985)

Risen Christ,
you have raised our human nature to the throne of heaven:
help us to seek and serve you,
that we may join you at the Father's side,
where you reign with the Spirit in glory,
now and for ever.

COLLECT

Reflection by **David Hoyle**   165

Monday 30 May

Psalms **93**, 96, 97 *or* **98**, 99, 101
Numbers 27.15-end
I Corinthians 3

Numbers 27.15-end

'You shall give him some of your authority' (v.20)

Frodo Baggins, in the *Lord of the Rings* trilogy by J. R. R. Tolkien, is the quiet and humble hobbit, who, though repeatedly injured and burdened by carrying the One Ring to the fires of Mount Doom in Mordor, is steadfast in his purpose. The ring is destroyed, and Aragorn is crowned King of Gondor, but, for Frodo, this new beginning does not include him. His wounds cannot be healed except by him letting go of his life and sailing with the elves to the Undying Lands.

Moses, so important in leading his people from the destructiveness of slavery, knows that he will never reach the Promised Land. His life's work has not shaped him for the next chapter in the life of his people; he knows God does not call him there. Moses, like Frodo, accepts the burden of his own personal history and lets go of his place in the story when the future is secured, his part played and his energy spent.

It can be shocking to pray for your church, workplace or family and realize you are not called to play the part you thought was yours. Moses is our example. He sees God's spirit at work in Joshua, so passes on some of his authority, ensuring stability in transition.

May we pray for the humility to let go of some of our authority and the insight to point where God's spirit leads.

COLLECT

O God the King of glory,
you have exalted your only Son Jesus Christ
with great triumph to your kingdom in heaven:
we beseech you, leave us not comfortless,
but send your Holy Spirit to strengthen us
and exalt us to the place where our Saviour Christ is gone before,
who is alive and reigns with you,
in the unity of the Holy Spirit,
one God, now and for ever.

| *Reflection by* **Justine Allain Chapman**

Psalms 85, 150
I Samuel 2.1-10
Mark 3.31-end

Tuesday 31 May
Visit of the Blessed Virgin
Mary to Elizabeth

Mark 3.31-end

'Whoever does the will of God is my brother and sister and mother'
(v.35)

My father was taken ill, miles from us but in the city where my daughter was at university. She visited her grandfather and told me that he had spoken of the enduring influence that I have had over his life. Hearing about that visit was the catalyst in me to see my father and my daughter as people who influence me and I them, because of who we are, not just in terms of family relationships.

Visits, especially those made out of concern or vulnerability, can bring personal insight and a renegotiation of the relationship. Mary visited her cousin Elizabeth when both were unexpectedly pregnant. The visit expressed their care for one another and brought reassurance. Elizabeth, the older woman, pointed Mary to God by proclaiming God's blessing for Mary personally as well as being used by God for his wider purposes. Much later, Mary visited Jesus having heard reports that he was out of his mind. Jesus, like Elizabeth, points her to look beyond her immediate concerns to God. He teaches her that he will draw human beings together with spiritual bonds that make them part of the same family – God's.

Every visit, into someone's home, to a ward or an office, holds the potential for relating in a way that opens us to God's spirit moving within and between us. Hold the visits of this week in prayer that you may be as open as Mary to the will of God.

COLLECT

Mighty God,
by whose grace Elizabeth rejoiced with Mary
and greeted her as the mother of the Lord:
look with favour on your lowly servants
that, with Mary, we may magnify your holy name
and rejoice to acclaim her Son our Saviour,
who is alive and reigns with you,
in the unity of the Holy Spirit,
one God, now and for ever.

Reflection by **Justine Allain Chapman** | 167

Wednesday 1 June

Psalms 2, **29** *or* 110, **111**, 112
1 Kings 19.1-18
Matthew 3.13-end

1 Kings 19.1-18

'What are you doing here, Elijah?' (v.9)

Legacy fever can drive a leader, near the end of their time of office, to focus on what history will say of them. It can take over and cloud their judgement. Accustomed to success and praise, they want what they have achieved handed on with their name attached.

Elijah, having won the contest with the prophets of Baal, has to flee for his life after his fellow prophets are all slaughtered. This isn't what he's expected, and in a state of nervous agitation, he prays for death because he has ended up no better than his ancestors. Restored by sleep and food, he travels and retreats to a cave on Mount Horeb to pray again.

At times of danger and of fear, we can get restless, preoccupied and unable to focus on what matters now. The Lord asks Elijah twice what he is doing in the cave, and both times Elijah starts by justifying himself, indignant at the way things have turned out. Elijah takes a while to settle and hear the voice of God. The noise of his success, his fear, the wind, earthquake and fire need to pass; there needs to be silence before he emerges from the cave, realizing he has come to hear what the Lord will say.

Elijah's legacy to us is that, in the fever of life, should we retreat to pray and wait, we will hear the still small voice of calm.

COLLECT

O God the King of glory,
you have exalted your only Son Jesus Christ
with great triumph to your kingdom in heaven:
we beseech you, leave us not comfortless,
but send your Holy Spirit to strengthen us
and exalt us to the place where our Saviour Christ is gone before,
who is alive and reigns with you,
in the unity of the Holy Spirit,
one God, now and for ever.

Reflection by **Justine Allain Chapman**

Psalms **24**, 72 *or* 113, **115**
Ezekiel 11.14-20
Matthew 9.35 – 10.20

Thursday 2 June

Ezekiel 11.14-20
'... heart of flesh' (v.19)

A heart of flesh is not a stubborn or proud heart, as cold and rigid as stone. A heart of flesh is alive and responsive, beating faster to rise to the challenges the body faces, slower when at rest. We don't tell our hearts how to do this. In fact, our physical hearts often tell us about ourselves – that we are afraid, nervous or in love.

Ezekiel prophesies that God will restore the nation from exile and give them a heart of flesh. This heart will make them responsive to God. It will tell them about themselves, that they belong to God who has provided them with what they need to live as his people, obeying his ordinances. One heart and a new spirit are promised. Those who were scattered will return, but as a unified and restored people.

The spiritual goal of the early monastic tradition was described as purity of heart. Purity of heart is a focus and direction of love towards God. It is an energy that integrates our life so that it is made whole, one in our purpose to love, like the constant pulse of energy that the heart ensures so that blood can flow in the right direction enabling us to live.

Spend a while listening to your heart of flesh and with purity of heart pray that God will make Christ's Church whole and one.

Risen, ascended Lord,
as we rejoice at your triumph,
fill your Church on earth with power and compassion,
that all who are estranged by sin
may find forgiveness and know your peace,
to the glory of God the Father.

COLLECT

Reflection by **Justine Allain Chapman**

Friday 3 June

Psalms **28**, 30 *or* **139**
Ezekiel 36.22-28
Matthew 12.22-32

Ezekiel 36.22-28

'... through you I display my holiness before their eyes' (v.23)

Pentecost is often referred to as Whitsun, short for 'White Sunday', after the colour worn for baptisms and confirmations, so often celebrated at the Feast. Individuals and families mark a new chapter of life on these occasions, pledging themselves to living as Christians. When you put on a white garment, a shirt or a shawl, fresh, clean and specially chosen, your dignity is made new as you are clothed in Christ.

Ezekiel declares that God's name will be honoured and known among the nations, not because God's people are punished for their profanity, but because God will gather them again and teach them how to live. God's rehabilitation programme resonates with Christian baptism. God will sprinkle them with water so that they are cleansed from the past, turning from idols to trusting in God. They receive a new spirit and are to follow God's ordinances, knowing they belong to God.

God's holiness is revealed by steadfast love that draws people back into a relationship with him. It is not a show of force that reveals God's nature, but that the people receive a gift of a new start and the gift of the Holy Spirit.

Might you wear white for Pentecost and show you honour God's name by the way in which you welcome, forgive and provide so that lives can be made new?

COLLECT

O God the King of glory,
you have exalted your only Son Jesus Christ
with great triumph to your kingdom in heaven:
we beseech you, leave us not comfortless,
but send your Holy Spirit to strengthen us
and exalt us to the place where our Saviour Christ is gone before,
who is alive and reigns with you,
in the unity of the Holy Spirit,
one God, now and for ever.

| *Reflection by* **Justine Allain Chapman**

Psalms 42, **43** *or* 120, **121**, 122
Micah 3.1-8
Ephesians 6.10-20

Micah 3.1-8

'But as for me, I am filled with power' (v.8)

Rosa Parks, on 1 December 1955, in Montgomery, Alabama, rejected the order of the bus driver to relinquish her seat in the 'colored' section of the bus to a white passenger after the whites-only section was filled. On that day, Rosa was weary from her hours working as a seamstress, and she acted out of an inner conviction of her dignity. She was 'tired of giving in' to injustice, but through the simplicity of her action, a pivotal moment in the civil rights movement was reached. Rosa was prepared to follow through, to be a controversial figure, her place in the community and church meaning she was the best candidate to see through a court challenge.

Micah lived in a nation where he could see leaders rule unjustly so that the wicked prospered and the prophets were complacent while people suffered. He declared that God will not answer the wicked, for he hides his face from them. They cannot, because of their sin, see God and so they and the nation as a whole cannot prosper. But God does not go silent, and Micah found himself filled with the power of God's spirit.

When we despair of the world and even the Church, look for God's irrepressible spirit. Through Micah's realization that he was compelled to speak the truth and Rosa Parks' tiredness and sense of dignity, the Holy Spirit found a home. As for you?

Risen, ascended Lord,
as we rejoice at your triumph,
fill your Church on earth with power and compassion,
that all who are estranged by sin
may find forgiveness and know your peace,
to the glory of God the Father.

COLLECT

Reflection by **Justine Allain Chapman**

171

Monday 6 June

Joshua 1

'... you shall put this people in possession of the land' (v.6)

Joshua is the first of the six history books, the others being Judges, 1 and 2 Samuel, and 1 and 2 Kings. History is written from the perspective of the victors, and in a post-colonial era the claiming and successful conquering of land and peoples can make for uncomfortable reading.

Generations of wisdom are needed to realize the impact of a nation's effect on others. Many nations have reassessed much in the last century, and some continue to be challenged by their past actions and assumptions. The legacy of conflict our sacred texts have passed down to the Promised Land rightly makes us pause as we read. An important question to ask is: who benefits from the story that is told?

Here we have a founding story for a people who needed to unite under new leadership for a new situation. Joshua led a displaced people of refugees needing to settle. The narratives of the book of Joshua reminded them of who they were and that they belong, when life was difficult with new ways of living to learn. As God's people, they had been given the land, claimed it successfully and would prosper if they kept their traditions, obeying their God.

One benefit this text can give us is to invite us to look at the stories we tell ourselves of our successes, personal or corporate. Do we acknowledge the hand of God? Have we become wise enough to consider the impact of our success on others at the time, or as we tell the story now?

COLLECT

O Lord, from whom all good things come:
grant to us your humble servants,
that by your holy inspiration
we may think those things that are good,
and by your merciful guiding may perform the same;
through our Lord Jesus Christ,
who is alive and reigns with you,
in the unity of the Holy Spirit,
one God, now and for ever.

| *Reflection by* **Justine Allain Chapman**

Psalms **132**, 133
Joshua 2
Luke 9.28-36

Tuesday 7 June

Joshua 2
'Our life for yours!' (v.14)

I don't think my mother would have been very pleased or believed me had I told her that I thought God would use me for his purposes as a prostitute or a spy. Neither are respectable ways of living since both are caught up in relationships that are disposable, laced with deceptions, promising what they can't give.

But the heroes who enable the capture of Jericho are the prostitute Rahab, from the enemy city, and the two spies sent by Joshua. Rahab betrayed her people to save her life and the life of her family in exchange for hiding the spies, saving their lives and furthering their mission.

When we live in secure and prosperous times, we are troubled when Jesus seems to commend dishonesty in the parable of the shrewd manager (Luke 16.1-15) or recommend that we be as wise or cunning as a serpent (Matthew 10.16). A snake, though a surprising role model, waits, poised for the right moment to strike.

Rahab and the spies are honoured because they take a risk and trust outsiders so that they can save the lives they need to and secure a future. War forces choices we might be grateful we don't have to make.

Does your Christian faith lead you to a desire to be respectable above all else? Can wisdom lead you to trust an outsider, compromise and take risks for the sake of life?

O Lord, from whom all good things come:
grant to us your humble servants,
that by your holy inspiration
we may think those things that are good,
and by your merciful guiding may perform the same;
through our Lord Jesus Christ,
who is alive and reigns with you,
in the unity of the Holy Spirit,
one God, now and for ever.

COLLECT

Reflection by **Justine Allain Chapman** | 173

Wednesday 8 June

Psalm 119.153-end
Joshua 3
Luke 9.37-50

Joshua 3

'... you have not passed this way before' (v.4)

When we watch a romantic film and see a groom carrying a bride over the threshold, we know that we are being told that married life has begun. It's an old tradition, and we see that the bride is supported, prevented from tripping, eased by care into a new stage of life.

For the people of Israel, often described as a bride, the threshold is the River Jordan. As they cross, they know God is with them, ahead of them as they follow the Ark of the Covenant. Their journey is eased by the rising up of the waters, so that they can cross on dry land.

This generation had not passed that way before, but they knew that the previous generation had crossed the Red Sea escaping from slavery. This was a different river, a leaving-behind of wandering to becoming settled and free.

The resonances of the story are a reminder of the past, assuring them and us that God leads his people as they cross new boundaries in their lives. The story points to the future in the same way. The River Jordan became the place where Jesus, accompanied by John the Baptist, entered the water and received the Holy Spirit for the beginning of his public ministry.

Where are the thresholds in your life or church where reminders of God's intimate presence are needed?

COLLECT

O Lord, from whom all good things come:
grant to us your humble servants,
that by your holy inspiration
we may think those things that are good,
and by your merciful guiding may perform the same;
through our Lord Jesus Christ,
who is alive and reigns with you,
in the unity of the Holy Spirit,
one God, now and for ever.

| *Reflection by* **Justine Allain Chapman**

Psalms **143**, 146
Joshua 4.1 – 5.1
Luke 9.51-end

Thursday 9 June

Joshua 4.1 – 5.1

'What do these stones mean to you?' (4.6)

I have noticed that families who move into a much bigger house often report a change in the way family members relate to each other. More rooms and more space mean they do not come across each other in the way they did before; they can live more separate lives. A new place needs settling into, and a household has to develop new ways of ensuring there is the opportunity of sharing life and love as well as passing on values to the younger generation.

As the nomadic Israelites prepared to settle and their tribes separate to get more space to live, Joshua knew they would need reminders that they were all God's people, brought out of slavery and given a covenant that would ensure their wellbeing and protection. So Joshua asked for one person in each tribe to choose a stone on which the priests had stood holding the Ark while the people crossed over the river and to take it to their camp. Huge stones were to act as a physical memorial for each tribe, and the twelve who had chosen them were entrusted with being the story bearers. They were to ensure that the people feared the Lord.

In a household or a community, there are some who can seem to go on a bit about the past. Authentic story bearers are those who, in new spaces, remind us of God's faithfulness and help in finding ways to show and pass on our life and love.

O Lord, from whom all good things come:
grant to us your humble servants,
that by your holy inspiration
we may think those things that are good,
and by your merciful guiding may perform the same;
through our Lord Jesus Christ,
who is alive and reigns with you,
in the unity of the Holy Spirit,
one God, now and for ever.

COLLECT

Reflection by **Justine Allain Chapman** | 175

Friday 10 June

Joshua 5.2-end

'I have rolled away from you the disgrace of Egypt' (v.9)

Within any demanding time, such as war or personal crisis, we have to prioritize survival. The Israelites were a displaced people and, though free from the slavery of Egypt, they were refugees. The sense of who they were as God's people was eroded by not being safe enough to carry out the religious ritual of circumcision, as well as not being able to pass on their culture and customs to the next generation.

Without status, respect of other nations and land, a people is brought into disgrace and lacks self-determination. Arrival in the Promised Land gave the Israelites hope and a future. Energy no longer spent on fear and constantly moving on could be given to culture and creativity, such as completing the story of their freedom by celebrating Passover. Having land brought the benefit of its varied produce but with it came the responsibility of farming, for they no longer needed to be dependent on manna.

Any freedom and security we enjoy goes with responsibility to use our energy to invest in the next generation and those in need. It is a disgrace to the human race when individuals and peoples are not safe or free enough to be who they are, have agency over their lives and enjoy what the world has to offer.

How might you, through the grace of God, speak out or give to roll away disgrace from those who suffer?

COLLECT	O Lord, from whom all good things come:
	grant to us your humble servants,
	that by your holy inspiration
	we may think those things that are good,
	and by your merciful guiding may perform the same;
	through our Lord Jesus Christ,
	who is alive and reigns with you,
	in the unity of the Holy Spirit,
	one God, now and for ever.

| *Reflection by* **Justine Allain Chapman**

Psalms 100, 101, 117
Jeremiah 9.23-24
Acts 4.32-end

Saturday 11 June

Barnabas the Apostle

Acts 4.32-end

'... son of encouragement' (v.36)

When my children started to share houses with other students, I encouraged them not to buy a toaster or a microwave jointly with flatmates, but to buy something they would share for the year and then still own afterwards. This bit of wisdom came out of my experience of difficult conversations about how to divide shared possessions.

Joseph from Cyprus sold a field and laid the money at the apostles' feet and the church gave him the nickname of Barnabas, meaning 'son of encouragement'. Barnabas trusted in God and in the leadership of the Church, and this enabled him to leave at least some security behind and invest in a shared future. He gave unreservedly, without conditions, not expecting to receive either a nameplate, a perk or a return of his cash if he no longer agreed with any decisions made.

Encouragement is not a centre-stage quality, but it is a virtue that has the capacity to transform lives. Openly placing your trust in a cause can give credibility to a venture. Your example encourages others to follow suit and so builds up a community. Such open-handed generosity of resources, including time and words, encourages leaders to move forward with vision for a new time.

Where today might you encourage your brothers and sisters in Christ, by your example of giving or speaking out of an open heart?

COLLECT

Bountiful God, giver of all gifts,
who poured your Spirit upon your servant Barnabas
and gave him grace to encourage others:
help us, by his example,
to be generous in our judgements
and unselfish in our service;
through Jesus Christ your Son our Lord,
who is alive and reigns with you,
in the unity of the Holy Spirit,
one God, now and for ever.

Reflection by **Justine Allain Chapman**

Monday 13 June

Joshua 7.1-15

'But the Israelites broke faith ...' (v.1)

For the writer of Joshua, disobedience to God's commandment is a breaking of faith. To our ears, 'breaking faith' sounds peculiar. We can *lose* our faith; we can *deepen* our faith; we can *find* faith. At times of crisis, we urge one another to *keep* the faith. But we cannot *break* faith, can we?

Moreover, we tend to think of faith as personal, even private: this is *my* faith; that is *yours*. Or we use faith as a way of defining a group; we talk about members of a faith community or 'people of faith'.

Writing from the experience of exile, the author of Joshua imagines faith differently, not as personal commitment, or as group identity, but as an expression of a solemn, binding agreement between Israel and God. The Israelites are defeated at Ai or dragged into exile by the Babylonians because they have transgressed the terms of a bond. They have broken something vital: faith.

Even worse than that, God says the Israelites have *become* that thing to which they have devoted themselves (v.12). Where we fix our faith is who we are. So am I a person, or a thing? The difference is faith. At the heart of these harsh and often rebarbative Deuteronomistic writings is the idea that faith is shared and breakable, like a promise. Faith in God is a living relationship. Outside that mutually faithful relationship is nothing. The choice is ours: thingdom or kingdom.

COLLECT

Almighty and everlasting God,
you have given us your servants grace,
by the confession of a true faith,
to acknowledge the glory of the eternal Trinity
and in the power of the divine majesty to worship the Unity:
keep us steadfast in this faith,
that we may evermore be defended from all adversities;
through Jesus Christ your Son our Lord,
who is alive and reigns with you,
in the unity of the Holy Spirit,
one God, now and for ever.

Reflection by **Colin Heber-Percy**

Psalms **5**, 6 (8)
Joshua 7.16-end
Luke 10.38-end

Tuesday 14 June

Joshua 7.16-end

'Tell me now what you have done; do not hide it from me' (v.19)

Confronted by texts like this, it is tempting to listen to Euripides when he argues, 'If the gods do anything base, they are not the gods!' We ask, this is not God, surely?

Or we can follow Marcion (c.85 – c.160) who believed the jealous, vengeful God of the Old Testament was not to be identified with the merciful, loving Father of our Lord Jesus Christ. Marcion was excommunicated as a heretic in 144. No, like it or not, we must wrestle with the God of Joshua, somehow come to terms. And make no mistake, they will be God's terms. This is not a negotiation. As Jacob found at Peniel (Genesis 32.22-32), wrestling with the Lord may leave us limping, wounded, but blessed.

Biblical accounts like the story of Achan force us to wrestle with our own devoted things. And what are they? Could they be our cosy theological preconceptions, our tendency to mould God to fit our own moral norms and standards, to render God manageable and predictable?

Like Achan, we have hidden our 'devoted things,' but in plain sight. They are the ethical air we breathe, our uninvestigated moral codes and mores. We are called, like the tribes, to recognize them among us, to hold them up for inspection, for accounting.

If this passage bothers us, good. Let it muddle us and mess up our comforting presumptions and biases, the idols of our own making. The bothering is the blessing.

Holy God,
faithful and unchanging:
enlarge our minds with the knowledge of your truth,
and draw us more deeply into the mystery of your love,
that we may truly worship you,
Father, Son and Holy Spirit,
one God, now and for ever.

COLLECT

Reflection by **Colin Heber-Percy**

Wednesday 15 June

Joshua 8.1-29

'Stretch out the sword that is in your hand' (v.18)

'THIS SENTENCE IS FALSE.' If this sentence expresses a truth, then what it expresses is its own falsity: impossible. If the sentence expresses a falsehood, then it is true: impossible again. Joshua 8 is an impossible text. It forces us into the most uncomfortable position, an impossible position: we feel forced to sit in moral judgement on God. God's actions are surely indefensible?

In Plato's *Euthyphro*, Socrates poses a question: is a given action holy because God commands it? Or does God command us to perform a particular action because it is holy? We might well feel our standards of right and wrong derive from the commands and prohibitions of an all-good God. And yet in this passage, God orchestrates mass murder. Are we to suppose that under certain circumstances mass murder is morally acceptable, God's will, righteous?

Even to ask that question is to try to make sense of an impossible text. Are we able to wriggle off the hook by interpreting away the problem as scholars, as archaeologists, as critics? Or should we accept the text as a divinely inspired factual account of a real event? Both approaches are flawed, human attempts at rendering the text tractable, making it possible. But it is impossible.

Confronted by a passage like this, all we can do is allow it to disrupt, to disturb, to rub us up the wrong way. Be troubled. There is grit in this oyster.

COLLECT

Almighty and everlasting God,
you have given us your servants grace,
by the confession of a true faith,
to acknowledge the glory of the eternal Trinity
and in the power of the divine majesty to worship the Unity:
keep us steadfast in this faith,
that we may evermore be defended from all adversities;
through Jesus Christ your Son our Lord,
who is alive and reigns with you,
in the unity of the Holy Spirit,
one God, now and for ever.

| *Reflection by* **Colin Heber-Percy**

Psalm 147
Deuteronomy 8.2-16
I Corinthians 10.1-17

Thursday 16 June

Day of Thanksgiving for the Institution
of Holy Communion (Corpus Christi)

Deuteronomy 8.2-16

'... and in the end to do you good' (v.16)

Today is the feast of Corpus Christi, the celebration of Christ's presence in the eucharistic elements. And while we leave the book of Joshua, we remain in the world of the Deuteronomistic writer.

According to Matthew and Luke, when the devil encourages Jesus to turn desert stones to bread, Jesus answers: 'One does not live by bread alone, but by every word that comes from the mouth of God' (Matthew 4.4). We are reflecting here on a passage Jesus knew well and from which he quoted. This passage and the moment in the Gospel narrative where it is quoted, are concerned with testing. The association of bread and the wilderness goes deep. The Israelites are fed in the desert on manna sent by God. The widow at Zarephath feeds Elijah with the last of her flour and oil (1 Kings 17.12-15). Bread saves.

The bread is both test and testament to our relationship with God. And central to this idea is the *givenness* of the bread. It is not for us to exalt ourselves in our ingenuity, but the grace of God in his generosity. What Christ does with this tradition is outrageous. He identifies himself neither with the giver nor with those who receive, but with the given, with bread – 'I am the bread of life' (John 6:35).

When Christ breaks and *gives* his body for the sake of us all, he becomes the end that does us ultimate good: our redemption. Bread saves.

Lord Jesus Christ,
we thank you that in this wonderful sacrament
you have given us the memorial of your passion:
grant us so to reverence the sacred mysteries
of your body and blood
that we may know within ourselves
and show forth in our lives
the fruits of your redemption;
for you are alive and reign with the Father
in the unity of the Holy Spirit,
one God, now and for ever.

COLLECT

Reflection by **Colin Heber-Percy**

Friday 17 June

Psalms 17, **19**
Joshua 9.3-26
Luke 11.29-36

Joshua 9.3-26

'We have sworn to them by the Lord' (v.19)

There is something comic about the Gibeonites' ruse. They use disguise and flattery to deceive the Israelites, who prove peculiarly gullible. I say 'I have come from a far country', but why should you believe me? What if I swear to the truth of my words? In law we pledge to speak the truth, placing our hand on a holy book and swearing an oath. My words may be weak, but my guarantor God is strong.

The leaders of the Israelites have to remind the congregation that the devious Gibeonites are not to be attacked; they are protected by an oath: 'We have sworn to them by the Lord, the God of Israel.'

Some scholars maintain that the first purpose of religion was its power to indemnify a sworn oath. Today, the working of our currencies, the entire global economy, is underpinned by 'the promise to pay the bearer' of the note. And that promise is secured: 'In God we trust', it says on every US dollar bill. The English philosopher, John Locke claims 'oaths, which are the bonds of human society, can have no hold upon or sanctity for an atheist'. Religion secures our civic and corporate lives.

Yet we are called not just to swear to the truth, but to stay true. For Christians, staying true to the Word is not a command or a function of religion; it *is* religion, and it is to live. Jesus Christ *is* the truth (John 14.6).

COLLECT	Almighty and everlasting God, you have given us your servants grace, by the confession of a true faith, to acknowledge the glory of the eternal Trinity and in the power of the divine majesty to worship the Unity: keep us steadfast in this faith, that we may evermore be defended from all adversities; through Jesus Christ your Son our Lord, who is alive and reigns with you, in the unity of the Holy Spirit, one God, now and for ever.

| *Reflection by* **Colin Heber-Percy**

Psalms 20, 21, **23**
Joshua 10.1-15
Luke 11.37-end

Saturday 18 June

Joshua 10.1-15

'... for the Lord fought for Israel' (v.14)

As a schoolboy, I loved reading accounts of battles in the ancient historians. What fascinated me was how just a few short paragraphs of Polybius or Livy could be a source for contemporary strategists. So, German General von Schlieffen's plan to annihilate the French Third Republic in 1914 by invading France through Belgium and Luxembourg is supposed to have had its genesis in careful study of Hannibal's tactics at the battle of Cannae in 216 BC.

Can we read the book of Joshua in the way we read the ancient historians? Yes and no. Yes inasmuch as what we are reading purports to be an historical account of an invasion; we have a narrative filled with incident and character and named places. There are stratagems, victories and defeats, alliances and deceptions. In this passage we also find typical ingredients of ancient history writing: portents and a description of unusual meteorological conditions.

But there is one crucial difference: reading Joshua, we have skin in the game. We are invested, implicated. The protagonists in Livy's account of the Punic Wars are all dead and gone. The protagonist in Joshua is God, alive and well.

In 2003, the chief adviser to the British Prime Minister is supposed to have said, 'We don't do God,' meaning there is no place for faith in politics. He forgot to let God know. Because the truth is, as Joshua reminds us, God definitely does politics, the transcendent, living context of our unfolding history.

Holy God,
faithful and unchanging:
enlarge our minds with the knowledge of your truth,
and draw us more deeply into the mystery of your love,
that we may truly worship you,
Father, Son and Holy Spirit,
one God, now and for ever.

COLLECT

Reflection by **Colin Heber-Percy** | 183

Monday 20 June

Psalms 27, **30**
Joshua 14
Luke 12.1-12

Joshua 14

'... yet I wholeheartedly followed the Lord my God' (v.8)

I vividly remember an illustration from a Bible I had as a child: two Israelite spies are carrying a vast bunch of grapes suspended from a pole between them. The pole sags, the muscles in the men's arms strain with the effort; it is as much as they can bear (Numbers 13.23).

The names of the Israelite spies are given in that chapter from Numbers, which recounts their mission into hostile Canaan. Among them are a young Joshua, still subordinate to Moses, and Caleb son of Jephunneh. Some forty years later, the two men meet again, now in their eighties, veterans of the long and gruelling campaign. Caleb reminds Joshua of their earlier daring exploits, scouting out the Promised Land for Moses.

There is something touching about this reunion. It reminds me of Falstaff and Justice Shallow in Shakespeare's *Henry IV, Part II,* two old rogues recalling their youth: 'The days that we have seen!' (Act 3, scene 2). Caleb claims to be as strong at 85 as he was at 40. 'Go on, feel my muscles ...' Perhaps he was one of those labouring under the weight of plundered grapes?

But the scene offers us more than an account of two friends reminiscing and signing off on a deal; it movingly summarizes and humanizes the central theme of the entire invasion narrative. The key to your inheritance of the Promised Land is in following the Lord with your whole heart.

COLLECT

O God,
the strength of all those who put their trust in you,
mercifully accept our prayers
and, because through the weakness of our mortal nature
we can do no good thing without you,
grant us the help of your grace,
that in the keeping of your commandments
we may please you both in will and deed;
through Jesus Christ your Son our Lord,
who is alive and reigns with you,
in the unity of the Holy Spirit,
one God, now and for ever.

| *Reflection by* **Colin Heber-Percy**

Tuesday 21 June

Joshua 21.43 – 22.8

'... the Lord gave to Israel all the land' (v.43)

After generations of slavery and wandering in the wilderness, the Israelites are suddenly settled. They find themselves in a radically new situation, and now the real test begins.

Tellingly, Joshua's speech here is more about covenant than it is about conveyance. Yes, the land is passing into your ownership: 'Well done, good and trustworthy slave' (Matthew 25:23), but remember, this land is given you with conditions. Observe the commandments; love the Lord your God; serve him with all your heart.

I love it in pirate movies when the 'X' on the map has been reached, the treasure dug up, a casket hacked open to reveal heaped doubloons and jewels. Go on, delve in and throw handfuls of loot into the air! It is a natural human tendency. At last, we are rich and free!

As Joshua reminds the Israelites, precisely the opposite is the case. It is a deep, scriptural truth: 'From one to whom much has been entrusted, even more will be demanded' (Luke 12.48). Taking possession of the Promised Land does not release the Israelites from their obligation, but ratifies it. Whatever we feel about the invasion narrative in Joshua, it is not a land grab; it is a land gift.

In our freewheeling and piratical-*parvenu* world, we are taught to think of possession and ownership as inoculation against being controlled and as authorization to exercise control over others. The God of Israel is here to tell you otherwise.

God of truth,
help us to keep your law of love
and to walk in ways of wisdom,
that we may find true life
in Jesus Christ your Son.

COLLECT

Wednesday 22 June

Joshua 22.9-end

'... to be a witness' (v.27)

At stake here is a law delivered to the Israelites concerning the altars, pillars and sacred poles of the Canaanites. They must be destroyed by fire or hewn down. And the people of Israel are not to worship God anywhere except in 'the place that the Lord your God will choose out of all your tribes as his habitation' (Deuteronomy 12.5). Have the Reubenites, Gadites and half-tribe of Manasseh broken the law?

Opened in 2005, the Holocaust Memorial in Berlin is a grid of blocks. You can lose yourself in its 'streets'. Some of the stelae are altar-sized; others tall as shipping containers or even houses. It is like walking through the stacks of a library or a mini Manhattan, or a morgue. Glimpses of others become sacralized: a bare arm, a peeping child playing hide-and-seek, a couple kissing.

The designers of the memorial could have taken a cue from the tribes, however: this is not actually a memorial at all. It is a *witness*. Silent, yet singing, like a psalm.

A memorial looks back, but the altar in this passage from Joshua – like the site in Berlin – is designed to stand as a testament for posterity. The idea of witness is far richer and more demanding than the idea of memorial. A memorial fixes; a witness watches, and sees.

We are called not to be memorials, but to be Christ's *witnesses* 'to the ends of the earth' (Acts 1.8).

COLLECT

O God,
the strength of all those who put their trust in you,
mercifully accept our prayers
and, because through the weakness of our mortal nature
we can do no good thing without you,
grant us the help of your grace,
that in the keeping of your commandments
we may please you both in will and deed;
through Jesus Christ your Son our Lord,
who is alive and reigns with you,
in the unity of the Holy Spirit,
one God, now and for ever.

| *Reflection by* **Colin Heber-Percy**

Thursday 23 June

Joshua 23

'... hold fast to the Lord your God' (v.8)

Someone steals your bank account details, your national insurance number, or starts using your email address, and we say you are a victim of identity theft. Your identity has been stolen. Really? Do these strings of numbers and letters actually constitute your identity? Of course not. Our identities cannot be stolen. But perhaps they can be lost or given away.

This passage is about holding on to an identity, ensuring it is not lost. Prohibitions on intermarriage and apostasy are ways, familiar from our own mobile and diverse cultures, of preventing identity loss or leakage.

While we find phrases like 'identity theft' absurd, we feel that *losing* or *changing* our identity might be possible and possibly be injurious. In Joshua's final speech to the Israelites, the Deuteronomist compounds a deep conservatism with a theology of covenant: the land that has been given you comes with conditions. Fail to satisfy those conditions and the land will be removed from you. Writing from exile, the Deuteronomist knows what it is to live with a threatened identity. Perhaps we all do. If your identity is not threatened by hackers, what is it threatened by? Are there aspects of our own prevailing culture that are Canaan?

The emphasis in Joshua's speech on racial purity and violence may unsettle, reminding us of more recent horrors, but use this passage to ask yourself: what actually *is* my identity? What could I not lose without losing myself?

God of truth,
help us to keep your law of love
and to walk in ways of wisdom,
that we may find true life
in Jesus Christ your Son.

COLLECT

Reflection by **Colin Heber-Percy** | 187

Friday 24 June

Birth of John the Baptist

Psalms 50, 149
Ecclesiasticus 48.1-10
or Malachi 3.1-6
Luke 3.1-17

Malachi 3.1-6

'I am sending my messenger to prepare the way before me' (v.1)

News of a messenger coming to prepare the way of the Lord is proclaimed right at the very close of the Old Testament. In the opening of the New Testament, at the beginning of the earliest of the synoptic gospels we hear: 'John the baptizer appeared in the wilderness' (Mark 1.4). Today is the feast of the Birth of John the Baptist.

John is a hinge on which the Bible turns. Without hinges, a door neither opens nor closes, but falls out of its frame. John is a turning point, certainly, but he is also an anchoring, a fixing. If the Bible were to be reupholstered, John would be a tufting button, holding the testaments together.

In the opening chapter of John's Gospel, priests and Levites are sent to ask the Baptist, 'Who are you?' John is able only to say who he is not. Tellingly, the only positive assertion he makes about himself is a quotation: 'I am the voice of one crying out in the wilderness' (John 1.23). He is a paradoxical figure, pointing forward by urging us to turn back, to repent. He sings of what is to come by reminding us of something ancient: Elijah and the prophets. We know what he wears, what he eats, when he's conceived and how he dies. And yet John himself remains a mystery. Hinged, John stands before us. 'Knock, and the door will be opened for you' (Matthew 7.7).

COLLECT

Almighty God,
by whose providence your servant John the Baptist
   was wonderfully born,
and sent to prepare the way of your Son our Saviour
by the preaching of repentance:
lead us to repent according to his preaching
and, after his example,
constantly to speak the truth, boldly to rebuke vice,
and patiently to suffer for the truth's sake;
through Jesus Christ your Son our Lord,
who is alive and reigns with you,
in the unity of the Holy Spirit,
one God, now and for ever.

| *Reflection by* **Colin Heber-Percy**

Psalms 41, **42**, 43
Joshua 24.29-end
Luke 12.49-end

Saturday 25 June

Joshua 24.29-end

'After these things...' (v.29)

Back when Israel was just Jacob, a plot of land was purchased for a hundred coins (Genesis 33.18-20). Outside Shechem, this patch of ground on which Jacob pitched his tent is now where Joseph's bones are laid to rest. In a profoundly moving gesture, Joshua has brought Israel full circle. Through it all, place persists as a theme, encircling the story, driving it on, like God. The association is not accidental. In the book of Joshua, God is a God of places, of promised places.

Throughout our reading of Joshua, we have taken care to remember that this account is written from an experience of landlessness, of exile. When we first meet Israel in the Bible, it is embodied in people 'passing through', in a context of movement and searching, place to place. Moses is 'an alien residing in a foreign land' (Exodus 2.22). The Israelites are slaves, then wanderers, then invaders. Then exiles. Their experience of being a landed people is brief and uneasy.

For the Israelites, place is not a staying put, but a promise. For us too, the promised place is before us all, still to come: the kingdom of God.

Like the Israelites, we are a restless, rootless people. And yet God abides and journeys with each of us, steadfast, his promise true.

Wanderer, there is a plot of land with an altar, just outside Shechem. Find it. And rest.

COLLECT

O God,
the strength of all those who put their trust in you,
mercifully accept our prayers
and, because through the weakness of our mortal nature
we can do no good thing without you,
grant us the help of your grace,
that in the keeping of your commandments
we may please you both in will and deed;
through Jesus Christ your Son our Lord,
who is alive and reigns with you,
in the unity of the Holy Spirit,
one God, now and for ever.

Reflection by **Colin Heber-Percy**

Monday 27 June

Psalm **44**
Judges 2
Luke 13.1-9

Judges 2

'I will never break my covenant with you' (v.1)

Finalized during the Babylonian exile, the book of Judges records the history of the people of Israel, following entry into the Promised Land. Today's passage covers several centuries and depicts the pattern of Israel's relationship with God. It's a cycle: God's people forget God's ways, turn to worship idols, are dominated by foreign powers, and then cry out, lamenting their predicament. In response to their pain, God sends a charismatic leader, who delivers the people. This is the office of Judge, held by a series of individuals. Throughout, God remains constant and faithful. God's side of the covenant is kept – unbroken – despite the faithlessness of the people.

In this long season of Ordinary Time, it's good to examine our relationship with the living God, revealed to us as Creator, Redeemer and Sanctifier. What is it in your life, or our world today that may make you turn away from the love of God offered to you? Where are you in danger of giving up on God? Which contemporary idols catch your attention?

If you or others are currently in a situation of oppression or coercion, cry out to God, calling for rescue and justice. Take time to lament situations of concern. There is good precedent: Jesus wept over Jerusalem (Luke 19.41); Paul wept for those who turned away from Christ (2 Corinthians 2.4). Remember, in all circumstances, God promises to be with us and for us.

COLLECT

Lord, you have taught us
that all our doings without love are nothing worth:
send your Holy Spirit
and pour into our hearts that most excellent gift of love,
the true bond of peace and of all virtues,
without which whoever lives is counted dead before you.
Grant this for your only Son Jesus Christ's sake,
who is alive and reigns with you,
in the unity of the Holy Spirit,
one God, now and for ever.

| *Reflection by* **Catherine Williams**

Psalms **48**, 52
Judges 4.1-23
Luke 13.10-21

Tuesday 28 June

Judges 4.1-23

'If you will go with me, I will go' (v.8)

Deborah, Judge and prophet, sits under a palm tree in the hills between settlements. There she waits, and there the people go to consult her and receive her guidance and wisdom. In that place of waiting, she listens to the Lord, speaks with authority of the things she has heard and sends for those whom the Lord is calling. Barak is one, summoned into battle against the mighty Sisera, oppressor of the Israelites. Barak will only go if Deborah goes with him, which she does, though adding enigmatically that it will be a woman who wins the victory, not him.

The dramatic and astonishing saga of the murder of Sisera at the hands of Jael and her tent-peg unfolds. A mixture of strategy, intuition, fellowship, opportunism and courage enable the Israelites to gain the upper hand. The Song of Deborah in Chapter 5 celebrates the victory.

We all need to be able to wait on God in order to discern the Holy Spirit's directing, which may be full of surprises. Trust is required of us to take time in stillness and wait patiently for the Spirit to lead and guide, for this will be in God's timing not ours. God's surprises may mean that events unfold in a way that we cannot possibly imagine, and over which we have little control. And sometimes others get the praise and recognition for something we have engineered and worked for. How do you handle all these facets of serving God? Which song are you singing?

Faithful Creator,
whose mercy never fails:
deepen our faithfulness to you
and to your living Word,
Jesus Christ our Lord.

COLLECT

Reflection by **Catherine Williams** | 191

Wednesday 29 June
Peter the Apostle

Psalms 71, 113
Isaiah 49.1-6
Acts 11.1-18

Isaiah 49.1-6
'... he made me a polished arrow' (v.2)

Today, the Church celebrates St Peter and St Paul, two great pillars of the faith, remembered together on this, the anniversary of their joint martyrdom in Rome around AD 64. Our passage speaks of the Lord's calling of the servant who will be the light to the nations. In the context of that, the writer of Isaiah speaks of this messenger as one who is like a polished arrow hidden in God's quiver waiting to be shot into flight. Peter and Paul would have known these verses by heart. I wonder if they identified themselves as God's polished arrows, carrying the good news of Jesus.

Arrows are precision instruments, beautifully crafted, often by hand. Arrows are streamlined to fly swiftly and accurately. Arrows are strong, but not rigid, flexing to the will of the archer. On its own, the arrow can do little – it is useless – but with the skill and the power of the archer, it comes to life and can be swift and accurate. Peter, Paul, you and I are these polished arrows, made by God the Archer. Hand-crafted, individual, unique, called and known by name. We each have a special relationship with God who spends time crafting and polishing us until we gleam with the light of Christ – a light for the nations.

God's arrows do not fly alone. We follow God's topflight arrow, Jesus Christ, and fly in the slipstream of the saints and apostles.

COLLECT

Almighty God,
who inspired your apostle Saint Peter
to confess Jesus as Christ and Son of the living God:
build up your Church upon this rock,
that in unity and peace it may proclaim one truth
and follow one Lord, your Son our Saviour Christ,
who is alive and reigns with you,
in the unity of the Holy Spirit,
one God, now and for ever.

Thursday 30 June

Judges 6.1-24

'I am the least in my family' (v.15)

When God calls, either as an initial calling into discipleship or a further calling to some form of service or ministry, it's not unusual to feel unworthy or inadequate. God's calling usually requires some growing into. God already knows who we will become, but we often need reassurance, affirmation and considerable Godly persuasion before we believe it.

This is certainly the case for Gideon called to deliver the Israelites from the Midianites. Gideon has questioned why, if the Lord is with the people, such dreadful things are happening. He wonders why God's wonderful deeds are no longer in evidence. The Lord replies to this challenge by commissioning Gideon, who hesitates, trying to find excuses to get out of God's calling.

Throughout the Bible, we encounter people of all walks of life, genders, ages and abilities being called by God to challenging tasks and roles. People respond in a variety of ways: questioning God's wisdom, pointing out their flaws and faults, running away, or suggesting that someone else would be a better choice. Gideon asks for a sign and gets more than he bargains for – seeing the angel of the Lord face to face. So, excuses, evasion, procrastination and fear are not unusual initial reactions to God's calling on our lives. Humble acknowledgement of our weakness and unsuitability is a fertile ground in which the grace of God flourishes to bring the plans of the Holy Spirit to fruition.

Lord, you have taught us
that all our doings without love are nothing worth:
send your Holy Spirit
and pour into our hearts that most excellent gift of love,
the true bond of peace and of all virtues,
without which whoever lives is counted dead before you.
Grant this for your only Son Jesus Christ's sake,
who is alive and reigns with you,
in the unity of the Holy Spirit,
one God, now and for ever.

COLLECT

Reflection by **Catherine Williams**

193

Friday 1 July

Judges 6.25-end

'… the spirit of the Lord took possession of Gideon' (v.34)

God regularly calls us to things that we believe to be completely beyond us, or that require us to trust deeply, taking risks with faith and courage. In today's passage, God asks Gideon to challenge the culture and worldview of his community by destroying the altar to Baal, replacing it with a new altar and worshipping God at it. It's a dangerous and subversive act, and Gideon is afraid. So, he does it by night. It reminds me of the Pharisee Nicodemus who met with Jesus under cover of darkness, fearful of being discovered by the Sanhedrin (John 3).

Once Gideon has carried out God's commission, he grows in stature and confidence. He puts on God's spirit like a new set of clothes and, standing tall, he summons and directs others to join with him. He still has his doubts, though, and tests God twice just to make sure he has God's blessing and is fulfilling God's will.

As followers of Jesus, we are clothed with Christ (Galatians 3.27) and filled with the Holy Spirit, who possesses us not just for a particular task or season but continually, leading and guiding us on our journey of faith. What do you sense God might be asking of you that you are currently too frightened to explore or undertake? Allow the Holy Spirit to take possession of your fear and bring to light your confidence to serve in whatever capacity God calls you to.

COLLECT

Lord, you have taught us
that all our doings without love are nothing worth:
send your Holy Spirit
and pour into our hearts that most excellent gift of love,
the true bond of peace and of all virtues,
without which whoever lives is counted dead before you.
Grant this for your only Son Jesus Christ's sake,
who is alive and reigns with you,
in the unity of the Holy Spirit,
one God, now and for ever.

Psalm **68**
Judges 7
Luke 14.25-end

Saturday 2 July

Judges 7
'For the Lord and for Gideon!' (v.18)

Gideon is ready to serve the Lord. He has amassed everything he needs to fulfil the task. But the Lord isn't impressed. The resources gathered mean that Gideon can win the battle in his own strength with no need to lean on God for deliverance. God shakes the resources and Gideon is left with a tiny fraction of his original troops. Now Gideon has to listen to God, trust that he will receive the courage and creativity he needs to lead his tiny forces against the huge destructive swarm that lies in wait. With not much to hand – a few trumpets, jugs and torches – Gideon's noisy army terrifies the Midianites and wins the day.

God can do extraordinary things with very little. Elderly parents can have descendants beyond number; a shepherd boy can become a king; a teenage mum can give birth to God's son. That son, Jesus, can feed thousands from a small packed lunch, tame the weather, and raise the dead. His small band of followers can grow a worldwide religion.

Very often we try to amass resources for ministry, agonizing over statistics and anxiously recording Church decline. We think that if we have more of everything, God's work will flourish. Perhaps God's shaking of our resources at this current time is a call to listen to God, walk with Jesus and trust afresh in the Holy Spirit's provision. With God at the helm, nothing is impossible.

Faithful Creator,
whose mercy never fails:
deepen our faithfulness to you
and to your living Word,
Jesus Christ our Lord.

COLLECT

Reflection by **Catherine Williams**   195

Monday 4 July

Psalm 71
Judges 8.22-end
Luke 15.1-10

Judges 8.22-end

'… it became a snare to Gideon and to his family' (v.22)

Oh dear! It was all going so well. The battle won, the people rescued and Gideon resisting their desire to make him and his family rulers: 'the Lord will rule over you', says Gideon. But success can be problematic, leading to complacency once life calms down and reliance on God becomes less urgent. Gideon sends mixed messages to the people. His act of piety in raising a golden ephod looks like idolatry, not dissimilar to the golden calf of Exodus 32. He refrains from being king but begins to behave like one: holding court, keeping many wives and concubines, and growing a dynasty. Following his death, the Israelites quickly turn from God, back to worshipping Baal.

There are many examples of success, fame or fortune leading to someone's downfall. Adulation by others is heady stuff, and being placed on a pedestal can be hard to resist. The particular message for us in Gideon's story is that his lack of integration leads others to turn away from God. As Christians, we witness to Jesus in every part of our lives – through words, actions, thoughts and behaviour. Dissonance between what we say and what we do, or in the inner and outer expressions of ourselves, causes people to be wary or disbelieving of the God we claim to follow.

What makes you trip up in your faith? Where are the snares that mean you might unwittingly lead others away from God?

COLLECT

Almighty God,
you have broken the tyranny of sin
and have sent the Spirit of your Son into our hearts
    whereby we call you Father:
give us grace to dedicate our freedom to your service,
that we and all creation may be brought
    to the glorious liberty of the children of God;
through Jesus Christ your Son our Lord,
who is alive and reigns with you,
in the unity of the Holy Spirit,
one God, now and for ever.

| *Reflection by* **Catherine Williams**

Psalm **73**
Judges 9.1-21
Luke 15.11-end

Tuesday 5 July

Judges 9.1-21

'... let fire come out of the bramble' (v.15)

Gideon's extravagant lifestyle and lack of integrity have far-reaching consequences. Abimelech, Gideon's son by his slave-girl, wheedles, begs and slaughters his way to the throne. Only one of Gideon's 70 sons – Jotham – survives. He speaks out against Abimelech through the parable of the trees. The olive, fig and vine refuse the call to leadership, not wishing to lay down their current life-giving production. Space is thereby created for the more pervasive and thornier bramble to accept the crown. Whether the bramble will be a place of refuge or destruction hangs in the balance.

A call to leadership by God and others can be a challenging and demanding vocation, often not sought, and sometimes unwanted, especially if one is already happily engaged in valuable and generative work for the kingdom. But some are called to lay down one form of work in order to lead and have oversight, enabling others to grow and flourish. As we see from the parable, refusing to accept leadership may result in a risky or precarious appointment, which could lead to fiery damage for all, leader and led alike. We're reminded that the flourishing of evil only requires good people to do nothing.

In Jesus, we have a model of leadership shaped by self-emptying, humility, appropriate strength, and sacrificial love for others, underpinned by a deep, trusting and passionate relationship with God. Let's pray for leaders who engender and encourage these qualities.

God our saviour,
look on this wounded world
in pity and in power;
hold us fast to your promises of peace
won for us by your Son,
our Saviour Jesus Christ.

COLLECT

Reflection by **Catherine Williams** | 197

Wednesday 6 July

Judges 9.22-end

'... he razed the city and sowed it with salt' (v.45)

Abimelech's usurped reign runs into trouble after only three years. In-fighting, lack of loyalty and ridicule of Abimelech break out. Confidence in Abimelech's ability to lead is waning. Factions occur; allegiances are transferred. The threatened Abimelech lashes out, amassing troops and burning the city of Shechem. As prophesied, the wood is being devoured by fire from its bramble leadership. In scenes reminiscent of both *Macbeth* and *The Lord of the Rings*, devastating battles are fought and thousands killed. It's a passage of destruction and terror wrought by a leader, not chosen by God, unfit for office and out of control.

Like Jael with her tent-peg, it's a woman with another domestic implement – a millstone – who brings down Abimelech. As he killed his 70 brothers on a stone, so a stone kills him. It's a neat device to bring about a satisfying (if horrific) end to a story of oppression and violence.

Hardly mentioned in Chapter 9, God's brief interventions eventually lead to the downfall of Abimelech and the restoration of justice. In the cycle, the people have again turned away from God's ways and disaster has overtaken them. Did the people notice the absence of God? Did you notice that God was barely present in this chapter? It's a reminder and warning to us that it can be all too easy to turn gradually from God, especially when immediate pressures hijack our attention, and we become threatened or self-absorbed.

COLLECT

Almighty God,
you have broken the tyranny of sin
and have sent the Spirit of your Son into our hearts
    whereby we call you Father:
give us grace to dedicate our freedom to your service,
that we and all creation may be brought
    to the glorious liberty of the children of God;
through Jesus Christ your Son our Lord,
who is alive and reigns with you,
in the unity of the Holy Spirit,
one God, now and for ever.

| *Reflection by* **Catherine Williams**

Psalm **78.1-39***
Judges 11.1-11
Luke 16.19-end

Thursday 7 July

Judges 11.1-11

'... the people made him head and commander of them' (v.11)

The people have again abandoned God and turned to worship idols. Consequently, they find themselves oppressed by both the Philistines and the Ammonites. True to the cycle, they cry out to God, admit their sinfulness and pray for deliverance. They look for someone to lead them into battle. Enter Jephthah, who has been driven away from Gilead and rejected. He's been living with outlaws as a bandit, but is wooed and coaxed back by the elders of Gilead to command the fight against the Ammonites. Through the power of God's spirit, Jephthah will lead the people to freedom, but as we'll see tomorrow, a huge error of pride and judgement will ruin his life and the lives of those around him.

The son of a prostitute, rejected by his half-siblings, and with no inheritance, Jephthah's life has been challenging. He learns to survive on his wits using violence and is naturally suspicious when his countrymen try to win his favour. They want him only because he is a great warrior. It's what he can do that matters, not who he is.

How do we interact with those around us? Are there times when we are guilty of using people because of what they can do rather than getting to know and appreciate the person they are? God accepts us unconditionally, irrespective of anything we achieve. We are loved beyond measure just as we are. We have nothing to prove.

God our saviour,
look on this wounded world
in pity and in power;
hold us fast to your promises of peace
won for us by your Son,
our Saviour Jesus Christ.

COLLECT

Friday 8 July

Psalm **55**
Judges 11.29-end
Luke 17.1-10

Judges 11.29-end

'... and there was his daughter coming out to meet him' (v.34)

There's no getting around it. This passage is horrific, and sadly, Jephthah's actions are all so unnecessary. His lack of understanding both of God and the faith of the Israelites he is commanding has tragic consequences. There's no need for a sacrificial vow. God has already placed his spirit on Jephthah and assured him of victory. There's no need to bribe or placate God; only trust is required. When Jephthah's daughter runs to greet him, the ramifications of his vow become clear. Jephthah has a way out. Mosaic Law makes provision for such vows to be rescinded and expressly bans child sacrifice. Jephthah blames his daughter for his actions and she is compliant to her father's will, merely requesting a two-month stay of execution. Time for Jephthah to come to his senses. But when she returns from the hills, Jephthah kills her. Why did no one stop him? Why didn't she run away? And where was God – the God who stayed Abraham's hand, saving Isaac from sacrifice?

Sadly, this story is not unique. Every day women and children are abused, coerced and sacrificed to satisfy human pride and 'honour'. Like Jephthah's daughter, they are unnamed, objectified – with little freedom to make choices in the shaping of their lives, often blamed for others' violent actions and insecurities. Where love should be, pride, domination and violence hold sway. And sometimes God seems absent. It is crucial, then, that the Bible records such a story.

COLLECT

Almighty God,
you have broken the tyranny of sin
and have sent the Spirit of your Son into our hearts
    whereby we call you Father:
give us grace to dedicate our freedom to your service,
that we and all creation may be brought
    to the glorious liberty of the children of God;
through Jesus Christ your Son our Lord,
who is alive and reigns with you,
in the unity of the Holy Spirit,
one God, now and for ever.

| *Reflection by* **Catherine Williams**

Psalms **76**, 79
Judges 12.1-7
Luke 17.11-19

Saturday 9 July

Judges 12.1-7

'... he said, "Sibboleth", for he could not pronounce it right' (v.6)

The Ephraimites are angry that Jephthah's forces went into battle against the Ammonites without them. The violence between the groups is escalating and breaking out in internal skirmishes, with both physical and verbal attacks. Communication between the various tribes within Jephthah's army is problematic. Gilead fights against Ephraim and the men of Gilead decide who's in and who's out by the way they pronounce the word 'shibboleth'. The Ephraimites reveal their ethnicity by being unable to pronounce the letter 'h'. For this small matter, 42,000 are slaughtered.

The way we communicate with one another matters. Taking time to listen, understand and iron out small disputes and misunderstandings, before they get out hand, can be crucial in family, work and church settings. Major disputes can turn on the smallest detail, escalating quickly and causing division, damage and hurt, sometimes running on for years. 'There's always a thing behind the thing' is one of the maxims in our household – meaning that it's necessary to delve a little deeper into an issue before it can be satisfactorily resolved for all parties.

This episode in Judges is one of power and privilege. Who is it in your context who chooses the 'correct' pronunciation or procedure? Who needs to check their privilege? If it's you, how are you going about that? All people are made in the image of God and loved beyond measure. Equity must be an essential component of both the Church and the world.

God our saviour,
look on this wounded world
in pity and in power;
hold us fast to your promises of peace
won for us by your Son,
our Saviour Jesus Christ.

COLLECT

Monday 11 July

Judges 13.1-24

'Let the woman give heed to all that I said to her' (v.13)

The events in today's passage mirror those of other miraculous birth announcements in the Bible: that of Isaac to Abraham and Sarah; Samuel to Hannah and Elkanah; John the Baptist to Zachariah and Elizabeth; and, of course, Jesus to Mary and Joseph. All these children, we're told, are miraculous gifts to barren, elderly or unmarried women, but more than that, the unusual circumstances indicate the special nature of the child to be born and the part each will play in God's plans. Today, Samson's birth is foretold to Manoah and his wife. It is a story of trust but also of the unexpected people through whom God speaks and acts.

Of all the birth announcements, this is the only one where the mother-to-be remains unnamed. Referred to only as Manoah's wife or 'the woman', she never doubts God or the angel's message, though her husband, unable to take her word, needs to hear the news for himself. At a time when the witness of women counted for less than that of men, the angel of God nonetheless appears first to her and, throughout, her faith contrasts with Manoah's anxiety and doubt. In verse 22 particularly, Manoah fears they will die because they have seen God, but his wife reassures and encourages him.

Perhaps this very day God is speaking to you, either directly or through someone unexpected. Do you have trust and faith enough to hear and receive the message?

COLLECT

O God, the protector of all who trust in you,
without whom nothing is strong, nothing is holy:
increase and multiply upon us your mercy;
that with you as our ruler and guide
we may so pass through things temporal
that we lose not our hold on things eternal;
grant this, heavenly Father,
for our Lord Jesus Christ's sake,
who is alive and reigns with you,
in the unity of the Holy Spirit,
one God, now and for ever.

| *Reflection by* **Guli Francis-Dehqani**

Tuesday 12 July

Judges 14

'In hot anger he went back to his father's house' (v.19)

Today we encounter a whole range of emotions and behaviours that reflect the shadow side of human nature. Among them are greed and lust, hubris, trickery, deceit, betrayal, coercion, threats and intimidation. At the core of this episode in Samson's life, what might have been a light-hearted riddle with a bet attached, turns into a dark tale with a bitter ending.

The story is a reminder that when human passions go unchecked, the results can be disastrous and bleak, and the ripple effects can be far reaching. By the end of our passage, a marriage has ended, thirty men have lost their lives and all Samson is left with is a wild, all-consuming rage.

Each apparently small action we take can have far-reaching consequences. We do well, regularly to ask ourselves where our true loyalties lie, what our motivations are and who are those who can help us make wise decisions.

So, who are those who accompany you through life, who know you, love you, have your best interests at heart and, crucially, will be honest with you, even when it's hard? Who are those you work alongside who might gently warn you when you're going off track, losing sight of the bigger picture or stepping on the toes of others? Take a moment to pray for them and give thanks for them – and make sure you make time to listen to them.

Gracious Father,
by the obedience of Jesus
you brought salvation to our wayward world:
draw us into harmony with your will,
that we may find all things restored in him,
our Saviour Jesus Christ.

COLLECT

Wednesday 13 July

Psalm **119.105-128**
Judges 15.1 – 16.3
Luke 18.15-30

Judges 15.1 – 16.3

'... the spirit of the Lord rushed on him' (15.14)

The life story of Samson is a perplexing one, full of violence and destruction. He seems to be a man of extremes, whose anger is easily triggered and whose rage causes untold damage, resulting in the killing of hundreds. And yet, Samson is also a man of God, one who is used by God and to whom God listens and responds, as in verses 18-19.

The Old Testament is full of stories that are difficult for us to comprehend or to square with our understanding of God as the source of love. Through the narrative, we encounter different aspects of God that often have to be seen within the wider context of God's covenantal relationship with the people of Israel. But still, there are dark and horrific episodes lurking, ones that the scholar Phyllis Tribble calls, 'texts of terror', impossible to explain or justify, when innocent people seem to get caught in the crossfire of divine drama. For example, what purpose could the burning of Samson's former wife and her father possibly serve?

We may not always have the answers, but incidents such as these, recounted almost as an aside, make me stop and ponder... As I seek to serve God and be faithful, who are the people that may unknowingly get hurt in the process? Overconfidence in pursuing even the most God-given of causes is a path beset with dangers.

COLLECT

O God, the protector of all who trust in you,
without whom nothing is strong, nothing is holy:
increase and multiply upon us your mercy;
that with you as our ruler and guide
we may so pass through things temporal
that we lose not our hold on things eternal;
grant this, heavenly Father,
for our Lord Jesus Christ's sake,
who is alive and reigns with you,
in the unity of the Holy Spirit,
one God, now and for ever.

| *Reflection by* **Guli Francis-Dehqani**

Psalms 90, 92
Judges 16.4-end
Luke 18.31-end

Judges 16.4-end

'But the hair of his head began to grow again' (v.22)

In the illustrated Bibles of my childhood, pictures of Samson razing the temple to the ground had an almost superhero quality about them, providing a terrifying denouement to his colourful story. Now, as an adult, I can't help feeling that the real horror – the tragedy for Samson, if you like – wasn't so much in the final devastating scenes of his life but occurred while he slept on Delilah's lap, which became a place of betrayal. For surely here lies one of our greatest fears: to be let down by those who claim to love us. And for Samson, the desolation is compounded on waking when he discovers his strength has gone and God too, it seems, has left him.

We can't escape the fact that the destructive end of the story is a violent one that sits uneasily with our desire for peace. It's a dramatic example of the Judges' concern with national pride rather than reconciliation. However, go back a few verses. At the height of Samson's humiliation, when he is seized, blind and bound, what do we read? The hair of his head began to grow again. It turns out that the mark of Samson's identity, which was in his relationship with God, was not removed by Delilah's betrayal.

Whatever your story, even at the most painful times, your preciousness is preserved in God's ongoing presence and relationship with you.

COLLECT

Gracious Father,
by the obedience of Jesus
you brought salvation to our wayward world:
draw us into harmony with your will,
that we may find all things restored in him,
our Saviour Jesus Christ.

Reflection by **Guli Francis-Dehqani**

205

Friday 15 July

Judges 17

'From where do you come?' (v.9)

This Danite founding myth contains an allusion to place and identity that's shaped and informed my own faith story. After the events surrounding the making of the idol and the installation of his own son as a priest, Micah has an encounter with the sojourner from Bethlehem. The meeting begins with the question, 'Where do you come from?' I'm asked this often, and it's easy to answer simply, 'I am from Iran', but, in truth, much more lies behind this factual response.

The Levite priest from Bethlehem brings special status to Micah's shrine, and his designation as 'father' shows respect and intimacy. However, I'm drawn not to his status as a Levite, his Bethlehem origins or his fatherly care. Rather, I'm drawn to his response which was to live wherever he could find a place. That has been my calling too, unexpectedly leaving birthplace and security but always with a desire to find my place. This is the path of many a migrant person, but it's also a calling for each of us – to find a place of belonging and worth. In this passage, as in life, establishing regular religious practice and devotion is one of the surest ways of finding a place of security.

For many years, as a refugee family we had a precarious status. I once remember my father being asked his nationality; he paused and replied, 'I am a citizen of heaven'.

COLLECT

O God, the protector of all who trust in you,
without whom nothing is strong, nothing is holy:
increase and multiply upon us your mercy;
that with you as our ruler and guide
we may so pass through things temporal
that we lose not our hold on things eternal;
grant this, heavenly Father,
for our Lord Jesus Christ's sake,
who is alive and reigns with you,
in the unity of the Holy Spirit,
one God, now and for ever.

| *Reflection by* **Guli Francis-Dehqani**

Psalms 96, **97**, 100
Judges 18.1-20, 27-end
Luke 19.11-27

Saturday 16 July

Judges 18.1-20, 27-end

'Go in peace. The mission you are on is under the eye of the Lord'
(v.6)

My husband grew up during the troubles in Northern Ireland, and I lived through an Islamic revolution. We cannot help reading accounts such as today's without bristling at the idea that the conquest of land and the subjugation of peoples is 'under the eye of the Lord'. And yet, the migration of the Danites, their defeat of Laish, the battles and the foundation of the city of Dan are all events recorded as part of the overarching narrative of God's relationship with the people of Israel.

We can opt to read these texts as one-dimensional, heroic histories – literal or mythical – of God's chosen people. Alternatively, we can look beyond the obvious, search for deeper meaning and ask how they relate to our own stories.

Right at the end of the passage, when the city of Dan is well founded, we read that 'the house of God was at Shiloh' – a reference to where the Ark of the Covenant, which represented God's presence, was housed. Perhaps the writer is suggesting that what the Danites had established was a poor substitute for where God was truly to be encountered.

We do well to ponder the question of what makes us sure that the eye of the Lord is upon our endeavours? In the end, regardless of success or failure, it is only when we keep close to the place of right worship that we can truly 'go in peace'.

Gracious Father,
by the obedience of Jesus
you brought salvation to our wayward world:
draw us into harmony with your will,
that we may find all things restored in him,
our Saviour Jesus Christ.

COLLECT

Reflection by **Guli Francis-Dehqani** | 207

Monday 18 July

1 Samuel 1.1-20

'I have asked him of the Lord' (v.20)

My eldest child was born after nine years of difficult waiting. They were complex, busy and at times traumatic, comprising intrusive medical investigation and intervention as well as several miscarriages.

Hannah is loved deeply by her husband, and yet she is bereft and longing for a child. When we are in uncertain situations, full of pain, loss and distress, it's easy to seek only a solution. Through medical skill, dogged determination and by God's grace I have been blessed with children. However, I often remind myself that, in the story of Hannah, there are seeds of hope evident even during her visit to the temple while she was distraught and the outcome was unknown. Hannah brings to God the depths of her longing, and she is heard. Initially, Eli misunderstands her distress, but Hannah defends herself and invokes from Eli a warm commendation to 'go in peace'. All her pain is held within the regular rejoicing of her family (she 'ate and drank with her husband'), and the life of the temple. Furthermore, this very human story is played out in Shiloh: the ancient place of meeting and worship. Despite her pain, Hannah is held at the heart of her community, both familial and faith.

We, too, can take our stories of loss and regret to the 'doorpost of the temple' knowing that we will be heard and met with kindness.

COLLECT

Almighty and everlasting God,
by whose Spirit the whole body of the Church
     is governed and sanctified:
hear our prayer which we offer for all your faithful people,
that in their vocation and ministry
they may serve you in holiness and truth
to the glory of your name;
through our Lord and Saviour Jesus Christ,
who is alive and reigns with you,
in the unity of the Holy Spirit,
one God, now and for ever.

| *Reflection by* **Guli Francis-Dehqani**

Psalm **106*** (*or* 103)
1 Samuel 1.21 – 2.11
Luke 19.41-end

Tuesday 19 July

1 Samuel 1.21 – 2.11

*'... he lifts the needy from the ash heap, to make them sit
with princes' (2.8)*

Although we read, 'Hannah prayed and said ...', verses 1-10 of
chapter 2 are more often described as the *Song* of Hannah,
reminding us that singing is perhaps the most appropriate response
to the gift of a longed-for child. Here we have a model and heartfelt
response to God's goodness. In Judaism, this passage is read on the
first day of Rosh Hashanah, beginning the Jewish New Year. In the
Revised Common Lectionary, we read it on the penultimate Sunday
of the year. At beginnings or endings, it seems, people of faith sing
of praise for God's faithfulness.

Scholars suggest that Hannah's song is based on an existing public
hymn of Israel. Its standard hymnic elements include many parallels
with Psalm 113. Throughout the song, Hannah's personal
remembrance and thanksgiving are generalized into a communal
remembrance of who God is.

Whether we see the song as a personal outpouring of a transformed
woman or a national exultation of God's deliverance, one thing is
sure: the God we encounter is one who reverses the expected order.
Verse 8 is an almost direct quotation of Psalm 113 vv. 7-8, and we
cannot but hear the parallel song of Mary too from Luke chapter 1:
'He has brought down the powerful from their thrones, and lifted up
the lowly' (Luke 1.52). The psalmist, Hannah, Mary and the faithful
in every age transform thankfulness into a call for reversal, so the
humble and meek may be exalted.

Almighty God,
send down upon your Church
the riches of your Spirit,
and kindle in all who minister the gospel
your countless gifts of grace;
through Jesus Christ our Lord.

COLLECT

Reflection by **Guli Francis-Dehqani**

Wednesday 20 July

1 Samuel 2.12-26

'... the boy Samuel continued to grow both in stature and in favour with the Lord and with the people' (v.26)

In May 1980, during the Iranian Revolution, my mother awaited news of her son which, within hours, would confirm his murder. She wrote in her diary: 'O God I have daily committed our son into your hands for the past twenty-four years – and do so again.'

Likewise Hannah, fulfilling her vow, entrusts Samuel to God to minister in the temple. This shouldn't be misunderstood as a forsaking of her son, alien though it may be to our style of parenting. Hannah's yearly visits are recorded tenderly not least in her taking him 'a little robe'). Nor should we see bargaining between Hannah and God. There's no sense that the gift of further children comes because Hannah handed over her firstborn. She entrusts him as pure gift to God who also gives freely and expansively.

Public exposure of the Church's all-too-recent failures to protect children from abuse fills us with shame. By contrast, here is a wonderful story of Samuel's safety and nurture in the heart of the temple. Contrary to the wickedness of Eli's sons, presumed heirs to his priestly office, Samuel ministers faithfully and securely. He learns what it means to be a priest but is no slave to ministerial duty. Through his service, guided by kindly, wise Eli, he grows physically and spiritually. Today, too, the Church must be a place where children can grow in safety to become the adults God intends them to be.

COLLECT

Almighty and everlasting God,
by whose Spirit the whole body of the Church
is governed and sanctified:
hear our prayer which we offer for all your faithful people,
that in their vocation and ministry
they may serve you in holiness and truth
to the glory of your name;
through our Lord and Saviour Jesus Christ,
who is alive and reigns with you,
in the unity of the Holy Spirit,
one God, now and for ever.

| *Reflection by* **Guli Francis-Dehqani**

Thursday 21 July

1 Samuel 2.27-end

'... those who honour me I will honour' (v.30)

Today's passage continues the narrative in the early chapters of 1 Samuel where the ground is being prepared for the emergence of Samuel as a prophet of God. Repeatedly, Samuel is presented favourably and in contrast to the Elides (household of Eli), including his sons – and today even Eli himself. The story includes descriptions of their sins and their stubborn refusal to accept reproof, and culminates in today's announcement of judgement.

There is the odour here of a 'sense of entitlement' that the Elides seem to have about their place in the life of the temple, as priests and prophets. Their position was assured, they felt, for their ancestors had been called to serve God in this way, and so it would always be. The verdict seems a bit harsh on Eli, who surely is a rather more complex character than his sons. But at the same time, it serves as a forceful reminder that there's no accounting for who can be used in God's economy; it is an aide-memoire, if you like, that we should never judge a person by their family credentials, their status in society nor any other external attribute but only by their inner character and qualities.

Are there those whom you have overlooked because they didn't look or sound the part? And when have you underestimated your own calling and considered yourself unfit? May God forgive our short-sightedness when judging others and give us courage to fulfil our vocation.

Almighty God,
send down upon your Church
the riches of your Spirit,
and kindle in all who minister the gospel
your countless gifts of grace;
through Jesus Christ our Lord.

COLLECT

Reflection by **Guli Francis-Dehqani** | 211

Friday 22 July
Mary Magdalene

Psalms 30, 32, 150
1 Samuel 16.14-end
Luke 8.1-3

Luke 8.1-3

'... as well as some women' (v.2)

To our contemporary ears, these four verses don't sound too surprising and we might easily pass by them without a second thought. We know the Christian story well and have absorbed the fact that women were present from the start, among Jesus' travelling band. In reality, however, while it wasn't uncommon for wealthy women in particular to support rabbis financially or from their property, it was unheard of for them to leave home and travel with a religious leader. Indeed, it's notable that this account is specific only to Gospel of Luke, who, by its inclusion, seems to be underlining the important role he assigns to women more generally.

The presence of Mary Magdalene and other women is a reminder of the scandalous nature of Jesus' ministry and the new community he was envisioning. Women, and by extension, other outsiders and marginalized groups, also have a place. This was shocking back then, but perhaps the real surprise today is that, over 2000 years later, we still have to be reminded of this truth. Women were welcome alongside Jesus in his earthly ministry and are still called to serve in many and diverse ways today.

Mary Magdalene, much maligned and around whom assumptions, stories and myths abound, is our foremother in faith. As you commemorate her life today, spare a thought too for the countless other women who have influenced and inspired you, and give thanks to God for them.

COLLECT

Almighty God,
whose Son restored Mary Magdalene to health of mind and body
and called her to be a witness to his resurrection:
forgive our sins and heal us by your grace,
that we may serve you in the power of his risen life;
who is alive and reigns with you,
in the unity of the Holy Spirit,
one God, now and for ever.

Reflection by **Guli Francis-Dehqani**

Psalms 120, **121**, 122
1 Samuel 4.1*b*-end
Luke 20.27-40

Saturday 23 July

1 Samuel 4.1*b*-end

'Let us bring the ark of the covenant of the Lord ... so that he may come among us' (v.3)

Today's passage sees the final demise of Eli and his sons. The narrative is heavy with foreboding, but beyond the immediate story itself, there are cautionary notes that reverberate down the centuries, signalling with remarkable clarity for us to take heed, pause and reflect.

The Israelites – God's chosen people – were losing in battle against the Philistines. As a last resort, they bring God onto the scene and claim divine protection. But still they are defeated, and the Ark of the Covenant is captured. The Israelites are left humiliated; Eli and his sons destroyed.

We may not be involved in literal battles today, but how often are we tempted to claim God for ourselves: to win an argument or prove a point, to justify our actions or convince ourselves that we are deserving recipients of some benefit or another – 'God is with me and so all will be well', we whisper to ourselves.

Truth is that all will be well, but not necessarily as we intend. The ways of God remain a mystery, of which we only glimpse a part and in which we are only bit players. In the words of Carl Jung, 'Bidden or not bidden, God is present', but not always active in ways we desire or understand. Faith is to embrace the unknown and welcome the unfolding of truth, which is sometimes disclosed in unexpected and surprising ways.

COLLECT

Almighty and everlasting God,
by whose Spirit the whole body of the Church
is governed and sanctified:
hear our prayer which we offer for all your faithful people,
that in their vocation and ministry
they may serve you in holiness and truth
to the glory of your name;
through our Lord and Saviour Jesus Christ,
who is alive and reigns with you,
in the unity of the Holy Spirit,
one God, now and for ever.

Reflection by **Guli Francis-Dehqani**

Monday 25 July

James the Apostle

Psalms 7, 29, 117
2 Kings 1.9-15
Luke 9.46-56

Luke 9.46-56

'... the least among all of you is the greatest' (v.48)

Santiago de Compostela in north-western Spain has been a centre of pilgrimage since at least the 11th century, with people making their way across Europe to visit the shrine of the apostle James, which has given its name to the city. The connection between St James and that place is tenuous, but he became in the Middle Ages a symbol of the gradual Christian reconquest of Spain from Islam, being known as 'St James, the Moor-slayer', depicted riding a white horse and holding a blood-dripping sword.

This warlike image might seem to fit with James' suggestion to Jesus, in the verses following today's reading, that the disciples should call down fire on a village of Samaritans that had refused to welcome them. However, this side of his character is clearly out of step with the nature of the kingdom of God that Jesus proclaims, in which the first shall be last, and the least is the greatest.

For many thousands today, the experience of following one of the several routes to James' shrine is more in tune with Jesus' upside-down vision of the kingdom than the world view of James, one of the Sons of Thunder (Mark 3.17). Walking and talking with fellow pilgrims from around the world, and sharing accommodation, food and blisters is a great leveller. In turn, this leads to the humility, peace and joy that are at the heart of Christian discipleship.

COLLECT

Merciful God,
whose holy apostle Saint James,
leaving his father and all that he had,
was obedient to the calling of your Son Jesus Christ
and followed him even to death:
help us, forsaking the false attractions of the world,
to be ready at all times to answer your call without delay;
through Jesus Christ your Son our Lord,
who is alive and reigns with you,
in the unity of the Holy Spirit,
one God, now and for ever.

| *Reflection by* **Brother Samuel SSF**

Psalms **132**, 133
1 Samuel 6.1-16
Luke 21.5-19

Tuesday 26 July

1 Samuel 6.1-16

'The cows went straight in the direction of Beth-shemesh' (v.12)

We are given the striking picture of the Ark of the Covenant, mounted on a cart drawn by two oxen and watched anxiously by those who are only too pleased to be rid of it. The procession makes its way slowly through the countryside, guided seemingly by a homing instinct back to its own community. The Lord returns to his wayward people who run out joyfully to welcome him.

It's a scene, mirrored in obverse by the parable in Luke's Gospel (15.11-end), in which the recalcitrant son, coming to his senses, returns home from a far country and is met by his father who runs out to embrace him.

Does God return to us or do we return to God? Either way there is a deep longing – of God for his people and of ourselves for God – to be in fellowship and to be at home together. 'You have made us for yourself O Lord', writes St Augustine in his *Confessions*, 'and our heart is restless until it finds its rest in you'.

There is in Israel's history, and in the story of our own lives, a restlessness that sometimes leads us away from home to be held captive like the Ark in an alien place. The same restlessness leads us on the journey back to the source and giver of life, who, in turn, is ever seeking to make his home with us. God is both our gracious host and our humble guest.

COLLECT

Merciful God,
you have prepared for those who love you
such good things as pass our understanding:
pour into our hearts such love toward you
that we, loving you in all things and above all things,
may obtain your promises,
which exceed all that we can desire;
through Jesus Christ your Son our Lord,
who is alive and reigns with you,
in the unity of the Holy Spirit,
one God, now and for ever.

Reflection by **Brother Samuel SSF** | 215

Wednesday 27 July

1 Samuel 7

'Then Samuel took a stone and set it up' (v.12)

Now that the Ark has returned to its homeland, Samuel calls upon the people to address the cause of its capture in the first place: the worship of 'foreign gods'. The first and second commandments given at Mount Sinai – to have no other gods besides the Lord and the prohibition of idolatry – are not simply negative injunctions to stay clear of dabbling in other religions; they are a call to keep the heart fixed on the one who has rescued the people out of slavery in Egypt and who has made them into a nation. Any turning away from that bedrock, any distraction from that focus, threatens the very existence of the community. The setting up by Samuel of a pillar of witness – 'Ebenezer', 'Stone of Help' – is to establish a landmark in the consciousness of the people. They can only survive as a nation, surrounded as they are by hostile forces, if they remember that help comes not from their own strength but from their covenant relationship with the Lord.

We need 'pillars of witness' today in a society that tends to cling to its own sovereignty and in which self-determination and self-sufficiency are esteemed. Such pillars may not always be built out of stone. Faithful individuals and communities witness powerfully to our essential dependence on one another and on the one whose love and mercy upholds and sustains the world.

COLLECT

Merciful God,
you have prepared for those who love you
such good things as pass our understanding:
pour into our hearts such love toward you
that we, loving you in all things and above all things,
may obtain your promises,
which exceed all that we can desire;
through Jesus Christ your Son our Lord,
who is alive and reigns with you,
in the unity of the Holy Spirit,
one God, now and for ever.

Thursday 28 July

1 Samuel 8

'... appoint for us ... a king to govern us, like other nations' (v.5)

Choosing a new form of government is never simply a matter of tweaking the political system, for a nation's politics demonstrates how that community understands itself. From the early days of their occupation of Canaan, the people of Israel had been a loose federation of tribes, held together by a common narrative – a story of shared ancestors, of a miraculous escape from slavery, of the gift of a promised land. They were united more closely in times of danger by a succession of charismatic figures, but there was little sense of hierarchy among them. Such ad hoc, light-touch governance was never a trouble-free arrangement. Inter-tribal rivalry often led to fragmentation and to defeat at the hands of external enemies. It's easy to see how a strong central authority modelled on that of the surrounding nations could be an attractive alternative.

As Samuel recognizes, Israel's covenant relationship with the Lord has been an expression of its national identity. The demand for a king to rule over them indicates the loss of that vision on which the nation was founded – of themselves as a holy people, upheld and guided by the Lord. Throughout the prophetic books of the Old Testament, there is an on-going argument about kingship in Israel and how it relates to, or undermines, the Lord's sovereignty over the people and the land. Samuel's warning about the corruption of power speaks to us today just as much as it did to God's people then.

Creator God,
you made us all in your image:
may we discern you in all that we see,
and serve you in all that we do;
through Jesus Christ our Lord.

COLLECT

Reflection by **Brother Samuel SSF** | 217

Friday 29 July

1 Samuel 9.1-14

'Come, let us go to the seer' (v.9)

It's strange how setting out to look for one thing – in the case of today's reading, a family's lost donkeys – can sometimes lead to the discovery of something quite unexpected.

Saul and the boy decide to approach 'the man of God' to help them fulfil the object of their journey, unaware that this will lead to quite a different conclusion. Samuel himself comes to the town unaware that the man who can fit the bill of kingship is arriving at the same time. Behind the words of the story, Samuel is mulling over and worrying about the people's request for a king. Where on earth is he to find the right person – especially since he doesn't really believe in the idea of kingship at all?

It was once suggested to Archbishop William Temple that answers to prayer were just coincidences. He replied that 'coincidences' seemed to happen much more frequently when he prayed. Perhaps something of the same is happening in this story. The description of Samuel as a 'seer' – one who has insight – is significant. The person who 'sees', who is attentive to the natural world and to people, who is awake to the signs of the times and who is alert to the Lord in their own life, is more likely to be able to discern what God is doing between the lines of the ordinary daily lives and concerns of others.

COLLECT

Merciful God,
you have prepared for those who love you
such good things as pass our understanding:
pour into our hearts such love toward you
that we, loving you in all things and above all things,
may obtain your promises,
which exceed all that we can desire;
through Jesus Christ your Son our Lord,
who is alive and reigns with you,
in the unity of the Holy Spirit,
one God, now and for ever.

| *Reflection by* **Brother Samuel SSF**

Saturday 30 July

1 Samuel 9.15 – 10.1

'I have seen the suffering of my people' (9.16)

The words of the Lord to Samuel are the same as those spoken to Moses at the burning bush at Mount Horeb (Exodus 3.7). God sees the suffering of his people and acts in faithful and compassionate response. As often in the Bible, God's choice of a person to carry out his purpose isn't the obvious one. Saul, the donkey-seeker, may be tall and handsome, but he hails from the least important of the twelve tribes and his family is almost unknown. As if to signify that the colour of blood isn't important in this matter, Saul is given the top seat at the banquet that Samuel has arranged, along with a king-sized portion of meat on his plate. The real purpose of this munificent hospitality is revealed only the next morning when the two of them are alone so that Samuel can make known God's word – his intention to save his people through Saul's agency.

This isn't going to be a straightforward business, as is revealed in the saga of Saul's kingship that unfolds over the following chapters, for it will end in tragedy and loss. But the purpose of God to save remains constant. As is experienced in the life of individuals and of the Church, the God of Israel and of Jesus Christ uses all the components of our lives, suffering and failure as well as success, to bring his people and his creation back to fellowship and fullness of life with him.

Creator God,
you made us all in your image:
may we discern you in all that we see,
and serve you in all that we do;
through Jesus Christ our Lord.

COLLECT

Reflection by **Brother Samuel SSF**   219

Monday 1 August

Psalms 1, 2, 3
1 Samuel 10.1-16
Luke 22.24-30

1 Samuel 10.1-16

'God gave him another heart' (v.9)

The heart in Hebrew thought is not so much the seat of emotion as the place where the human will resides. It's when our will is brought into harmony with God's will that a profound conversion transforms and empowers our lives, and through us transforms the lives of others.

Saul's anointing as king by Samuel is the outward sign of commissioning for the task ahead, but it isn't until Saul turns away from this ceremony that the inward transformation takes place. This is the point when Saul puts himself at the disposal of the Lord. The spirit-possession that leads him momentarily to join the band of prophets in their frenzied dancing causes his friends and acquaintances to wonder what has come over this formerly hesitant young man. However, the real substance of change was in Saul's willingness to be part of the Lord's purpose to save his people and in the gift of leadership for this task, though as yet it's unclear how it is to be fulfilled.

Our transformation by the power of the Spirit may not take place instantaneously as with Saul. It happens more often in a long process of heart-shaping through patient attention, humble service and steadfast longing. We pray with the psalmist: 'knit my heart to you, that I may fear your name' (Psalm 86.11).

COLLECT

Lord of all power and might,
the author and giver of all good things:
graft in our hearts the love of your name,
increase in us true religion,
nourish us with all goodness,
and of your great mercy keep us in the same;
through Jesus Christ your Son our Lord,
who is alive and reigns with you,
in the unity of the Holy Spirit,
one God, now and for ever.

| *Reflection by* **Brother Samuel SSF**

Tuesday 2 August

1 Samuel 10.17-end

'Samuel told the people the rights and duties of the kingship' (v.25)

This appears to be a second, alternative, account of how Saul comes to be chosen as king. To our minds the casting of lots may seem a somewhat random, not to say undemocratic, way of finding the right person to rule over a nation, but it does avoid the strife of a contested election. It also prevents the seizure of power by an ambitious clan or individual. Nobody could say that a man who hides among the baggage is gagging for the job. As with the events that led up to Saul's anointing, this method makes clear that he is God's candidate and choice, even if some are still reluctant to accept the result.

The rights and duties of the kingship spelled out by Samuel involve three parties. Saul is to be responsible for preserving the covenant life of the community; the people are to unite under his leadership in times when the nation is under threat; and both king and people are bound in covenant with the Lord, who has not surrendered his ultimate sovereignty over the community and land. The same reciprocal responsibilities between citizens and those in authority, and the recognition that both are responsible to a higher authority – to truth and justice if not to God – makes for wise and stable government in any age. If just one of these rights and duties is missing, a nation is in trouble.

Generous God,
you give us gifts and make them grow:
though our faith is small as mustard seed,
make it grow to your glory
and the flourishing of your kingdom;
through Jesus Christ our Lord.

COLLECT

Wednesday 3 August

Psalm 119.1-32
1 Samuel 11
Luke 22.39-46

1 Samuel 11

'Tomorrow, by the time the sun is hot, you shall have deliverance'
(v.9)

Saul's authority and ability are soon put to the test when two of the Israelite tribes send an urgent appeal for rescue from impending capture and humiliation at the hands of a neighbouring king. The siege of Jabesh-gilead seems to have been a deliberate provocation by Nahash to Israel's new leader. A failure by Saul to respond effectively would have quickly led to the collapse of his standing within the covenant community. As it turns out, a rapid and complete victory over the Ammonites re-affirms his authority, silences the doubters and grumblers, and seals the establishment of the kingship.

The brutal slaughter of the Ammonites at the hands of the Israelites, led by Lord's newly chosen servant, raises for us – not for the first or last time in these books of the Bible – some difficult questions about how this can be reconciled with the will and nature of God that we see revealed in Jesus Christ. The stories are set in a culture in which tensions between neighbours over land, water and food supply often graduate to a violent conflict for survival. The underlying theme running through them is how God works in and through the events and crises of Israel's life – and there are some spectacular defeats as well as victories – to bring his people, and ultimately all people, to salvation. Before we rush to judgement on these narratives, we should reflect on the violence of our own times.

COLLECT

Lord of all power and might,
the author and giver of all good things:
graft in our hearts the love of your name,
increase in us true religion,
nourish us with all goodness,
and of your great mercy keep us in the same;
through Jesus Christ your Son our Lord,
who is alive and reigns with you,
in the unity of the Holy Spirit,
one God, now and for ever.

| *Reflection by* **Brother Samuel SSF**

Psalms 14, **15**, 16
1 Samuel 12
Luke 22.47-62

Thursday 4 August

1 Samuel 12

'I have listened ...' (v.1)

From his earliest years, Samuel has been a listener to the word of God – 'Speak, for your servant is listening' (1 Samuel 3.10) – and as judge over Israel, he has listened to the people with a discerning ear. Now in old age, in a valedictory address, he urges upon them the need to 'heed the voice of the Lord'. The people's track record in this has not been a good one. Again and again, once the immediate crisis has passed, they have turned away from the one who has rescued them. Samuel reiterates his belief that their demand for a king to rule over them – perhaps in his mind a call for someone who will be more malleable to their wishes than he has been – is just the latest example of a pattern of disobedience, of not listening, that goes back to the birth of the nation.

The Franciscan medieval theologian, St Bonaventure, says that our primary sin is inattention. Disobedience is at root a failure to listen attentively to God's word – not just to the words of Scripture, but to what God is saying and doing in our world today. To ignore the needs of our neighbour, the cry of the poor and the cry of the earth, not to listen to the voice of conscience or to heed God's song of loving mercy upholding all creation, is to invite disaster upon us and all our institutions.

Generous God,
you give us gifts and make them grow:
though our faith is small as mustard seed,
make it grow to your glory
and the flourishing of your kingdom;
through Jesus Christ our Lord.

COLLECT

Reflection by **Brother Samuel SSF** | 223

Friday 5 August

Psalms 17, **19**
1 Samuel 13.5-18
Luke 22.63-end

1 Samuel 13.5-18

'You have done foolishly' (v.13)

Short cuts are not always a good idea. One cannot but feel sorry for Saul, in a tight spot with a large Philistine army massing against Israel and the danger of his own troops drifting away from the approaching conflict. Who wouldn't have done just what he did, stepping forward to present the offering of wellbeing in place of the absent Samuel? One might even suspect that Samuel, eventually rolling up and expressing his disapproval, is just rather jealously guarding his own sacerdotal position against the kingship to which he is still not fully reconciled.

Another way of looking at it, however, is that Saul, taking matters into his own hands in his impatience to get stuck into the battle with the enemy, has demonstrated a lack of trust in the ability and purpose of God to get him and the people out of this hole in which they find themselves. It's a fulfilment of Samuel's words that, in choosing a king to rule over them, the people have rejected the Lord's kingship. It's a fatal flaw that crops up many times in Israel's history. The people and their kings look for help anywhere but in the place where it is to be found. 'Waiting on the Lord', whether in major decision-making or in day-to-day choices, involves an act of trust in God's sovereignty that includes his faithfulness to his promises towards us and towards his creation.

COLLECT

Lord of all power and might,
the author and giver of all good things:
graft in our hearts the love of your name,
increase in us true religion,
nourish us with all goodness,
and of your great mercy keep us in the same;
through Jesus Christ your Son our Lord,
who is alive and reigns with you,
in the unity of the Holy Spirit,
one God, now and for ever.

Psalms 27, 150
Ecclesiasticus 48.1-10
or 1 Kings 19.1-16
1 John 3.1-3

Saturday 6 August
Transfiguration of Our Lord

1 John 3.1-3
'... we will be like him' (v.2)

The Transfiguration of Our Lord, one of the greatest festivals of the Church's year, shares its feast day with the anniversary of the dropping of the first nuclear bomb on the city of Hiroshima, Japan, on 6 August 1945. Whether or not one accepts the argument that the shortening of the Second World War and the saving of the lives of many allied troops justified the huge destruction of civilian lives – between 129,000 and 226,000 were killed by the two bombs dropped on Hiroshima and Nagasaki – there is poignant significance in this coincidence of dates. On the day when we remember what might be considered among the greatest of human-caused disfigurations, we celebrate the transfiguration not just of humanity but of the whole of creation in and through Jesus Christ.

The words 'we will be like him' from today's reading are the assurance that we are called to the same transfigured glory that was revealed to the disciples on the mountain. Karl Barth, the great Protestant theologian of the last century, said that when God looks at each one of us, he sees 'only Jesus'. That is, he already sees us as we are to become in and through his Son. We and every creature are already God's beloved children in whom is all his delight. To glimpse ourselves, each other and the whole of creation in the light of Jesus' glory is the only vision that can transform our often terribly disfigured world.

> Father in heaven,
> whose Son Jesus Christ was wonderfully transfigured
> before chosen witnesses upon the holy mountain,
> and spoke of the exodus he would accomplish at Jerusalem:
> give us strength so to hear his voice and bear our cross
> that in the world to come we may see him as he is;
> who is alive and reigns with you,
> in the unity of the Holy Spirit,
> one God, now and for ever.

COLLECT

Reflection by **Brother Samuel SSF** | 225

Monday 8 August

Psalms 27, **30**
I Samuel 14.24-46
Luke 23.13-25

1 Samuel 14.24-46

'... his eyes brightened' (v.27)

Jonathan is illuminated, as he sees and challenges the fallacy in his father's thinking. It is a calculated risk based on his hope that his relationship with his father will outweigh the rule of the king. How many times do we serve some arbitrary rule that diminishes wellbeing for fear of the system bearing down on us?

This passage demonstrates ways we can bring about sustainable change. First, we notice what is needed, and yet not offered. Second, we ask the difficult questions in the company of a supporter. Third, we align our gifts with the gaps. In this way, we can learn to live with greater purpose and deeper integrity.

One word for this type of ongoing courageous living is *vocation*. American philosopher and theologian Frederick Buechner describes it in this way: 'Vocation is where your greatest passion meets the world's greatest needs.' While Jonathan's commonsense approach does not win over his father, it does win over the army, and they switch allegiance.

We can all encounter Sauls in the kingdoms of our homes, our places of work or education, and within our families and neighbourhoods. They can appear intimidating and irrational. Jonathan chose to nourish himself in order to nurture the others. When we choose love over fear, we can be assured that God is our first ally; others will follow in time when we act in love, for liberation.

COLLECT

Almighty Lord and everlasting God,
we beseech you to direct, sanctify and govern
    both our hearts and bodies
in the ways of your laws
    and the works of your commandments;
that through your most mighty protection, both here and ever,
we may be preserved in body and soul;
through our Lord and Saviour Jesus Christ,
who is alive and reigns with you,
in the unity of the Holy Spirit,
one God, now and for ever.

| *Reflection by* **Azariah France-Williams**

Psalms 32, **36**
1 Samuel 15.1-23
Luke 23.26-43

1 Samuel 15.1-23

'Though you are little in your own eyes, are you not the head of the tribes of Israel?' (v.17)

You may be familiar with the term 'imposter syndrome': finding yourself in a context with a set of responsibilities that you feel you are unable to meet, and fearing everyone around you knows that you are pretending. In this situation, it is tempting for us to put on a show of strength, not realizing we are fooling no one. It can be hard to take responsibility for our mistakes.

Samuel doesn't have to activate his prophetic lie detector when he encounters Saul, as the noisy sheep give the lie away. Saul then blames the people, but Samuel is not buying it. Saul then claims the animals were for sacrifice for God – like the child caught with their hand in the biscuit tin asking 'Would you like a biscuit too?'

What of our old world and worldview do we need to leave behind? Which mementos are we tempted to keep even if all they do is tie us to the past and remind us of former bullies, addictions, obsessions? It is easier to trust in what we can see, instead of trusting the God we cannot. If we fear we are not enough, we can never have enough. Let us learn to see ourselves through the eyes of a loving God who says: we are loved, and we are enough.

Lord God,
your Son left the riches of heaven
and became poor for our sake:
when we prosper save us from pride,
when we are needy save us from despair,
that we may trust in you alone;
through Jesus Christ our Lord.

COLLECT

Reflection by **Azariah France-Williams**

Wednesday 10 August

1 Samuel 16

' ... skilful in playing, a man of valour, a warrior, prudent in speech, and a man of good presence; and the Lord is with him' (v.18)

David was Jesse's youngest son, but he was already a man. In this mini-biography, we learn he's an accomplished artist, an established fighter, an orator with charisma – and that the Lord is with him. He has already lived a life and achieved a reputation.

However, when I think of David, the image of the little boy with the sling comes into my mind because of the way I learnt the story. It is such a strong image it blocks out what is actually there in black and white; this is the *man* who would later take on Goliath and enter into politics, eventually becoming king. If we look with clear eyes at David, he was already powerful having lived many stories before he arrives in this one.

We all have a combination of interests and skills; we may be walkers, artists, accountants, parents, bloggers, scientists, goalies or cricket fans. Can you think of times when you went home to the place you grew up? Have you ever felt people's old view of you was limited and limiting?

What life challenges are preoccupying you now? If you take stock and recognize the variety of your interests, historical or current, you may find clues to help unlock current dilemmas. The Lord is with you; you are already powerful; your life stories so far, your skills and passions are all important right now and will be the foundation of your next chapter.

COLLECT

Almighty Lord and everlasting God,
we beseech you to direct, sanctify and govern
    both our hearts and bodies
in the ways of your laws
    and the works of your commandments;
that through your most mighty protection, both here and ever,
we may be preserved in body and soul;
through our Lord and Saviour Jesus Christ,
who is alive and reigns with you,
in the unity of the Holy Spirit,
one God, now and for ever.

228 | *Reflection by* **Azariah France-Williams**

Psalm 37*
1 Samuel 17.1-30
Luke 23.56b – 24.12

1 Samuel 17.1-30

'David left the things in charge of the keeper of the baggage ...' (v.22)

Many of us have responsibilities towards others: caring for a child, a parent in ill health, an unwell partner or a neighbour in need. We understand the sacrifice and willingly give, yet we can notice our own needs and desires going unanswered.

David looked after the sheep, which were a key source of income and wealth. His father was an important figure in the community and there were family obligations. He had a significant duty to fulfil.

When the superpower that were the Philistines made their challenge through their champion Goliath, David could have thought, 'I will sit this one out' – the equivalent of watching the television news of some event that you feel stirred by. You want to do something to help, but you feel duty bound by your home, or job, or the 'to do' list.

Have you considered the idea of a 'keeper'? A keeper is someone – or a group – who can share your responsibilities with you so that you can play your part in the battles around you that you might be particularly suited to address.

David leaves the sheep and later the provisions he has bought. On both occasions, he entrusts his obligations temporarily to someone else, enabling him to play a fuller role. Maybe a 'keeper' could promise to make contact with your ailing relative, or mind a child, giving you the freedom to create and craft opportunities so you can eventually topple some giants – or simply have a needed day off.

Lord God,
your Son left the riches of heaven
and became poor for our sake:
when we prosper save us from pride,
when we are needy save us from despair,
that we may trust in you alone;
through Jesus Christ our Lord.

COLLECT

Friday 12 August

1 Samuel 17.31-54

'Go, and may the Lord be with you!' (v.37)

This is undoubtedly one of the most famous single-combat battles of all time. It is usually billed as the underdog versus the bully. The odds are not in David's favour, yet he triumphs. However, it could be better understood as 'out of the box' thinking.

David was an experienced fighter. The ancient armies had a range of fighting units. One lesser-known, but well-established, group were the slingers. They were the artillery, using projectiles, bows and arrows, anything they could shoot, toss, or hurl. The stones of slingers could be the size of tennis balls made of flint, and the speed of a slung stone was equivalent to a bullet being shot. David was a slinger.

David would have lost if he had fought Goliath on Goliath's terms. Goliath was heavy artillery, a one-man tank, slow and devastating. David tore up the script of slugging it out at close range, which had been the expectation. David works smarter not harder; he refuses armour that would slow him down and ironically make him more vulnerable.

It can feel like a risk to go into battle, to face any challenge, without following the formula of your peers or your betters. If the Lord is with us, who we already are and what we already have might just be all we need to overcome.

COLLECT

Almighty Lord and everlasting God,
we beseech you to direct, sanctify and govern
    both our hearts and bodies
in the ways of your laws
    and the works of your commandments;
that through your most mighty protection, both here and ever,
we may be preserved in body and soul;
through our Lord and Saviour Jesus Christ,
who is alive and reigns with you,
in the unity of the Holy Spirit,
one God, now and for ever.

| *Reflection by* **Azariah France-Williams**

Psalms 41, **42**, 43
1 Samuel 17.55 – 18.16
Luke 24.36-end

Saturday 13 August

1 Samuel 17.55 – 18.16
'So Saul eyed David from that day on' (18.9)

There is an intriguing term I have come across, which is 'frenemy'. A friend is supportive most of the time, and you can trust them. An enemy is unsupportive most of the time, and you know where you are with them. A frenemy, however, is someone who flips between friend and enemy. This is very disorientating because you don't know when this might happen. They might offer encouragement personally as you try a new task, but then ridicule you when other friends are around, in order to make themselves look good.

David knows the headless giant to be his enemy; in Jonathan, he has a friend; but Saul is a frenemy. A frenemy is easily jealous of your success and will attempt to undermine you. Saul, eager to meet David and have David move in, grows green with envy as the women, his own son and the soldiers grow more devoted to David than to him.

A frenemy will attack when you least expect it, like Saul trying to pin David to the wall, or they will leave you overexposed or overwhelmed in a setting where you're forced to sink or swim.

Who are the frenemies in your life – the people who demonstrate they are not worthy of your trust? Do not ignore that feeling; look instead for 'Jonathans', with whom the love shared can be mutual and reciprocal.

Lord God,
your Son left the riches of heaven
and became poor for our sake:
when we prosper save us from pride,
when we are needy save us from despair,
that we may trust in you alone;
through Jesus Christ our Lord.

COLLECT

Reflection by **Azariah France-Williams** | 231

Monday 15 August
The Blessed Virgin Mary

Psalms 98, 138, 147.1-12
Isaiah 7.10-15
Luke 11.27-28

Luke 11.27-28

'While he was saying this, a woman in the crowd raised her voice'
(v.27)

One of my closest friends is a comedian. I love seeing him juggling funny anecdotes, sharp insights and one-liners. However, I become anxious when someone in the crowd heckles. I worry that it will disrupt the show and interrupt his flow. It does neither. He simply catches the ball of their comment and keeps on juggling their 'wit' with the words of his established routine.

Jesus has been teaching a growing crowd, debating and responding, and following an argument through. The heckler crashes into the conversation blurting out seeming praise. But Jesus was skilled at discerning the private commentary behind the public comment.

Jesus is pushing forwards, increasing the number of messengers to this movement. The heckler has the potential to wrap, package, stamp and post the full responsibility of shaping a loving society back to Jesus. In effect she is saying: 'Jesus, you are the special one. What a lucky mum you had! Go for it my boy!'

Jesus was the sender of the package in the first place; there is no return label. Hence, the challenge to the heckler is that she needs to take responsibility for shaping her world. The root of the word 'obey' is 'listen and respond'. If we can learn to listen to Jesus' life, as well as his lines, we can be born anew and become the source of life for others too.

Almighty God,
who looked upon the lowliness of the Blessed Virgin Mary
and chose her to be the mother of your only Son:
grant that we who are redeemed by his blood
may share with her in the glory of your eternal kingdom;
through Jesus Christ your Son our Lord,
who is alive and reigns with you,
in the unity of the Holy Spirit,
one God, now and for ever.

| *Reflection by* **Azariah France-Williams**

Psalms **48**, 52
I Samuel 20.1-17
Acts 1.15-end

Tuesday 16 August

Acts 1.15-end

'Lord ... Show us which one of these two you have chosen' (v.24)

Imagine you are a follower of Jesus in the time period referenced. You were wowed by the stories and miracles of Jesus. You were devastated when you witnessed him executed by the state. Then you were confused, but confusion turned to joy when you met Jesus after he was raised from death. After Jesus' departure into the skies, you are struggling to make sense of all this. Now you are with the others gathered in the busy upper room. These 120 people are members of Jesus' family, his siblings and their families, devoted men, women and children.

You are all hushed as Peter stands and declares that there is to be a replacement for Judas. A couple of people look at you and nod. You look down and feel a little faint. Before you know what is happening, you and Justus are being ushered to the front. Lots are drawn and Peter slowly shakes his head looking at Justus, who looks relieved and begins to pat you on the back ... what is happening? The room erupts with your name 'Matthias, Matthias!'. The apostles are smiling warmly. Peter embraces you and whispers in your ear: 'Are you any good with accounts?'

We are chosen as disciples of Christ. Fear not, we have a role to play. Let's trust God to reveal the next right thing.

COLLECT

Almighty God,
who sent your Holy Spirit
to be the life and light of your Church:
open our hearts to the riches of your grace,
that we may bring forth the fruit of the Spirit
in love and joy and peace;
through Jesus Christ your Son our Lord,
who is alive and reigns with you,
in the unity of the Holy Spirit,
one God, now and for ever.

Reflection by **Azariah France-Williams**

Wednesday 17 August

Psalm 119.57-80
1 Samuel 20.18-end
Acts 2.1-21

Acts 2.1-21

'... speaking in the native language of each' (v.6)

I am Black British with a West Indian heritage. I remember a religious conversation with a zealous young man, in a library of all places. He was an African missionary of this faith of which I was unfamiliar. When he saw I was immune to his persuasion, he abruptly finished the conversation saying: 'Anyway, you West Indians don't know your mother tongue, your true country or your tribe!' And with that unforgettable blow, he left me to seek another target.

My paternal family tree stretches back to Aki a West African slave, but then the trail goes cold. The young missionary's comment left me cold and empty. Yet in the Scripture reading, we learn there is a deeper language, an ancient language, a forming of a new tribe that includes and redeems all the tribes we come from, the beginning of a new country.

We have a phrase when we connect with another human – we say, 'You're speaking my language'. This suggests a bonding of ideas and common understanding even if the conversation partners are working with interpreters. This connection spells new possibilities for humans to find God speaking through them and others, speaking a better word, for a fairer world.

In this world, all of our individual histories are bound up in our new collective future as God draws us forward into the last days, which will make sense of the first.

COLLECT

Almighty God,
who sent your Holy Spirit
to be the life and light of your Church:
open our hearts to the riches of your grace,
that we may bring forth the fruit of the Spirit
in love and joy and peace;
through Jesus Christ your Son our Lord,
who is alive and reigns with you,
in the unity of the Holy Spirit,
one God, now and for ever.

| *Reflection by* **Azariah France-Williams**

Thursday 18 August

Acts 2.22-36

'... you will not abandon my soul to Hades' (v.27)

Some years ago, I had a stint of attending a 5-kilometre Saturday morning run called 'Park Run'. I would dread it, but it was needed exercise. I would always end up near the back of the group. On one occasion, I fell so far behind, I got lost and ended up by a horse's paddock, well off track. I despaired and couldn't locate any of the stewards who were usually dotted about. Another runner who'd arrived late and knew the route saw me in my dazed confusion; she called me over to the right path and got me back to a point where I could see the finish line and continue alone.

She could have run on to chase a personal best – and I could have been there floundering until this day! However, she did not abandon me, and I was deeply grateful.

A favourite mantra of my parents was: 'Keep on keeping on.' Whatever season of life we find ourselves in – waiting for exam results, waiting for a diagnosis, waiting to be forgiven – our momentum can slow, and our direction can be lost. Let us pause, catch our breath and listen for the call back to the pathway, confident in the companionship of a loving God who will accompany us to the next stage and then remain ahead until we find our stride and can move forward once more.

Gracious Father,
revive your Church in our day,
and make her holy, strong and faithful,
for your glory's sake
in Jesus Christ our Lord.

COLLECT

Reflection by **Azariah France-Williams**

Friday 19 August

Acts 2.37-end

'Save yourselves from this corrupt generation' (v.40)

'How you boil a frog?' The concept is that you place it in a pot of cold water and heat so gently that it fails to realize it is becoming a delicacy. No doubt if the frog knew what you were doing, it would be hopping mad!

We can find ourselves in families, workplaces, churches where the temperature has slowly changed: a once-welcoming church becomes a 'members only' club; a joyful family grows ever more resentful; an ambitious workplace becomes overly focused on the bottom line.

The people in today's passage have turned to Christ and have been baptized. But that is not all that is needed; they have to actively escape the corruption around them. This is the hot water that is killing them. How can we take stock of the contexts within which we find ourselves? How can the cold fresh waters of baptism cool the harmful stale waters of toxic religion and broken relationships?

Peter did not say 'Save yourselves from this generation', as the command is not an escape from life; rather it is the opposite, an invitation to escape to life and a renewed world. Let us come alive and awaken to God's call to redeem the places and the spaces where we exist. Become aware of the pot inside which you, the frog, might be sitting – and when no one is watching, hop it!

COLLECT

Almighty God,
who sent your Holy Spirit
to be the life and light of your Church:
open our hearts to the riches of your grace,
that we may bring forth the fruit of the Spirit
in love and joy and peace;
through Jesus Christ your Son our Lord,
who is alive and reigns with you,
in the unity of the Holy Spirit,
one God, now and for ever.

| *Reflection by* **Azariah France-Williams**

Psalm **68**
1 Samuel 23
Acts 3.1-10

Saturday 20 August

Acts 3.1-10

'... and they recognized him' (v.10)

Or did they? In this story, the dis-ability was in the society who could not perceive the man's needs and gifts as he was. The miracle of recognition is what was needed for him to be a human among humans. A friend of mine, a priest called Eva, lives with a disability. She helped me understand the focus here being on the apostles giving him what they thought he needed. So yet again, he was ignored and unrecognized.

Those of us living with disabilities can be ostracized by miracle stories such as these, which, on the surface, can seem to point to physical and mental normalcy as the ideal. We even hear from Church leaders that the majority's version of our embodied selves is God's ideal too.

In the time of this passage, holding to a conventional physicality was the doorway into the social, economic and religious dimensions of life. In that society, the miracle enabled access to what should always have been his: love, connection, equality and justice. But we can do better, as we learn to encounter each other as God does. The apostles and the worshippers might not have recognized the man, but the man could no doubt have recognized them. Maybe in his delight he still recognized he was a prop to the apostles' popularity, and an anomaly to the crowd.

Let us acknowledge the ones so easily 'othered'. Maybe they can help us to begin to recognize ourselves.

Gracious Father,
revive your Church in our day,
and make her holy, strong and faithful,
for your glory's sake
in Jesus Christ our Lord.

COLLECT

Reflection by **Azariah France-Williams** | 237

Monday 22 August

Psalm **71**
I Samuel 24
Acts 3.11-end

Acts 3.11-end

'... times of refreshing' (v.20)

The healed man provokes the crowd's astonishment, and gives Peter and John an opportunity to witness to the power of Jesus not only to bring healing from suffering, but life from death. Confronting the crowd with their own complicity in the death of Jesus, Peter speaks words of truth and hope: the story has not ended with the death of Jesus, and neither need their story be defined by their complicity in it. Repentance is possible, and with it forgiveness and a different ending to their story than that they might have imagined.

This is a promise for us, too: our stories, our histories, can find their meaning and fulfilment in the crucified and risen Jesus. We are not defined by the worst thing we have done, or that has happened to us. The God who raised Jesus from the dead can breathe new life into old wounds, bringing times of refreshing and new life even into those parts of our lives and stories that feel hard and closed.

The story of our life is only truly told by Christ. What is the story of life from death, or of new creation, that he wants to tell in you? And where might he be asking you, like Peter, to tell this story so others can find in it hope for their story's fulfilment?

COLLECT

Let your merciful ears, O Lord,
be open to the prayers of your humble servants;
and that they may obtain their petitions
make them to ask such things as shall please you;
through Jesus Christ your Son our Lord,
who is alive and reigns with you,
in the unity of the Holy Spirit,
one God, now and for ever.

| *Reflection by* **Anna Matthews**

Psalm **73**
I Samuel 26
Acts 4.1-12

Tuesday 23 August

Acts 4.1-12

'... filled with the Holy Spirit' (v.8)

As with the teacher, so with the disciples: Jesus had been brought before Annas and Caiaphas in his travesty of a trial (John 18.12ff). Now Peter and John are hauled before the religious leaders to account for themselves, and for the power at work in them. There is a clash of authority here: the religious elite has the power to put the living to death. But in the Spirit-filled ministry of the disciples, they face the God who has the power to raise the dead to life.

As the religious authorities are confronted with the limits of their power, Peter and John learn that the Spirit at work in them brings courage and truth: the humble and meek are being lifted up (cf. Luke 1.52), and those who are used to meting out judgement are themselves being judged. Having killed Jesus as a way of trying to protect Israel's interests, the religious authorities are now faced with the truth that the stone they had rejected is the cornerstone on which God is building a holy nation. They think they are acting by God's authority. But God's power is at work here in the judged, not the judges.

As you read this passage, with whom do you stand? And for whom do you use the power or influence you have?

Lord of heaven and earth,
as Jesus taught his disciples to be persistent in prayer,
give us patience and courage never to lose hope,
but always to bring our prayers before you;
through Jesus Christ our Lord.

COLLECT

Reflection by **Anna Matthews** | 239

Wednesday 24 August
Bartholomew the Apostle

Psalms 86, 117
Genesis 28.10-17
John 1.43-end

Genesis 28.10-17

'Surely the Lord is in this place' (v.16)

John's Gospel (1.43ff) tells of Jesus meeting Nathaniel (whom tradition often identifies with Bartholomew), when Jesus draws on today's passage to show that in him, the gate of heaven stands open.

In the Genesis story, Jacob, having cheated his way to a blessing, thinks that all he had hoped for seems lost. He is an exile: the promised land lies far behind him, and with it hopes of offspring and the love of family. As he makes camp as night falls, Jacob does not expect to meet God. He has lied and swindled and fled from justice. In a straightforward morality tale, the lonely Jacob cut off from his family gets what he deserves. But this is not how God operates. Time and again, God chooses to deal with the weak, the second-best, the guilty, to bring hope and a future.

In his vision of the angels and the heavenly ladder, the blessing of Abraham is given to Jacob. When he wakes up, Jacob's situation doesn't look very different: he's still an exile; Esau is still angry enough to kill him; there's no prospect of an heir. But Jacob is changed. He recognizes a makeshift campsite as the gate of heaven, and his messed-up life as the sphere of God's action. 'Surely the Lord is in this place – and I did not know it!'

It's not just Jacob who trudges along not even thinking of the possibility that the Lord might be in *this* place – the places of our own fears or guilt or exile – making of our lives holy ground, and the very gate of heaven.

COLLECT

Almighty and everlasting God,
who gave to your apostle Bartholomew grace
    truly to believe and to preach your word:
grant that your Church
may love that word which he believed
and may faithfully preach and receive the same;
through Jesus Christ your Son our Lord,
who is alive and reigns with you,
in the unity of the Holy Spirit,
one God, now and for ever.

| *Reflection by* **Anna Matthews**

Psalm **78.1-39***
1 Samuel 31
Acts 4.32 – 5.11

Thursday 25 August

Acts 4.32 – 5.11

'... at the apostles' feet' (4.35)

The narrative now shifts to the ordering of the Christian community. From proclamation of the resurrection of Jesus from the dead we now see what this new life looks like in the common lives of the disciples as it is lived out 'at the apostles' feet'. In the new community formed through the death and resurrection of Jesus the rules of belonging and kinship are rewritten.

In this passage, private possessions find their purpose in the need of the community, and even cherished relationships (the marriage of Ananias and Sapphira) are re-ordered by the kinship effected through baptism. They no longer belong solely to themselves but to the community, which makes their withholding of some of the proceeds of the sale of their property not just a sin against God but against their brothers and sisters in Christ. At the feet of the apostles, Ananias and Sapphira stand with us in all the ways we are tempted to withhold gifts from God or the community – temptations we often justify because they are for our family, or for our security.

Here, in the community of the Spirit and at the feet of the apostles we are asked not just how we use the wealth and possessions we have, but how willing we are to live a common life where we are open to each other in our vulnerabilities and needs, as well as in our ability to give and to share.

Let your merciful ears, O Lord,
be open to the prayers of your humble servants;
and that they may obtain their petitions
make them to ask such things as shall please you;
through Jesus Christ your Son our Lord,
who is alive and reigns with you,
in the unity of the Holy Spirit,
one God, now and for ever.

COLLECT

Friday 26 August

Psalm **55**
2 Samuel I
Acts 5.12-26

Acts 5.12-26

'... they did not find them in the prison' (v.22)

Signs and wonders are done. Crowds of needy people press in, and the sick are healed by touch. The authorities' jealousy is aroused, and the apostles are arrested. We are meant to hear the echoes of Jesus' ministry here, for Luke's purpose in writing Acts is to show how Jesus is still present through his Spirit in the Church.

And it is not just in proclamation and ministry that the apostles imitate Christ: obedience to him will bring them before rulers and put them in prison (Luke 21.12), for the way of the cross will always lead into the places of sin and captivity so that Christ's resurrection may be made known. Death could not hold Jesus, as the empty tomb bears witness. So a locked prison door is no bar to the power of God at work in the apostles who are set free to go and continue what had got them arrested: telling the people 'the whole message about this life'.

The apostles, freed from their captivity at the hands of the Jewish authorities, but more significantly, set free from the prison of sin and death, are now empowered to go on proclaiming the good news. For where death no longer has dominion, neither does fear – and it is striking that as this passage ends, and the apostles are arrested again, it is the authorities who are afraid of the power they see at work in them.

COLLECT

Let your merciful ears, O Lord,
be open to the prayers of your humble servants;
and that they may obtain their petitions
make them to ask such things as shall please you;
through Jesus Christ your Son our Lord,
who is alive and reigns with you,
in the unity of the Holy Spirit,
one God, now and for ever.

| *Reflection by* **Anna Matthews**

Saturday 27 August

Acts 5.27-end

'... let them alone' (v.38)

Through whom does God speak? Through the religious elite, used to holding power and interpreting the law, or through the rabble-rousing Galilean nuisances who persist in proclaiming that God is doing a new thing in the world through the death and resurrection of Jesus? Peter's speech angers the members of the Council, even if it does not yet quite convict them. They want to react with violence, but Gamaliel's intervention stops them.

The God confessed by Gamaliel is the same God confessed by the apostles, but Gamaliel and the others are unable to hear the invitation to new life that the apostles preach. Imprisoned fishermen from the sticks make unlikely messengers of God to the learned and the powerful. For the apostles, the resurrection of Jesus and the gift of the Spirit draw them into God's action in the world. Salvation is unfolding and a new order is being established in which they are made participants.

Gamaliel, on the other hand, watches from the sidelines to see what will unfold. His power and position allow him this distance. But he has not so far recognised God at work in raising Jesus from the dead. Nor, in the witness of the apostles, does he hear God's voice calling to him, saying that the invitation is for him, too.

Through whom might God be speaking to you at this time? How is he calling you to join in with what he's doing in the world?

COLLECT

Lord of heaven and earth,
as Jesus taught his disciples to be persistent in prayer,
give us patience and courage never to lose hope,
but always to bring our prayers before you;
through Jesus Christ our Lord.

Reflection by **Anna Matthews**   243

Monday 29 August

Acts 6
'... the Hellenists complained against the Hebrews' (v.1)

Tensions arise between the Hebrews and the Hellenists – Jews who were native to Jerusalem and Judea, and Greek-speaking Jews who had lived in the diaspora and returned to Jerusalem. There were differences in language and culture, exacerbated, in this episode, by the perception of unfair treatment in the distribution of food.

This is a challenge to the growing, joyful community 'of one heart and soul' (4.32): the challenge of belonging to a community made up of more than simply 'people like us'. The apostles, all Hebrews, ask the community to select people fit for the task (that it includes more than serving at tables is evident from the second half of this chapter, where Stephen does 'great wonders and signs among the people', and from Philip's preaching, which extends the borders of the Church beyond Israel (8.4ff)). That the men chosen are all Hellenists is significant: they are from the group which has complained of not being treated fairly.

The community listens, and responds by raising up leaders from this underrepresented group, being recalled by their complaint to the vocation to treat the poor and disadvantaged with mercy and justice. And the community empowers these new ministers to enact this vocation – moving the community beyond narrow understandings of what it is to belong to Christ, and paving the way for the gospel to go out into all the world.

COLLECT

O God, you declare your almighty power
most chiefly in showing mercy and pity:
mercifully grant to us such a measure of your grace,
that we, running the way of your commandments,
may receive your gracious promises,
and be made partakers of your heavenly treasure;
through Jesus Christ your Son our Lord,
who is alive and reigns with you,
in the unity of the Holy Spirit,
one God, now and for ever.

Psalms 87, **89.1-18**
2 Samuel 5.1-12
Acts 7.1-16

Tuesday 30 August

Acts 7.1-16

'Are these things so?' (v.1)

Jesus had told his disciples that the Holy Spirit would give them words to say when they were brought before councils (Luke 12.11-12) and here we see this promise kept as Stephen defends himself against charges of heresy by interpreting the story of God and Israel in the light of the death and resurrection of Jesus.

Beginning with Abraham, who responds to the divine command to 'Go from your country and your kindred...' (Genesis 12.1), Stephen tells the story of Israel as the story of a people shaped by God's promise to be their God. It's a promise that requires the people to live in trust and expectancy – trust that God remains faithful through childlessness and famine and slavery, and expectancy that God will go on acting to save his people.

As Stephen tells it, this is a story to which he and the persecuted Christians are the faithful heirs: a people shaped by promise and expectancy, and responsive to God's ongoing call and faithfulness. The religious leaders see Stephen and the other Christians as a threat to Israel. But like the prophets before him, and like Jesus himself, Stephen uses the Scriptures to call the Council to a faithfulness shaped by God's promise – and to a recognition of the Spirit at work, bringing it to fruition. As the story continues, what might this sort of faithfulness look like in your life?

God of glory,
the end of our searching,
help us to lay aside
all that prevents us from seeking your kingdom,
and to give all that we have
to gain the pearl beyond all price,
through our Saviour Jesus Christ.

COLLECT

Wednesday 31 August

Acts 7.17-43

'Moses whom they rejected' (v.35)

Stephen is charged with speaking blasphemous words against Moses and God (6.11). Here he turns the charge back on his accusers by recounting the story of Moses and reminding the Council that the people of Israel rejected Moses' leadership and turned away from God by worshipping the golden calf.

How tempting it can be to tell the story so that we identify with Joseph and not his jealous brothers, or with faithful Moses rather than the grumbling Israelites. But the story of salvation is not the story of our faithfulness but of God's – who keeps his covenant with his recalcitrant people, loving them to the end and waiting for them to respond in love. The reminder is plain in Stephen's speech of God's faithfulness to his promise to be their God, through the bitter years of slavery and the wandering in the wilderness, and now, as the speech builds towards its climax, in the life, death and resurrection of Jesus.

It is in the name of faithfulness to God that Stephen is hauled before the Council. Though they do not recognize it as anything but a threat, Stephen is inviting them to respond to the ongoing faithfulness of God. As you reflect on the story of God's faithfulness down the ages, how might he be asking you to look anew at the story you tell of God and of your life with him?

COLLECT

O God, you declare your almighty power
most chiefly in showing mercy and pity:
mercifully grant to us such a measure of your grace,
that we, running the way of your commandments,
may receive your gracious promises,
and be made partakers of your heavenly treasure;
through Jesus Christ your Son our Lord,
who is alive and reigns with you,
in the unity of the Holy Spirit,
one God, now and for ever.

| *Reflection by* **Anna Matthews**

Psalms 90, **92**
2 Samuel 7.1-17
Acts 7.44-53

Thursday 1 September

Acts 7.44-53
'... stiff-necked' (v.51)

As Stephen's speech gathers pace, his rootedness in Israel's scriptures is obvious. When the ancient Israelites made the golden calf, God called them a stiff-necked people (Exodus 32.9). Now, on Stephen's lips, the same charge is levelled against the Council members whose response to Jesus and action against the Church is interpreted as opposition to the Holy Spirit.

Stephen is on dangerous ground: already accused of having spoken against the temple, the place of God's dwelling among his people, he now quotes from the Psalms and from Solomon's dedicatory prayer for the temple to provoke them to a bigger understanding of God and his purposes. Beyond the temple, the place God longs to dwell is among his people, drawing them into the relationship of love for which he made them. Persistently and patiently, through the story of divine love offered and rejected told by the prophets, God has been calling his people into relationship, even taking on flesh and dwelling among them so that he might share their life.

As Stephen tells it, like their ancestors who persecuted the prophets before them, the Council members are judged by their resistance to God's presence and purposes. Stephen's interpretation of Israel's history puts him firmly within the prophetic strand of the tradition. And it is witness offered not only with his lips but with his life, as the story of persecution continues, and the Church gains her first martyr.

God of glory,
the end of our searching,
help us to lay aside
all that prevents us from seeking your kingdom,
and to give all that we have
to gain the pearl beyond all price,
through our Saviour Jesus Christ.

COLLECT

Friday 2 September

Psalms **88** (95)
2 Samuel 7.18-end
Acts 7.54 – 8.3

Acts 7.54 – 8.3

'... do not hold this sin against them' (7.60)

The young man Saul, witness and approver of the violence unleashed on Stephen, will later write that 'I want to know Christ and the power of his resurrection and the sharing of his sufferings by becoming like him in his death, if somehow I may attain the resurrection from the dead' (Philippians 3.10-11). Now, it is Stephen who becomes like Jesus in his death: dragged before the religious authorities on trumped-up charges, he has a vision of the Son of Man standing at the right hand of God, and prays for the forgiveness of his persecutors.

He is like his Saviour in death, and his Saviour appears from the far side of death to hold out to Stephen the promise of glory and the power of his resurrection. Stephen is the first martyr of the new age begun in Christ, but he will not be its last, for severe persecution breaks out against the Church. There is lamentation for Stephen – the new age begun has not yet reached its completion in that time when there will be no mourning or tears (Revelation 21.4). But as the early Church affirmed, 'the blood of the martyrs is the seed of the Church' (Tertullian).

The power of Christ's resurrection is shown in the courageous and truthful witness of Stephen and the others persecuted for their faith in Christ, whose testimony will make of even the harshest enemy a friend of God.

COLLECT

O God, you declare your almighty power
most chiefly in showing mercy and pity:
mercifully grant to us such a measure of your grace,
that we, running the way of your commandments,
may receive your gracious promises,
and be made partakers of your heavenly treasure;
through Jesus Christ your Son our Lord,
who is alive and reigns with you,
in the unity of the Holy Spirit,
one God, now and for ever.

| *Reflection by* **Anna Matthews**

Saturday 3 September

Acts 8.4-25

'Give me also this power' (v.19)

The disciples are scattered to try to stamp out their faith, but they go on proclaiming the word. In Philip's preaching, the Holy Spirit moves into Samaria, joining to the body of the disciples the despised Samaritans.

Jesus had made a Samaritan woman the first preacher of the good news (John 4). He used the example of a good Samaritan to rebuke Israel's leaders (Luke 10.25ff). But until now in Acts the early Church has been Jewish. The joining of Jew and Samaritan through the preaching of Philip and the laying on of apostolic hands shows God's desire for his love to extend beyond Israel into the whole world.

But the Spirit poured out freely on Jew and Samaritan alike is withheld from Simon the magician. Simon is attracted by the power he sees at work in the apostles, but does not understand what he sees, thinking it a commodity that can be bought and traded like anything else. God wants relationship, but Simon wants power – and in every age of the Church there are those who will try to use faith for their own ends. Yet there is hope: Simon recognises the truth of Peter's rebuke. He asks for the help of his prayers. And in entering into the space of repentance and prayer, Simon can learn that what he sees to buy and control can only be received as a gift. The Holy Spirit can yet be for him, too.

God of glory,
the end of our searching,
help us to lay aside
all that prevents us from seeking your kingdom,
and to give all that we have
to gain the pearl beyond all price,
through our Saviour Jesus Christ.

COLLECT

Reflection by **Anna Matthews** | 249

Monday 5 September

Acts 8.26-end

'What is to prevent me from being baptized?' (v.36)

When I came to faith in my mid-twenties, I was terrified about going to church. As an LGBT person, I was convinced that all the 'holy people' inside the building would reject me. I actually received a warm welcome, but when I read this encounter between the Apostle Philip and the Ethiopian eunuch, I'm reminded about my anxieties about being accepted by the Church community. Many members of the LGBT community have seen the Ethiopian eunuch as an example of a biblical character who represents themselves – someone who does not fit the neat patterns of gender and sexuality.

Insofar as that is a fair claim, there is something reassuring and powerful about how Philip receives a prompt from God to be with this unnamed man, greeting him with acceptance rather than judgement. Philip finds the man reading the Scriptures, clearly hungry to know about whom Isaiah speaks when he says, 'Like a sheep he was led to the slaughter'.

I find Philip's moving response a model for welcoming those who might seem at the edges of the Church. Philip does not reject the man, but invites him into living faith in Jesus Christ. When they encounter a body of water, the Ethiopian asks: 'What is to prevent me from being baptised?' Philip places no bar in his way. It is surely a reminder that living faith in Jesus Christ is always primary, not whether we fit society's or the Church's neat and sometimes questionable norms.

COLLECT

Almighty and everlasting God,
you are always more ready to hear than we to pray
and to give more than either we desire or deserve:
pour down upon us the abundance of your mercy,
forgiving us those things of which our conscience is afraid
and giving us those good things which we are not worthy to ask
but through the merits and mediation
of Jesus Christ your Son our Lord,
who is alive and reigns with you,
in the unity of the Holy Spirit,
one God, now and for ever.

| *Reflection by* **Rachel Mann**

Tuesday 6 September

Acts 9.1-19*a*

'I am Jesus, whom you are persecuting' (v.5)

The story of the conversion of Saul is justly famous. His encounter with the profound and gracious power of God is so well known that the phrase 'Road to Damascus experience' has entered common parlance to represent any sudden change of worldview.

Yet for all its familiarity, this story should still shake us to our bones. The context for Saul's conversion is violence, hatred and persecution. He is a figure who inspires fear, even terror, in Jesus' early followers. He is a man who, seemingly, is so sure of the righteousness of his cause that he is prepared, like a secret police officer, to drag Christians out of their homes to face their end. Into the midst of Saul's righteous violence comes the humbling grace of God. Jesus' encounter with Saul is shattering in its simplicity and honesty. He presents Saul with a discomforting truth: that each time he persecutes a follower of Jesus, he persecutes Jesus (and therefore God) himself. I too am brought up short by this truth. I am reminded that when I treat others with disrespect or with aggression or meanness, my action echoes beyond itself. I do a 'violence' to Jesus and to God himself.

If this passage shows that God calls even the most violent to be obedient to God, all of us should be aware that our words and actions sting God as much as our neighbours. When we treat others badly, the Body of Christ itself is hurt.

> God of constant mercy,
> who sent your Son to save us:
> remind us of your goodness,
> increase your grace within us,
> that our thankfulness may grow,
> through Jesus Christ our Lord.

COLLECT

Wednesday 7 September

Psalms 110, 111, 112
2 Samuel 15.1-12
Acts 9.19*b*-31

Acts 9.19*b*-31

'... immediately he began to proclaim Jesus' (v.20)

There is something both charming and stunning about the way Paul moves so quickly from persecutor to evangelist. This shift is a testimony to the converting power of God.

Paul's behaviour reminds me of my own conversion experience in my twenties. At the time I was teaching and studying in a secular philosophy department. I recall a stand-up row I had in public one lunchtime with one my best friends as I sought to tell him about why I had gone from unbeliever to a follower of Jesus. I was desperate for him to know the power of the risen Christ in his life too. Ultimately, it was a fracture in a friendship, which eventually broke down for years and has never been the same.

This passage from Acts presents Paul as someone who confounds and enrages his audience so much that he has to be smuggled out of Damascus in a basket. Decades on from my conversion experience, I can see that how we share the good news is nearly as important as the good news itself. If it cannot be heard because we are bumptious or 'in your face', I'm not sure we should speak.

On reflection, I can see that my argument with my friend was not my finest hour. I was like a teenager who wanted to tell my friend about this amazing person with whom I'd just fallen in love and who insisted that my friend love them too. I wrote to my friend years later, apologizing for behaving like a teenager. I did not apologize for my faith and trust in the Author of the Universe.

COLLECT

Almighty and everlasting God,
you are always more ready to hear than we to pray
and to give more than either we desire or deserve:
pour down upon us the abundance of your mercy,
forgiving us those things of which our conscience is afraid
and giving us those good things which we are not worthy to ask
but through the merits and mediation
of Jesus Christ your Son our Lord,
who is alive and reigns with you,
in the unity of the Holy Spirit,
one God, now and for ever.

| *Reflection by* **Rachel Mann**

Psalms 113, 115
2 Samuel 15.13-end
Acts 9.32-end

Thursday 8 September

Acts 9.32-end

'Please come to us without delay' (v.38)

Today's passage includes two miraculous healings. They are interesting, not least because the healings of Aeneas and Dorcas hold deliberate echoes of Jesus' healings. What leaps out at me, however, is how Peter is impressively alert to the promptings of the Spirit. After healing Aeneas in Jesus' name, he receives a message from Dorcas' friends: 'Please come to us without delay.' Peter does not dawdle or sit back on his laurels; he goes and serves.

Peter's behaviour should challenge us all. While we all need time to rest and reflect, I am only too conscious how easy it is for any of us to act as if we are the authors of the hope and goodness we help bring into the world. We can act as if the call to serve is not the primary call on our lives. In Peter's case – as in Jesus' – there is no film-flam or hocus-pocus about the ministry he models: the healings of Aeneas and Dorcas take the form of invitations simply to get up. There is an ordinariness about the wonders that God brings about through Peter's ministry.

In my own limited and often exhausted ministry, this ordinariness encourages me to pay attention to the work of God in the everyday. The call to serve and allow God to work his miracles through our lives – whether that be via healing or, as in Dorcas' case, through simple good works – is not about signs and wonders. It is part of the everyday thread of our lives.

God of constant mercy,
who sent your Son to save us:
remind us of your goodness,
increase your grace within us,
that our thankfulness may grow,
through Jesus Christ our Lord.

COLLECT

Reflection by **Rachel Mann** | 253

Friday 9 September

Psalm 139
2 Samuel 16.1-14
Acts 10.1-16

Acts 10.1-16

'What God has made clean, you must not call profane' (v.15)

I am yet to meet a person without prejudice and bias. We all have lines beyond which we may feel it unsafe to transgress. As we have witnessed over the past decades, the Church has a seeming gift for tearing itself apart over matters of gender and sexuality. Much of the energy and heat generated by these disputes reflects deeply held views on what is permitted and not permitted.

The vision God gives to Peter is a powerful challenge when we become too entrenched in our sincerely and deeply held positions. Peter, the observant Jew, is presented with a vision that challenges his very picture of God's grace. It is worth reminding ourselves that for Jewish people, the law – including the dietary restrictions – is not a burden, but a gift and sign of God's profound blessing. Yet, Peter's deepest convictions are shaken by God's invitation to feast on unclean food.

We, the readers, know what Peter doesn't yet know: that this invitation to cross lines of taboo will lead to a revolution in the early Church's self-understanding: that God's gift in Jesus Christ is for gentiles like Cornelius as much as for observant Jews. God is bringing about a new thing in Jesus Christ. It strikes me that in our own time, as much as in Peter's, we should dare to be open to God's invitation to cross the lines of belief that we are sure are fixed for all time.

COLLECT

Almighty and everlasting God,
you are always more ready to hear than we to pray
and to give more than either we desire or deserve:
pour down upon us the abundance of your mercy,
forgiving us those things of which our conscience is afraid
and giving us those good things which we are not worthy to ask
but through the merits and mediation
of Jesus Christ your Son our Lord,
who is alive and reigns with you,
in the unity of the Holy Spirit,
one God, now and for ever.

| *Reflection by* **Rachel Mann**

Psalms 120, **121**, 122
2 Samuel 17.1-23
Acts 10.17-33

Saturday 10 September

Acts 10.17-33

'I should not call anyone profane or unclean' (v.28)

The encounter between Cornelius and Peter is extraordinary by any standard. It is a moment where new relationships and religious possibilities break open. It is a point where social, cultural and religious taboos between gentile and Jew are definitively challenged by God's abundant love.

This abundant love rightly continues to invite and challenge us in our own present contexts. When I was young, naively I imagined that many prejudices and cultural taboos were behind us in our society. I thought that the stains of racism and antisemitism, for example, would be wiped out in a generation. While I remain convinced that God's curve of love tends towards the breaking-down of hate and selfishness, I can see now how very naive I was.

The temptation to call people 'profane' or 'unclean' is as present in our time as in Peter's. Unlike the era of Peter and Cornelius, in our age technology and social media can spread hatred and prejudice at extraordinary speed. Fake news can be found within a couple of clicks on the internet. For us, Peter's words are the very model of our calling as Christians. God invites each of us to resist stereotyping as well as the conscious and unconscious bias that may be embedded in our upbringings. God is the boundary breaker who invites us to recognize others as our neighbours.

God of constant mercy,
who sent your Son to save us:
remind us of your goodness,
increase your grace within us,
that our thankfulness may grow,
through Jesus Christ our Lord.

COLLECT

Monday 12 September

Acts 10.34-end

'... the Holy Spirit fell upon all who heard the word' (v.44)

I suspect many are a little suspicious of the power of the Holy Spirit, perhaps because the Spirit disrupts and makes unanticipated things happen. Acts says that the Holy Spirit 'fell upon' those who heard the word of God shared by Peter. This sounds quite dramatic. Walls are the kind of things that fall on people!

Equally, the passage speaks of the Spirit being 'poured out'. This language takes us back to the day of Pentecost when the Spirit was poured out on the frightened disciples, enabling them to speak in the tongues of the nations. In today's passage, we witness how there is no division between brand-new followers of Jesus and those whom Jesus knew personally and called from his own community. What is crucial for God is not our heritage or background; what matters is our response to the good news of Jesus Christ. This is beautiful and revolutionary stuff.

While the encounters with the Spirit in the book of Acts are often dramatic, I've never been overly concerned when the Spirit works more quietly in our lives. I've long believed that God gives us what we need. Sometimes – as with Cornelius and his friends – what is needed is powerful and dramatic. More often, the Spirit's promptings are subtler. The way we know the Spirit is at work is when we are brought into deeper relationship with the Word of God, Jesus Christ, and find ourselves sent out in service.

COLLECT

Almighty God,
who called your Church to bear witness
that you were in Christ reconciling the world to yourself:
help us to proclaim the good news of your love,
that all who hear it may be drawn to you;
through him who was lifted up on the cross,
and reigns with you in the unity of the Holy Spirit,
one God, now and for ever.

Psalms **132**, 133
2 Samuel 18.19 – 19.8*a*
Acts 11.1-18

Tuesday 13 September

Acts 11.1-18

'... who was I that I could hinder God?' (v.17)

When I trained to be a spiritual director, two things were impressed on me by my tutors: first, there is only one true director, the Holy Spirit, and, second, that I should not get in the Spirit's way. I've often reflected on these 'rules' and sought to place them at the centre of my work and ministry.

There is something reassuring, then, to hear the 'head' of the early Church, Peter, be alert to our human, sinful instinct that wants to get in the way of God's work. He faces resistance from fellow leaders in the early Church to his obedience to the Spirit's promptings. He meets their ritual and cultural scruples with a strong sense that it was not for him to hinder the work of God.

I remember, a few years ago, telling a colleague that, despite working every hour that God sent, I felt I was failing in my pastoral charge. I felt I wasn't seeing enough parishioners or preaching good enough sermons and so on. I needed a break and was worried about taking one. She said that perhaps one reason I needed to go away on a break was to give God a chance to do something. It was a telling point.

While I suspect few of us deliberately wish to subvert God's love or get in his way, it is an ever-present temptation to identify what we want with what God desires. Ultimately, we are wise when we dare to let God lead.

Almighty God,
you search us and know us:
may we rely on you in strength
and rest on you in weakness,
now and in all our days;
through Jesus Christ our Lord.

COLLECT

Wednesday 14 September
Holy Cross Day

Psalms 2, 8, 146
Genesis 3.1-15
John 12.27-36*a*

John 12.27-36*a*

*'And I, when I am lifted up from the earth, will draw all people
to myself' (v.32)*

There is, as St Paul reminds us in the first chapter of 1 Corinthians,
something scandalous about the cross (1 Corinthians 1.23). Crucifixion
was used a means of torture and humiliation reserved for criminals
and rebels. Yet, as we know – and as we celebrate on Holy Cross Day
– the cross is, for Christians, a sign and means of salvation. Yet it is
also scandal in its earliest sense: a stumbling-block or tripwire. It can
be experienced as a block to faith.

Perhaps part of the strange beauty of the cross of Christ is its ironic
power. It is surely impossible to celebrate an instrument of violence
in and of itself. However, as Jesus' words indicate, his way of death
becomes the route to salvation. As Jesus is 'lifted up' physically on
an instrument of torture he is also 'lifted up' symbolically. The point
of his humiliation is the moment when he is raised up for all people
to see him in glory.

For those of us who have given our lives to Christ, it can be
challenging to appreciate just how much of a scandal this idea is. I
hope that meditating on the Holy Cross means that we are stopped
short. One of the meanings of 'holy' is 'set apart'. The cross sets Christ
apart, but all of us are called to find our salvation in him. How we
receive the holiness of the cross will be crucial to how we share the
good news of Jesus Christ.

COLLECT

Almighty God,
who in the passion of your blessed Son
made an instrument of painful death
to be for us the means of life and peace:
grant us so to glory in the cross of Christ
that we may gladly suffer for his sake;
who is alive and reigns with you,
in the unity of the Holy Spirit,
one God, now and for ever.

| *Reflection by* **Rachel Mann**

Psalms **143**, 146
2 Samuel 19.24-end
Acts 12.1-17

Thursday 15 September

Acts 12.1-17

'He had James, the brother of John, killed with the sword' (v.2)

We have all heard the phrase, 'God moves in a mysterious way'. We come face to face with its truth in Acts 12 in the contrasting fortunes of two of Jesus' original disciples. Peter seems, to use a modern phrase, 'Teflon coated'. He is briefly imprisoned and then led to safety by an angel; his chains fall off. James' fate is captured in one sentence: Herod has him put to death by the sword. I find the simple statement of James' death filled with a kind of pathos. This is the brother of John, who in Mark's Gospel is called, with his brother, 'a son of thunder'. He, along with Peter and John, is chosen to witness the transfiguration. He is, arguably, one of Jesus' inner circle, set aside for great things.

It is one of the mysteries of life why some have long lives and some lives are cut short. The Covid-19 pandemic has brought this truth into even sharper focus. We all know people for whom fervent prayer has been offered up, especially when ill, and still they have died. We have known others who, against the odds, have survived.

This mystery may lead us to conclude that God is capricious or unjust. That is understandable but not, in my view, correct. James, Peter, you and I – we all have our time on earth and each of us is invited to respond to God's gift of life. None of us knows the time of our departure. What we can do is seek to be like James and Peter and live in the fullness of the Spirit.

COLLECT

Almighty God,
who called your Church to bear witness
that you were in Christ reconciling the world to yourself:
help us to proclaim the good news of your love,
that all who hear it may be drawn to you;
through him who was lifted up on the cross,
and reigns with you in the unity of the Holy Spirit,
one God, now and for ever.

Reflection by **Rachel Mann** |

Friday 16 September

Acts 12.18-end

'... the word of God continued to advance' (v.24)

Sometimes I've met people who are romantic about the Church as described in Acts. There is a temptation to say: 'If only we were more like those early saints, the kingdom would draw closer to us.' I hear the power of that plea, but I'm not sure we should be romantic about the world in which the gospel took root.

Herod has just slaughtered St James. Now, in the shadow of Peter's escape, he kills the guards. Herod himself ultimately receives a grisly fate. These scenes are a striking reminder that the Bible is very honest about how God's work happens in the midst of often brutal and grubby human conditions. Given the way in which God brings salvation to the world – through Christ's crucifixion and resurrection – this should not surprise us.

We may feel that the world in which we live is less brutal than that of the Acts. I'm not so sure. Atrocities continue to be perpetrated in many parts of the world, and, if many of us in privileged countries feel insulated from their worst effects, that is no excuse for ignoring them. We have a gospel to proclaim, but it is not proclaimed in a vacuum. Surely part of our vocation as Christians is to support the work of the gospel in places more fragile than our own. More than that, we are surely called to be alert to the hidden brutalities in our own settings and challenge them. God's word will not be advanced if we are simply bystanders.

COLLECT

Almighty God,
who called your Church to bear witness
that you were in Christ reconciling the world to yourself:
help us to proclaim the good news of your love,
that all who hear it may be drawn to you;
through him who was lifted up on the cross,
and reigns with you in the unity of the Holy Spirit,
one God, now and for ever.

| *Reflection by* **Rachel Mann**

Psalm **147**
2 Samuel 24
Acts 13.1-12

Saturday 17 September

Acts 13.1-12

'... you enemy of all righteousness' (v.10)

One of the most shocking things about Paul is his blunt willingness to speak the unvarnished truth. I almost draw in a sharp intake of breath as he calls the false prophet Bar-Jesus/Elymas, 'You son of the devil, you enemy of all righteousness'. Paul may only be speaking the truth, but I am still stunned by the way he just does not hold back. If he were a judge on a TV talent show, he'd be the brutal one who delivers waspish notes to the candidate, claiming that he's only speaking the words the candidate needs to hear. I would not want to be on the receiving end of Paul's assessment!

Elymas, of course, is no talent show contestant and surely he gets his just deserts. However, this encounter raises questions about how we, as modern Christians, embody and speak the 'gospel truth'. Surely we are called to speak truth to power when it departs from the requirements of the gospel and also be prepared to challenge phenomena such as 'fake news' and 'alternative facts'.

How we communicate our commitment to the truth of Jesus Christ is much trickier. In the modern era, Paul's direct style may not always be the most effective. It runs the risk of being unnecessarily confrontational and off-putting. Perhaps that old dictum, attributed to St Francis, may be helpful: 'Always preach the gospel and when necessary, use words.'

Almighty God,
you search us and know us:
may we rely on you in strength
and rest on you in weakness,
now and in all our days;
through Jesus Christ our Lord.

COLLECT

Reflection by **Rachel Mann** | 261

Monday 19 September

Acts 13.13-43

'Look, you scoffers! Be amazed and perish' (v.41)

Perhaps when Paul was in the major Roman town of Pisidian Antioch, he climbed the twelve steps up to the Augusteum. In front of him at the portico of the Temple, he would have seen four massive columns, each standing 8.72 metres tall (roughly 28 feet), and a huge stone on which were carved the 'Deeds of the Divine Augustus', a record of all the Emperor's achievements. That stone referred to kings who had sent emissaries to the Emperor, including surprisingly, two kings of the Britons, Dumnobellaunus and Tincommius. It's quite a thought that if Paul had read the words on that monument, he might have wondered who these two British kings were. That Augustus had such a geographically wide-ranging set of contacts makes Paul's journeys seem tiny by comparison.

When Paul was addressing the synagogue, he was in a small building tucked away in the town, a town dominated by its temples and by the political might of the Empire. Paul mentions none of this. His message is tightly focused and is delivered to Jews and God-fearers only. He rehearses the history of Israel and finishes with a great biblical flourish: a quotation from the prophet Habakkuk. Clearly, some of his audience were impressed; they asked for more.

No one listening to Paul's peroration could have imagined that his words would radically change the world. No matter how noisy and assertive power-politics may be, it is the word of God that transforms.

COLLECT

Almighty God,
whose only Son has opened for us
a new and living way into your presence:
give us pure hearts and steadfast wills
to worship you in spirit and in truth;
through Jesus Christ your Son our Lord,
who is alive and reigns with you,
in the unity of the Holy Spirit,
one God, now and for ever.

| *Reflection by* **Christopher Herbert**

Psalms **5**, 6 (8)
I Kings 1.32 – 2.4; 2.10-12
Acts 13.44 – 14.7

Tuesday 20 September

Acts 13.44 – 14.7

'But the residents of the city were divided' (14.4)

Archaeologists are a sub-genre of 'detectives'. They dig and delve, find things, scrape off the mud, compare the evidence with similar pieces found nearby and try hard not to leap to conclusions ... Several teams of archaeologists have worked at Iconium over the years, including ones who have excavated coins minted in the town at roughly the time that Paul and Barnabas were there. The question for them is whether there were two dominant political groups in the town represented by different coin-issuing mints: the *polis* (Greeks) and the other from the *colonia* (Roman veterans). If there were, then it is likely that tensions between those two groups might sometimes have bubbled over.

When Paul and Barnabas went to the synagogue in Iconium it was almost foreseeable that in that small community nestled inside the larger community, their message would cause divisions. Some Jews and God-fearers sided with the apostles and became believers, while others, both Jews and God-fearers caused such a disturbance that Paul and Barnabas had to flee for their lives. The good news was, ironically, a cause of deep division.

We speak much of the role of the Church as reconciler, and quite rightly. But will there be times when our message splits people apart rather than drawing them together? And if that happens, what should we do?

Merciful God,
your Son came to save us
and bore our sins on the cross:
may we trust in your mercy
and know your love,
rejoicing in the righteousness
that is ours through Jesus Christ our Lord.

COLLECT

Reflection by **Christopher Herbert** | 263

Wednesday 21 September

Matthew, Apostle and Evangelist

1 Kings 19.15-end

'... what have I done to you?' (v.20)

There was no request for a CV, no interviews, no demand for three references. All that happened was the casting of the cloak upon Elisha. But then, after fulfilling the command of God to anoint Elisha in his place, Elijah suddenly has a moment of indecision: '... what have I done to you?' It is all too human, that moment when, having taken a major decision, doubts suddenly crowd in.

Might the same have happened to Jesus after he had called his disciples? There was Matthew, sitting at a table in the Galilean sunshine doing his accounts when Jesus calls him. Matthew responds immediately.

Why? Had Jesus known him for a while? After all, Matthew might have been a citizen of Capernaum, though this is implied rather than being explicitly made clear. Had Jesus been observing him for some time before approaching him? Or had Jesus sought the advice of Peter, James and John, local men who might have known Matthew? Or was it a sudden hunch that here was a man in whom he could see great potential?

Once the Twelve were living and working together, sitting at Jesus' feet, listening to his teaching, did Jesus ever look out at them and wonder if he had asked too much of them? If he could foresee the likely consequences for himself at the hands of the authorities, was he right to have hand-picked those twelve men to be with him? Catching Matthew's eye at the Last Supper, what did Jesus think?

COLLECT

O Almighty God,
whose blessed Son called Matthew the tax collector
to be an apostle and evangelist:
give us grace to forsake the selfish pursuit of gain
    and the possessive love of riches
that we may follow in the way of your Son Jesus Christ,
who is alive and reigns with you,
in the unity of the Holy Spirit,
one God, now and for ever.

| *Reflection by* **Christopher Herbert**

Psalms 14, **15**, 16
I Kings 4.29 – 5.12
Acts 15.1-21

Thursday 22 September

Acts 15.1-21

'The apostles and the elders met together to consider this matter' (v.6)

The sequence is clear: first there is general debate; then Peter speaks; he is followed by Paul and Barnabas; James summarizes the situation and comes to a decision. It could have been a testy and heated meeting, but the careful process ensured that all the people had a voice, the experts were listened to carefully, and the authoritative James concluded with a clinching quotation from the prophet Amos – end of meeting. Time for a glass of wine and conversation with friends – often the best and most enlightening part of such meetings.

What Luke fails to tell us is what happened before the meeting. Who drew up the agenda? Who decided on the running order of speakers? Who took the minutes? And after the meeting, what was going on in the small, informal groups? Who completely agreed with the decision? Who still had reservations? Who fell into the 'sitting-on-the-fence' category?

Perhaps this meeting in Jerusalem set the tone for every future meeting of every church throughout the centuries that followed. That is an exaggeration, of course, but the fact is, no church can survive and flourish without meetings. Dozens of them. Why? It is something to do with taking every member seriously, recognizing that even the quietest and least confident member of the church deserves to be heard. When that underlying trust is ignored, serious trouble begins to brew.

We aren't always good at handling dissent in our meetings. So, how can we explore truth and trust together, creatively?

COLLECT

Almighty God,
whose only Son has opened for us
a new and living way into your presence:
give us pure hearts and steadfast wills
to worship you in spirit and in truth;
through Jesus Christ your Son our Lord,
who is alive and reigns with you,
in the unity of the Holy Spirit,
one God, now and for ever.

Reflection by **Christopher Herbert**   265

Friday 23 September

Acts 15.22-35

'When they gathered the congregation together, they delivered the letter' (v.30)

On 22 April 1855, Florence Nightingale sent a letter from Scutari to her family. In it she explained that when two of her supportive friends returned to Britain, it would be all the more reason for her to stay – otherwise, as she explained 'this Hospital will become the bear garden which Kullali and Smyrna are – where ladies come out to get married – where the nurses come out to get drunk ...' Although her letters were addressed to her immediate family, she knew that they would be shared with all her many cousins, uncles and aunts. Her letters were not really private.

Similarly, when the Jerusalem Council sent their letter to the church at Antioch, they would have known that it would be circulated widely. Luke quotes that letter in its entirety, which means either he had a copy beside him as he wrote, or he composed something that he thought would fit the bill.

The letter was particularly important because it was the first official attempt to clarify what the rules of behaviour were for the young church in Antioch and beyond. It was the first of many, because as the Church expanded, so it encountered new situations. That kind of ethical dialogue between Church and society has gone on ever since.

If you could write a letter to your church concerning a serious ethical dilemma, what would it be about?

COLLECT

Almighty God,
whose only Son has opened for us
a new and living way into your presence:
give us pure hearts and steadfast wills
to worship you in spirit and in truth;
through Jesus Christ your Son our Lord,
who is alive and reigns with you,
in the unity of the Holy Spirit,
one God, now and for ever.

| *Reflection by* **Christopher Herbert**

Psalms 20, 21, **23**
I Kings 8.1-30
Acts 15.36 – 16.5

Saturday 24 September

Acts 15.36 – 16.5

'The disagreement became so sharp that they parted company'
(15.39)

From time to time Luke gives us what appears to be the unvarnished truth. So, where he wants to show Paul in a heroic, pioneering light, it is telling when he mentions disagreements between Paul and close colleagues. On the other hand, we should note that today's reading is the last mention that Luke makes of Barnabas. He is written out of the story. Luke did the same with Peter, who, after he has spoken persuasively at the Council of Jerusalem (Acts 15.11), does not feature again in the narrative. In both cases, Luke rapidly switches the spotlight back onto Paul.

It would be fascinating to be able to question Luke about his motives. Perhaps he was so committed to the sweeping, exciting drama of the growth of the early Church that he had neither the time nor the inclination to explore anything else. He had his main character, Paul, and other players were therefore given only subsidiary and temporary parts in the action.

This is fine when you are composing a novel, but not so attractive when you are purporting to write history. It might, of course, be the result of hero-worship of a charismatic personality. Luke knew Paul well.

It raises a question for us: when we tell others of our life story, do we omit some bits so that the sweep of our story is not slowed down but remains exciting? If we do, what is the relationship between truth and drama?

Merciful God,
your Son came to save us
and bore our sins on the cross:
may we trust in your mercy
and know your love,
rejoicing in the righteousness
that is ours through Jesus Christ our Lord.

COLLECT

Reflection by **Christopher Herbert**   267

Monday 26 September

Psalms 27, **30**
I Kings 8.31-62
Acts 16.6-24

Acts 16.6-24

'... we immediately tried to cross over to Macedonia' (v.10)

There is a subtle shift here. Look at the passage carefully and you will see that it begins with references to 'they', but at verse 10, 'they' becomes 'we'. This is assumed to mean that Luke had now joined Paul and kept a kind of travel diary from time to time.

It begins with that haunting vision of a man calling out: 'Come over to Macedonia and help us'. It was one of those startlingly vivid dreams that stay with you for days. Paul, being an intrepid and excitable man himself, took the dream with great seriousness and, with no time to waste, decided to take a boat from the port of Troas and head for Europe.

Perhaps it was because he had felt thwarted in the previous few days that the dream came so intensely to him. Frustration, an amateur psychologist might suggest, led to the 'vision'. What we don't have from Luke the diarist is any description of the boat journey. There is no account of the conversations that accompanied the gentle slap of the waves against the wooden hull. Nor any description of the rocky island of Samothrace to which they initially travelled. Nor of Philippi, a Roman city on the Via Egnatia in the region of Macedonia where they stayed for a few days. What matters is the 'good news'. It resulted not in a meeting with a Macedonian man but with Lydia, the woman textile merchant, who was baptized.

Providence can take some unexpected and delightful turns ...

COLLECT

God, who in generous mercy sent the Holy Spirit
  upon your Church in the burning fire of your love:
grant that your people may be fervent
in the fellowship of the gospel
that, always abiding in you,
they may be found steadfast in faith and active in service;
through Jesus Christ your Son our Lord,
who is alive and reigns with you,
in the unity of the Holy Spirit,
one God, now and for ever.

| *Reflection by* **Christopher Herbert**

Psalms 32, **36**
I Kings 8.63 – 9.9
Acts 16.25-end

Tuesday 27 September

Acts 16.25-end

'... immediately all the doors were opened and everyone's chains were unfastened' (v.26)

Define what you mean by 'miracle'. Is it an unexpected and extraneous event that surprises the observer by its liberating, life-affirming consequences? Or is it a radical internal change of heart in someone who shifts from unbelief to belief? Or is something only a 'miracle' for those who believe that it is? What kind of characteristics must a 'miracle' have for us to describe it as originating from God?

Questions pile on questions. That is not to say that the problem of 'miracle' can be shunted off to one side as 'just one of those things'. To answer one of the questions posed above, for something to be a 'miracle', it could be argued that no matter how astonishing or awe-inspiring the event is, it must have the fingerprints of God all over it. And to go further, the 'miracle' must be marked by grace and power, but in such a way that it does not overwhelmingly compel the onlooker to believe in the divine originator.

In the story of Paul and Silas in prison, every prisoner had their chains unfastened, but not everyone concluded that the event was caused by God. In the same way, in Jesus' lifetime, many people witnessed his 'miracles', but not everyone became a disciple. Human choice and human perception entered into the equation.

The courteous self-limitation of God is astounding.

Lord God,
defend your Church from all false teaching
and give to your people knowledge of your truth,
that we may enjoy eternal life
in Jesus Christ our Lord.

COLLECT

Reflection by **Christopher Herbert**

Wednesday 28 September

Acts 17.1-15

'... on three sabbath days [Paul] argued with them from the scriptures' (v.2)

Luke does not tell us who Paul and Silas stayed with when they arrived in Thessalonica. He only says that they were there for at least three weeks. Further, he doesn't say how they managed financially. Nor does he tell us what they did when they were not debating, did they stroll idly along the waterfront? Did Paul explore the market looking for good quality canvas for his tent-making business?

Nor does Luke tell us which scriptural texts Paul used in his debates with the members of the synagogue. It would be really interesting to know, for it is clear that the core of his message was that Jesus had been crucified, had risen from the dead and was indeed the Messiah.

But if you read 1 Thessalonians alongside today's lectionary reading, two things are noticeable; first, that Paul felt a deep, affectionate bond with the people he had met in the city; and, second, that while with them, he had given them instructions about how they were to behave. There was to be no fornication; they should be people of self-control, loving each other; they should work with their own hands; and should behave properly towards outsiders.

After only three or four weeks, Paul and Silas were forced to leave their new church-plant, yet that small group of Christ-followers were sufficiently encouraged that they continued and flourished, sustained by letters from Paul, by their new faith – but little else. It was, under God, enough.

COLLECT

God, who in generous mercy sent the Holy Spirit
   upon your Church in the burning fire of your love:
grant that your people may be fervent
in the fellowship of the gospel
that, always abiding in you,
they may be found steadfast in faith and active in service;
through Jesus Christ your Son our Lord,
who is alive and reigns with you,
in the unity of the Holy Spirit,
one God, now and for ever.

| *Reflection by* **Christopher Herbert**

Psalms 34, 150
Tobit 12.6-end *or* Daniel 12.1-4
Acts 12.1-11

Thursday 29 September
Michael and All Angels

Daniel 12.1-4
'... shall shine like the brightness of the sky' (v.3)

There is a relatively new ritual in football: if a recently bereaved player scores a spectacular goal, they look heavenwards and raise the first finger of their right hand to the sky. It's touching. Private grief, for a few seconds, is given a public face – and then the game moves on.

It makes an interesting comparison with those theological scholars some years ago who tried to get rid of any notion that God might be 'up there' and instead offered us phrases for God such as 'Ground of Being'. It was an honourable thing to try to do. After all, no spatial metaphor whether 'up there' or 'down here', can possibly contain the otherness, the ineffability, the beauty and the holiness of God. Theological language is not a heavily strapped piece of luggage, the contents of which we spend our lives rummaging around in and re-organizing; rather, theological language is elusive and allusive, more like a friend who courteously points us in a promising direction. It suggests, it offers possibilities, it indicates, but it can never fully comprehend the mystery at the heart of things.

Perhaps this is why language about angels remains popular. Those images of wings delicately brushed with gold, of songs so deft that the very air is radiant with joy. What could be lovelier?

We should rejoice in our heritage of images of angels, not try, like arrogant clodhoppers to dismiss them as old-fashioned ideas that we no longer need. Their images point us towards God.

Everlasting God,
you have ordained and constituted
the ministries of angels and mortals in a wonderful order:
grant that as your holy angels always serve you in heaven,
so, at your command,
they may help and defend us on earth;
through Jesus Christ your Son our Lord,
who is alive and reigns with you,
in the unity of the Holy Spirit,
one God, now and for ever.

COLLECT

Reflection by **Christopher Herbert**

Friday 30 September

Psalm 31
1 Kings 11.26-end
Acts 18.1-21

Acts 18.1-21

'... his house was next door to the synagogue' (v.7)

Diplomacy was not one of Paul's gifts. He had been teaching in the Corinthian synagogue for a while, but something went wrong, and he fell out with the membership. So, he angrily announced that he had finished with them and was going to the gentiles instead. But what he actually did was to move into the house next door. It was a hot-headed thing to do, not least because the president of the synagogue also joined him.

This was an intense, local row. Despite Paul's declaration about going to the gentiles, Luke makes no mention of conversations Paul could have had with the leaders of gentile religious groups in Corinth. It was a city dominated by Greek temples, including an infamous one dedicated to Aphrodite high up on the Acropolis where, some alleged, temple prostitution was rife.

In the early part of his stay in Corinth, Paul had followed his normal pattern. Wherever he went on his missionary journeys, he concentrated on debating in synagogues. At least eight are mentioned in Acts as places where he taught. The rabbi in him could not move too far away from the comfort zone in which he had always operated. There are very few accounts of Paul directly engaging with a predominantly gentile audience – as in Athens, for example – otherwise, his natural milieu was the synagogue.

Before we feel too superior, we might humbly acknowledge that we all gravitate to the known rather than the unknown. It's called human nature.

COLLECT

God, who in generous mercy sent the Holy Spirit
    upon your Church in the burning fire of your love:
grant that your people may be fervent
in the fellowship of the gospel
that, always abiding in you,
they may be found steadfast in faith and active in service;
through Jesus Christ your Son our Lord,
who is alive and reigns with you,
in the unity of the Holy Spirit,
one God, now and for ever.

| *Reflection by **Christopher Herbert***

Psalms 41, **42**, 43
1 Kings 12.1-24
Acts 18.22 – 19.7

Saturday 1 October

Acts 18.22 – 19.7

'... altogether there were about twelve of them' (19.7)

In 1128, twelve monks and their abbot arrived on the shores of the south coast of England. They had set out some weeks earlier from the Cistercian abbey of Notre Dame de l'Aumône, twenty miles north of Blois in France. They made their way inland, arriving at a fairly remote meadow in south-west Surrey, where, on the banks of the River Wey, they founded the first Cistercian Abbey in England on land given to them by Wiiliam Giffard, the Bishop of Winchester.

Just four years later, the new Bishop of Winchester, Henri de Blois, founded the 'Hospital of St Cross and Almshouse of Noble Poverty' on the banks of the River Itchen in Winchester. It provided almshouse accommodation for thirteen poor men. Similarly, but over 300 years later, an almshouse for thirteen men was founded at Ewelme, Oxfordshire by William and Alice de la Pole.

You will have spotted the connection. In each case, these medieval foundations consisted of thirteen men. The number was chosen deliberately to represent Jesus and the Twelve Disciples.

Perhaps a similar idea was in the mind of Luke when he wrote today's passage about Paul baptizing twelve people at Ephesus and laying his hands on them. The unnamed twelve received the gift of the Holy Spirit, spoke in tongues and prophesied. The Church was increasing. The Way was being lived and proclaimed.

Recall twelve people who have influenced you in the faith – and give thanks for them.

Lord God,
defend your Church from all false teaching
and give to your people knowledge of your truth,
that we may enjoy eternal life
in Jesus Christ our Lord.

COLLECT

Reflection by **Christopher Herbert** | 273

Monday 3 October

Acts 19.8-20

'God did extraordinary miracles' (v.11)

The quest for healing is nothing new. The Covid-19 pandemic prompted a desperate race for an effective vaccine and treatments, alternative suggestions on diet, exercise and meditation that may, or may not, help, and of course prayer. Faith and doubt walked hand in hand, whether in doctors and health systems, friends and families, governments, or God's willingness to intervene. Illness is disempowering for sufferers, for their loved ones, for those fearing for themselves and others, so we look for cures and healing, using the faculties that God has endowed us with, just as people did in Acts.

They looked for miracles, through Paul and itinerant exorcists. The urge was the same; the results, vastly different. The exorcists used the name of Jesus like a magic formula, trying to control illness without relating to God. But God was doing miracles *through* Paul. Paul was not in control; God's free, untameable grace was. Paul had faith: openness to work with God, and let God act.

Did Paul have doubts? Probably. Without the possibility of doubt, there is no room for faith. The opposite of faith is certainty, control. It is knowing that outcomes are determined through our actions, rather than placed into the hand of God. Faith is trusting that this God will work through whatever means – medical or supernatural, expected or unexpected – to bring about his kingdom in the midst of us. How are you praying for God to show himself today?

COLLECT

O Lord, we beseech you mercifully to hear the prayers
    of your people who call upon you;
and grant that they may both perceive and know
    what things they ought to do,
and also may have grace and power faithfully to fulfil them;
through Jesus Christ your Son our Lord,
who is alive and reigns with you,
in the unity of the Holy Spirit,
one God, now and for ever.

| *Reflection by* **Isabelle Hamley**

Psalms **48**, 52
I Kings 13.11-end
Acts 19.21-end

Tuesday 4 October

Acts 19.21-end

'... most of them did not know why they had come together' (v.32)

Scripture is nothing if not realistic about human nature. Here, we see the power of a mob, with its usual corollary – scaremongering and scapegoating a minority. A downturn in business is blamed on Christians, with alarming claims about what their presence might mean in the future.

No need for facts, only emotion whipped up by speakers and the comfort of numbers. Negative emotions, grievances, fears and uncertainty, all get channelled into one, easy place. It is much easier to blame those who are different, who do not fit, than for the crowd to consider themselves in truth and vulnerability. Easier than considering their own responsibilities, easier than looking at what power they might have, however small, to effect change, easier than looking at what false gods they may serve, easier than working together to find a better way.

This human tendency to blame shapes the heart of the gospel. On the cross, everything that is wrong in the world, every negative emotion, is concentrated on Jesus. The cross begs us to look at ourselves and the world with complete honesty – and relief. Christ has already borne the weight of our blame and recriminations, and invites us to see the world with new eyes, to join him in relating differently. The catch is, just like for Paul, following in the footsteps of Jesus takes us the way of the cross. Are we ready to give up blame and embrace the cross instead?

Lord of creation,
whose glory is around and within us:
open our eyes to your wonders,
that we may serve you with reverence
and know your peace at our lives' end,
through Jesus Christ our Lord.

COLLECT

Wednesday 5 October

Psalm 119.57-80
1 Kings 17
Acts 20.1-16

Acts 20.1-16

'... they had taken the boy away alive and were not a little comforted' (v.12)

It is business as usual among the little Christian community in Troas, breaking bread, praying, studying the Scriptures. Well, mostly usual, as clearly an amazing event has gathered them late through the night: Paul, the great teacher, is with them, and nothing will deprive them from learning at his feet, not even a spectacular fall through a window and a miraculous healing.

I wonder how many of our meetings see us gathered with such eagerness and thirst? Or how much we expect God to be at work within them? The believers here are overjoyed and comforted by God's intervention, but not surprised. They had no expectation that God would necessarily heal, as if God always did. Neither did they assume that he would not. Their Christian imagination was large enough to hold the possibility of healing, and the reality of death and sorrow, and weave both through their life together.

I wonder how we shape such imagination today? How do we avoid the twin dangers around healing: to think it never happens, or that it always does. Both beliefs try to make life manageable by making God predictable, and in the process diminish him. But they reduce, rather than expand, our imagination. To live in the in-between, in the unknown, forces us into an open place with broad horizons, a place where mechanistic principles cannot replace relationship with God. Maybe today is a day to pray, 'expand our imagination'.

COLLECT

O Lord, we beseech you mercifully to hear the prayers
    of your people who call upon you;
and grant that they may both perceive and know
    what things they ought to do,
and also may have grace and power faithfully to fulfil them;
through Jesus Christ your Son our Lord,
who is alive and reigns with you,
in the unity of the Holy Spirit,
one God, now and for ever.

Psalms 56, **57** (63*)
1 Kings 18.1-20
Acts 20.17-end

Thursday 6 October

Acts 20.17-end

'I commend you to God and to the message of his grace' (v.32)

No word encapsulates Paul's message better than 'grace'. Time and again, his eagerness to share the gospel shows through, because it is good news that can 'build up'. His focus on grace is rooted in his personal experience, as a man of violence who persecuted Christians, yet, miraculously, was not written off but became a teacher and leader. How much grace! Not just from God, but from the early Church. For Paul, grace was a daily reality embodied in every Christian. Every preaching or teaching engagement, every letter he wrote, was born out of amazing, unexpected, undeserved grace.

And so Paul seeks to 'build up' the young community. His letters consistently praise what is good and beautiful in struggling churches. It does not stop him from holding them accountable – grace is not a free pass. But grace is where it always starts, and transformation is a response to being loved and accepted. How do we, and can we, nurture communities of grace today? Particularly in a world where social media is far keener to tear down than to build up, where virtual networks thrive on judging people we have never met.

Paul's experience of grace was personal. It is one thing to know that God forgives. It is quite another to experience this forgiveness in real relationships. At its best, isn't it exactly what the Church that God has 'obtained through the blood of his own Son' can be?

Lord of creation,
whose glory is around and within us:
open our eyes to your wonders,
that we may serve you with reverence
and know your peace at our lives' end,
through Jesus Christ our Lord.

COLLECT

Friday 7 October

Psalms **51**, 54
I Kings 18.21-end
Acts 21.1-16

Acts 21.1-16

'The Lord's will be done' (v.14)

In this story, these words could easily sound like a fatalistic acceptance of defeat. Paul won't listen, so let's leave it with God. Yet is this really about passive acceptance? These words are ones we say whenever we pray the Lord's Prayer, active words of trust and surrender. Paul refuses to let his actions be shaped by fear, rather than a sense of what is right. Fear would drive him to follow his own needs and emotions; prayer drives him to seek to align his life and purpose with the kind of life that God modelled in Christ.

Paul isn't actively pursuing martyrdom; rather, he seeks to serve God faithfully, loving the Church and proclaiming the gospel. Elsewhere, he says he has learnt to be content in every circumstance, and his reaction here is an expression of this frame of mind. His trust isn't wishful thinking; he does not think he is invulnerable, or that God will rescue him no matter what. Rather, it is trust that it is infinitely safer and better for him to walk in the ways of Jesus than to follow his own – after all, following his own way, however much he wanted it to be right, had led him to persecute Christians.

Committing ourselves to God's will is not committing ourselves to safety, or giving up, but saying, 'we choose to trust even when we cannot see the way'.

COLLECT

O Lord, we beseech you mercifully to hear the prayers
    of your people who call upon you;
and grant that they may both perceive and know
    what things they ought to do,
and also may have grace and power faithfully to fulfil them;
through Jesus Christ your Son our Lord,
who is alive and reigns with you,
in the unity of the Holy Spirit,
one God, now and for ever.

| *Reflection by* **Isabelle Hamley**

Psalm **68**
1 Kings 19
Acts 21.17-36

Saturday 8 October

Acts 21.17-36

'They have been told about you ...' (v.21)

Another day in Acts, another mob. Paul seems to be very adept at antagonizing crowds, and, as predicted in the previous passage, he is in danger in Jerusalem. The conversation with James makes it clear that there is a battle ahead between uninformed, misleading fear and gossip, and Paul's careful and sensitive approach to shaping faith anew.

It is significant that the crowd choose to focus on markers of difference: circumcision and customs, which is what defined identity and ethnicity. Paul challenges not just their understanding of faith, but their deep-rooted sense of identity. James' advice is therefore canny: for Paul to show his rootedness in tradition, in line with his own identity as a Jew, yet for the Church more widely to delineate clearly what properly belongs to Christian conduct, and what can be left aside by those of different ethnicities coming to faith.

Of course, the crowds are not won over by such a reasonable approach. They are fearful, and their fears tap into something much deeper, more primal than reason. The new faith taking root in their city challenges their very sense of self, the way in which they imagined the world, and their place within it.

What can be done, when deep fears threaten to stifle change and new-found truth? How can those fears be attended to without letting them shape the future?

COLLECT

Lord of creation,
whose glory is around and within us:
open our eyes to your wonders,
that we may serve you with reverence
and know your peace at our lives' end,
through Jesus Christ our Lord.

Reflection by **Isabelle Hamley** | 279

Monday 10 October

Acts 21.37 – 22.21

'I myself was standing by' (22.20)

In answer to the fears of the crowd, Paul tells a story – his story. He does appeal to reason, but it is reason born of an experience he invites them to share and explore. He does not sugar-coat the story, does not make it exciting, does not make himself look good. Instead, he shares the absolute paradox of his story: that as a Jew, he sought to follow God, and did his best to do all the things that his listeners care about. Yet what did this lead him to? His faith brought him to persecute the young Church, to stand by, while others were hurt.

Paul does not shy away from his responsibilities. He may not have cast a stone, but he knows that his presence meant he was guilty. What could he possibly say in response to the apparition of Jesus, identifying himself as the very God he thought he was serving? Paul had done everything by the book; he had followed every command, and directed his mind and heart to following God. Yet his own efforts led nowhere.

The story of Paul is one of grace alone: Paul is brought to the point of realizing that all his efforts cannot bring him closer to God. He will draw close to God because God draws close to him, and drew close by taking human form in Christ. What story of grace do you have to tell?

COLLECT

Almighty God,
you have made us for yourself,
and our hearts are restless till they find their rest in you:
pour your love into our hearts and draw us to yourself,
and so bring us at last to your heavenly city
where we shall see you face to face;
through Jesus Christ your Son our Lord,
who is alive and reigns with you,
in the unity of the Holy Spirit,
one God, now and for ever.

Reflection by **Isabelle Hamley**

Psalm **73**
I Kings 22.1-28
Acts 22.22 – 23.11

Tuesday 11 October

Acts 22.22 – 23.11

'You shall not speak evil' (23.5)

The crowd is not mollified by Paul's testimony, and he needs Roman protection. Protection however comes with questions, and both Roman soldiers and Jewish leaders seek to 'examine' Paul. The manner of examining is questionable, relying on violence. Did the leaders, Roman and Jewish, truly believe that violence can possibly bring out truth? Of course, this isn't an uncommon belief, even today. But I wonder what kind of worldview gives birth to such beliefs and behaviour. And what kind of view of fellow human beings justifies such actions?

It would be easy to distance ourselves from the questions. To think, well, we do not do this anymore. We have laws, charters of human rights. We do, and it is good, and right. Yet are our attitudes fundamentally different? Do we ever think that the end justifies the means? Do we treat every human being as made in the image of God, regardless of their ethnicity, creed, gender or any other characteristic? Do we ever use violence – in words, thought and deed, to gain what we want?

The Bible as a whole has as much to say about violent speech as it has about violent deeds, and much about violent thoughts as the root of both. How do we examine and guard our thoughts? How do we build habits of grace within us, so that violence does not take root in any part of our being?

Gracious God,
you call us to fullness of life:
deliver us from unbelief
and banish our anxieties
with the liberating love of Jesus Christ our Lord.

COLLECT

Wednesday 12 October

Psalm **77**
1 Kings 22.29-45
Acts 23.12-end

Acts 23.12-end

'[They] bound themselves by an oath ...' (vv.12,21)

Paul's wrangles with the religious establishment take a sinister tone, as they decide to kill him illegally if they cannot do it legally. He is saved, this time not through his privileged status, but through the care of his family. A group of men has taken an oath not to eat or drink until they kill him. I cannot help asking, what happened to them? Did they starve? Or give up? Clearly this was a gross misuse of fasting, as well as a very foolish vow. They were left with few options: keep trying to do something physically demanding (ambushing a Roman escort) whilst getting increasingly weaker; shamefully renege on their vow; or take upon themselves the tragic consequences of their unnecessary foolishness.

The Bible has much to say about rash speech in general, and unwise vows in particular. Jephthah's vow in Judges leads to his daughter's death. David's vow in Samuel endangers his son Jonathan. In both cases, as here, the vows are not just foolish on logical grounds; they are foolish because they are based on distorted desires and values. The men are trying to arm wrestle God into delivering the outcome they want, rather than creating space to seek the guidance and mind of God. The stories thereby work both as warnings, and prompts for us to ask, what do we desire, and what are we prepared to do to get our way?

COLLECT

Almighty God,
you have made us for yourself,
and our hearts are restless till they find their rest in you:
pour your love into our hearts and draw us to yourself,
and so bring us at last to your heavenly city
where we shall see you face to face;
through Jesus Christ your Son our Lord,
who is alive and reigns with you,
in the unity of the Holy Spirit,
one God, now and for ever.

| *Reflection by* **Isabelle Hamley**

Psalm **78.1-39***
2 Kings 1.2-17
Acts 24.1-23

Thursday 13 October

Acts 24.1-23

'I have a hope in God' (v.15)

The audience before Felix is a masterclass in rhetoric. First off, the accusers, whose tactic seems to be to ingratiate themselves with the governor, flattering him and implying the matter is beneath him to deal with. They suggest Felix 'examine' Paul, which, as the previous chapter showed, was not so much about questions but about physical violence to obtain predetermined answers.

Paul, in contrast, keeps his speech simple and to the point, addressing the facts rather than the person. Instead of abasing himself before Felix, he displays trust in the leader's good judgement, an equally powerful strategy. His speech is not limited to his personal defence. As always, he takes the opportunity to witness.

Shining through his words are the mention of joy ('I cheerfully make my defence') and hope ('I have a hope in God'). There is nothing fancy about his words, no amazing proclamation, but there is integrity, as his life matches his claims. In mentioning joy and hope, he does not just speak of his inner reality, but testifies to the truth of the faith he is on trial for. He would not have either joy or hope in his current predicament had he not full trust in the power of God. It is the correspondence between what he believes and how this is worked out that is so striking for all present, and deserves Felix's further consideration.

Gracious God,
you call us to fullness of life:
deliver us from unbelief
and banish our anxieties
with the liberating love of Jesus Christ our Lord.

COLLECT

Friday 14 October

Acts 24.24 – 25.12

'... he discussed justice, self-control, and the coming judgement'
(24.25)

This entire passage sits under the question, 'What is justice?' Just as Pilate had asked Jesus, 'What is truth', Felix speaks of justice with Paul, and is just as ambivalent. As a Roman official, Felix had official responsibilities for the administration of justice; his relationship to justice is complex however, as he was hoping for a bribe from Paul. His successor, Festus, is equally torn, and wants to please the Jews.

Both men struggle to maintain justice in the face of multiple other pressures, and it isn't surprising that Felix is scared after speaking with Paul: true justice goes hand in hand with self-control, so that it does not slide into revenge and vendetta; and human justice, imperfect as it always is, sits under the wider umbrella of divine justice and judgement, a frightening prospect for a man used to bend justice to suit his political needs.

Paul's life and words, in contrast, display the integrity that had struck Felix in the first place, accepting judgement for what he may have done wrong, but seeking justice against false accusations. It would be easy to gloss over Felix's dilemmas, saying he had power that most of us will never have. Yet justice is something we encounter in our everyday dealings. How do we use the power we do have? How do we understand justice in friendships, in workplaces, in families, in our use of money and resources?

COLLECT

Almighty God,
you have made us for yourself,
and our hearts are restless till they find their rest in you:
pour your love into our hearts and draw us to yourself,
and so bring us at last to your heavenly city
where we shall see you face to face;
through Jesus Christ your Son our Lord,
who is alive and reigns with you,
in the unity of the Holy Spirit,
one God, now and for ever.

Reflection by **Isabelle Hamley**

Psalms **76**, 79
2 Kings 4.1-37
Acts 25.13-end

Saturday 15 October

Acts 25.13-end

'I would like to hear the man myself' (v.22)

What a contrast between Agrippa, and all others around Paul! Felix and Festus had their own agenda, which prevented them from fully engaging with Paul. Jewish leaders were pursuing a vendetta, imputing false motives to Paul. All were eager to speak, with no intention to listen or examine the facts before them. Agrippa, instead, chooses to listen first. He is not swayed by multiple competing agendas. He does not pre-judge what Paul may have to say, or arrive with his mind made up already. Festus' wordy babbling seems superfluous in comparison with Agrippa's calm and measured, 'I would like to hear the man myself'.

How often do we choose to listen first? Do we ever come to a controversial topic, our ears already full of the arguments made by others, so that we fail to listen to the person in front of us? There are few gifts more precious than giving another person our full attention, with a completely open mind, listening to them, rather than to a version of them our mind has constructed from the words of others. It is only his kind of openness that can make a safe space of encounter.

True listening is transformative: here, it has the power to affect Paul's life deeply, while Agrippa may be changed himself. What opportunities might you have today to listen fully to another? And who may listen to you unreservedly?

Gracious God,
you call us to fullness of life:
deliver us from unbelief
and banish our anxieties
with the liberating love of Jesus Christ our Lord.

COLLECT

Reflection by **Isabelle Hamley**

Monday 17 October

Acts 26.1-23

'Saul, Saul, why are you persecuting me? It hurts you to kick against the goads' (v.14)

Paul's speech to Agrippa contains the last of Acts' three accounts of his 'conversion experience' on the Damascus road. The original is in chapter 9, and in chapter 22 Paul tells the story to hostile fellow Jews in Jerusalem. Here, he tells it to the gentile authorities in Caesarea, and he includes some words of Jesus that are absent from the previous accounts: 'It hurts you to kick against the goads.' Even though Paul heard the words in Aramaic, he communicates them using a Greek proverb. This was probably simple enough because they refer to a common rural phenomenon of the time, the self-inflicted pain of an ox that strains to move in a direction for which it is not destined by the ploughman.

Paul had thought that, in persecuting the followers of Jesus, he could wipe his memory from the earth and silence those insistent questions at the back of his own mind. But the more he strained, the more it hurt him, and he found himself dealing not with a memory but a person, not silencing thoughts but hearing a voice.

In v.6, Paul tells Agrippa that this is not just a dramatic story but the very basis of the hope by which he lives. It's the hope that comes from being called by name, having his hurt both named and healed, being raised to stand tall, and appointed to a unique role in the good purposes of God – as it is for each of us.

COLLECT

Almighty and everlasting God,
increase in us your gift of faith
that, forsaking what lies behind
and reaching out to that which is before,
we may run the way of your commandments
and win the crown of everlasting joy;
through Jesus Christ your Son our Lord,
who is alive and reigns with you,
in the unity of the Holy Spirit,
one God, now and for ever.

| *Reflection by* **Joanna Collicutt**

Psalms 145, 146
Isaiah 55
Luke 1.1-4

Tuesday 18 October
Luke the Evangelist

Luke 1.1-4

'... so that you may know the truth' (v.4)

These four verses, a single lengthy but elegant sentence in Greek, form the introduction to a two-volume work comprising what we know as Luke's Gospel and Acts. They are written to assure Luke's patron, Theophilus, that this work can be trusted, that the good news that it proclaims is not fake news. As Theophilus means 'one who loves God', we are to understand this assurance as extending to any reader who is genuinely seeking truth.

The assurance is communicated through Luke's reliance on eye-witness testimony; he did not know Jesus himself but has received his information from those who were with him from the beginning and can give a continuous first-hand account of his earthly life. But then, with the words 'I too', Luke steps into his own narrative, continuing with a phrase most naturally translated 'having closely followed it all for a long time' (v.3). He is identifying himself as a disciple and, in his own way, an eyewitness.

Luke's model of the Christian life is that of a journey; important encounters and discoveries are made *en route*, and he describes the first Christians as people who belong to 'The Way' (e.g. Acts 9.2; 18.25). He is following in the footsteps of Jesus as a historian who orders his source material faithfully; and he is following Jesus along The Way as a disciple who offers his personal testimony. Luke believes his sources to be reliable, but he also knows and trusts Jesus; that's what makes his 'orderly account' so compelling.

COLLECT

Almighty God,
you called Luke the physician,
whose praise is in the gospel,
to be an evangelist and physician of the soul:
by the grace of the Spirit
and through the wholesome medicine of the gospel,
give your Church the same love and power to heal;
through Jesus Christ your Son our Lord,
who is alive and reigns with you,
in the unity of the Holy Spirit,
one God, now and for ever.

Reflection by **Joanna Collicutt**

Wednesday 19 October

Acts 27.1-26

'We were being pounded by the storm so violently ...' (v.18)

Luke writes of himself in the first person in the introduction to his two-volume work but then steps back into the shadows. He emerges later in three passages in Acts, often referred to as the 'we' passages: Chapters 16, 21, and a passage that begins in today's reading, which tells of the last stages of Paul's fateful journey to Rome.

Whether or not Luke is using some literary licence in relation to 'we', it is clear that this is a meticulous first-hand report of a sea voyage. Several of the places mentioned are today pleasant destinations for Mediterranean cruisers in summertime, but this voyage took place after Yom Kippur (v.9) in the tempestuous autumn season and with winter relentlessly approaching (v.12).

Following his appeal to the emperor, Paul's case has been processed by the local imperial authorities and he is now being escorted to the capital, taking a route that at first hugged the southern coast of modern-day Turkey, offered a staging post in Crete, but now pushes out into an expanse of open sea where the ship is at the mercy of dreadful seasonal storms.

This is a vivid account of Paul's visionary, courageous and compassionate presence among a storm-tossed group of pagans, harking back to earlier events on Lake Galilee (Luke 8. 23-24). But it's also a universal human story for today, because it bears witness to the experience of thousands who take to the seas in unworthy vessels, even in winter, desperate for their own fair haven.

COLLECT

Almighty and everlasting God,
increase in us your gift of faith
that, forsaking what lies behind
and reaching out to that which is before,
we may run the way of your commandments
and win the crown of everlasting joy;
through Jesus Christ your Son our Lord,
who is alive and reigns with you,
in the unity of the Holy Spirit,
one God, now and for ever.

| *Reflection by* **Joanna Collicutt**

Psalms 90, **92**
2 Kings 9.17-end
Acts 27.27-end

Thursday 20 October

Acts 27.27-end

'... he took bread; and giving thanks to God in the presence of all, he broke it' (v.35)

Paul's role in being the point of stillness in the midst of a storm is patterned on Christ. An even closer connection is evident in today's reading in his action with the bread. The form of words used to describe this is an amalgam of those used for Jesus' actions at the last supper (Luke 22.19) and at the Emmaus inn (Luke 24.30). There are of course some differences; instead of giving the bread to his companions, Paul invites them to join him in eating it. Yet there are also further connections with the feeding of the 5,000; the number who ate is specified, and they are described as being satisfied.

Paul's actions in insisting that everyone eat something are a continuation of the leadership he has shown in urging them not to be afraid: eating not only gives nourishment, it is antithetical to fear. But Paul is being more than an effective leader here; he is demonstrating the same compassion shown by Jesus to the crowds who followed him to a 'deserted place' (Luke 9.12-13).

In his letters, Paul repeatedly returns to themes of being in Christ (2 Corinthians 5.17), having the mind of Christ (Philippians 2.5), being conformed to Christ (Romans 8.29). His most profound and mysterious statement is that 'it is no longer I who live, but it is Christ who lives in me' (Galatians 2.20). Now, like the Church he once persecuted, Paul is moving beyond resembling Jesus to becoming Jesus for these hungry folk.

God, our judge and saviour,
teach us to be open to your truth
and to trust in your love,
that we may live each day
with confidence in the salvation which is given
through Jesus Christ our Lord.

COLLECT

Friday 21 October

Psalms **88** (95)
2 Kings 12.1-19
Acts 28.1-16

Acts 28.1-16

'... the rest of the people on the island who had diseases also came and were cured' (v.9)

The presence of Christ in the person and ministry of Paul continues to be made manifest. The events in Publius' house in Malta reprise those in Peter's house in Capernaum a few years before (Luke 4.38-40): an elderly parent has been laid low by a fever, s/he is healed, the news spreads fast, and other sick and troubled people congregate, hopeful that they too will receive healing. And they do.

Earlier Paul has survived an attack by a snake, reminding us of Jesus' promise to the 70 that they would carry his 'authority to tread on snakes and scorpions' (Luke 10.19). When Jesus sent out the 70, he told them to do exactly what Paul is doing here: 'Whenever you enter a town and its people welcome you, eat what is set before you; cure the sick who are there, and say to them, "The kingdom of God has come near to you."' (Luke 10.8-9)

We tend to think of Paul as a purveyor of complex theological ideas, trying to manage recalcitrant congregations from a distance, arguing with opponents both within and outside the Church. Here, we instead see the heart of his calling as Christian apostle: to manifest God's kingdom of peace through the giving and receiving of hospitality and to participate in the transformation and liberation of lives blighted by sickness and oppression. This was the calling of the very first disciples, it continued for the first Christians after Jesus' resurrection, and it remains our calling today.

COLLECT

Almighty and everlasting God,
increase in us your gift of faith
that, forsaking what lies behind
and reaching out to that which is before,
we may run the way of your commandments
and win the crown of everlasting joy;
through Jesus Christ your Son our Lord,
who is alive and reigns with you,
in the unity of the Holy Spirit,
one God, now and for ever.

| *Reflection by* **Joanna Collicutt**

Saturday 22 October

Acts 28.17-end

*'... proclaiming the kingdom of God and teaching about
the Lord Jesus Christ' (v.31)*

The conclusion of the 'we' passage is signalled somewhat sadly by Paul being allowed to 'live by himself' (v.16) under house arrest in Rome; he is on his own and remains so until the end of the book.

Luke's Gospel begins in the temple in Jerusalem, the heart of Judaism, and his second volume ends in Rome, the centre of the gentile world. It recounts Jesus' mission statement at the beginning of his ministry as to 'proclaim the good news of the kingdom of God' (Luke 4.43); Luke's story ends with Paul's proclamation of this kingdom with Jesus as its Lord. Luke–Acts is literally bookended by the kingdom of God.

Even in Rome, Paul's message is offered first to the Jewish community. Paul remains a Jew, and for him it is always 'the Jew first' (Romans 1.16; 2.9,10). Some accept his message, but most appear to reject it, and Paul begins to contrast their lack of receptivity with the openness of the gentiles that he has experienced so often on his missionary journeys. Yet the salvation of the gentiles is not at the expense of the Jews. There is here a direct parallel with the father of the prodigal who invites the older brother to the feast with the words 'Son, you are always with me' (Luke 15.31). The door remains open; the young man just has to walk through it. In the same way, we are told that Paul, like the master he proclaimed, 'welcomed all who came to him'.

God, our judge and saviour,
teach us to be open to your truth
and to trust in your love,
that we may live each day
with confidence in the salvation which is given
through Jesus Christ our Lord.

COLLECT

Monday 24 October

Psalms **98**, 99, 101
2 Kings 17.24-end
Philippians 1.1-11

Philippians 1.1-11

'... that your love may overflow more and more with knowledge and full insight' (v.9)

Last week's readings from Acts tell a part of Paul's story. In today's reading and those that follow, he speaks for himself. Philippians is perhaps Paul's most beautiful and tender letter. It is written during a period of imprisonment and has the tone of someone who is facing imminent death at the end of a long period of fruitful ministry. This makes it likely (though not certain) that Paul is writing during his final period in Rome preluded in Acts 28 and with his execution under Nero on the horizon.

Paul writes to a Christian community he had founded some years before in the home of Lydia (Acts 16). His letter is marked by affection and yearning; the warm words tumble over each other. Paul is delighted with and proud of these people and, more than that, he is homesick for them. The word translated 'compassion' literally means urgent care that comes from the guts (v.8); crucially it is also used to describe Jesus (e.g. Matthew 9.36).

But amid all this visceral affection, Paul still appreciates and emphasizes head-sense. We are nothing without love (1 Corinthians 13.2), but love is not enough; we also need wisdom so that we can live out love in the complex and challenging situations that so often face us. There are no short cuts; study of the Bible, other sources of Christian learning, and the issues facing our world today must be prayerfully woven together with loving compassion if we are to fulfil our calling.

COLLECT

Blessed Lord,
who caused all holy Scriptures to be written for our learning:
help us so to hear them,
to read, mark, learn and inwardly digest them
that, through patience, and the comfort of your holy word,
we may embrace and for ever hold fast
    the hope of everlasting life,
which you have given us in our Saviour Jesus Christ,
who is alive and reigns with you,
in the unity of the Holy Spirit,
one God, now and for ever.

| *Reflection by* **Joanna Collicutt**

Psalms **106*** (*or* 103)
2 Kings 18.1-12
Philippians 1.12-end

Tuesday 25 October

Philippians 1.12-end
'Yes, and I will continue to rejoice' (v.18)

James 1.2 instructs the readers to 'consider it nothing but joy' in the face of hardship, threat and even worse, suggesting that joy is not primarily something we feel but a way of regarding events. Paul looks on helplessly as others proclaim Christ to get one up on him, but he decides not to get eaten up with bitterness and envy; instead, he takes his eyes off himself and focuses on the fact that Christ is being proclaimed, and it is this that enables him to rejoice. His emphatic 'Yes, and' – better communicated by the 'Yea' of the King James Version – expresses an act of determined will.

In many ways, Paul's world is crashing around him. His influence seems to be waning as others try and supplant him; he is cut off from his friends, worried about his fledgeling churches, and staring death in the face, yet he continues to rejoice. Indeed, the words 'joy' and 'rejoice' occur more in this short letter than anywhere else in Paul's correspondence.

Paul believes that he will be delivered, but he is not talking about bodily survival. He must have feared the physical process of death (especially if this was to be in the arena), but his main concern is that his last days will do justice to his Lord and the gospel, and be in accordance with his previous active ministry. To die true to oneself and one's deepest beliefs is to die with dignity.

Merciful God,
teach us to be faithful in change and uncertainty,
that trusting in your word
and obeying your will
we may enter the unfailing joy of Jesus Christ our Lord.

COLLECT

Reflection by **Joanna Collicutt** | 293

Wednesday 26 October

Psalms 110, 111, 112
2 Kings 18.13-end
Philippians 2.1-13

Philippians 2.1-13

'... not only in my presence, but much more now in my absence'
(v.12)

In yesterday's reading, Paul mentions one other concern relating to his death: what will the Philippians do without him? He begins to give them instructions for after he has gone. This is in its own way a 'farewell discourse' similar to Jesus' long goodbye to his disciples in John 13–17.

In 1.27, Paul begins to exhort the Philippians to live up to the gospel in a way that is not dependent on his presence or even his oversight from a distance. This continues into chapter 2 with a beautiful plea for unity of mind and spirit. Again, Paul talks of joy. Joy is a response to two main scenarios: reunion with loved ones after separation and the successful completion of labour of love. The Philippians are Paul's labour of love. Indeed, elsewhere he describes his ministry of planting and growing young churches as being in labour (Galatians 4.19).

In urging unity, Paul invokes an early hymn to Christ that would have been known to his hearers; perhaps it was one they had sung together. The astonishing theological sophistication of these few lines reminds us that a poem can hold more substance than a comparable prose passage. Poems are also better remembered, and this is important to Paul because it looks very much as if the Philippians will not be getting any more teaching from him in the future. They are going to have to grow up and, as a united and harmonious community, work out their salvation without him.

COLLECT

Blessed Lord,
who caused all holy Scriptures to be written for our learning:
help us so to hear them,
to read, mark, learn and inwardly digest them
that, through patience, and the comfort of your holy word,
we may embrace and for ever hold fast
    the hope of everlasting life,
which you have given us in our Saviour Jesus Christ,
who is alive and reigns with you,
in the unity of the Holy Spirit,
one God, now and for ever.

| *Reflection by* **Joanna Collicutt**

Psalms 113, 115
2 Kings 19.1-19
Philippians 2.14-end

Thursday 27 October

Philippians 2.14-end

'... in which you shine like stars in the world' (v.15)

Today's reading gives a glimpse of the darkness that is facing Paul. He talks of 'being poured out'; of letting go of Timothy who is like a son to him – a costly step but necessary to set his mind at rest about the Philippians; of his uncertainty about the future; of the near fatal illness of Epaphroditus; and of his own anxiety and grief.

Yet this part of the letter is also the most densely populated with 'joy' words ('rejoice', 'glad', 'joy'). They shine, not like a single beacon but like dispersed points of light in the darkness. So, the image of stars to describe the Philippians fits well with Paul's personal situation. He may also be drawing on the Book of Daniel, in which it is said that 'Those who are wise shall shine like the brightness of the sky, and those who lead many to righteousness, like the stars forever and ever' (Daniel 12.3).

The themes of wisdom and righteousness pick up on Paul's prayer in chapter 1. This Christian community in Philippi is made up of individuals who, as they go about their business in the surrounding pagan culture, are to enlighten their neighbours with lives in which knowledge, insight, and love are seamlessly woven together. Their joy in the face of hardships is their radiance. Each may feel that they can make little difference, but all are part of a bigger coherent constellation; all are part of something beautiful.

Merciful God,
teach us to be faithful in change and uncertainty,
that trusting in your word
and obeying your will
we may enter the unfailing joy of Jesus Christ our Lord.

COLLECT

Reflection by **Joanna Collicutt**   295

Friday 28 October

Simon and Jude, Apostles

Psalms 116, 117
Wisdom 5.1-16
or Isaiah 45.18-end
Luke 6.12-16

Luke 6.12-16

'... he spent the night in prayer to God' (v.12)

It is not until chapter 11 of Luke's Gospel that Jesus gives his disciples any teaching on prayer, and even then it is at their request rather than his initiative (11.1). An unnamed disciple has asked for instruction on the content and practice of prayer of the sort that a holy man (such as John the Baptist) might be expected to provide. Presumably, people knew which team you were on by the prayers that you favoured. Jesus has not so far provided this; it is almost as if the idea is strange to him, and he responds with a prayer of less than 40 words.

This does not mean that prayer is unimportant to Jesus. We are told that he was in the habit of withdrawing to 'deserted places and pray' (Luke 5.16), and in today's reading he goes up a mountain to spend the whole night in prayer. Clearly more than 40 words were exchanged. Or perhaps no words at all.

For Luke, Jesus is the 'prophet like Moses' promised in Deuteronomy 18.15. He is a journeying messiah whose mission is framed as an exodus. Like Moses, he goes up the mountain; like Moses, he communes directly with God; like Moses, he comes down and confirms a twelve-tribal form of governance (Exodus 24.4). But unlike Moses, he does not keep people away from the holy and fearful divine; he brings the divine to them, instructing them to approach with childlike trust and intimacy and the word 'Father' on their lips.

COLLECT

Almighty God,
who built your Church upon the foundation
 of the apostles and prophets,
with Jesus Christ himself as the chief cornerstone:
so join us together in unity of spirit by their doctrine,
that we may be made a holy temple acceptable to you;
through Jesus Christ your Son our Lord,
who is alive and reigns with you,
in the unity of the Holy Spirit,
one God, now and for ever.

| *Reflection by* **Joanna Collicutt**

Psalms 120, **121**, 122
2 Kings 20
Philippians 4.2-end

Saturday 29 October

Philippians 4.2-end

'I can do all things through him who strengthens me' (v.13)

If this letter was written during Paul's final imprisonment in Rome, then these are the last of his words that we have. They are some of his greatest: 'Rejoice in the Lord always'; 'whatever is true ...'; 'the peace of God, which surpasses all understanding'.

Paul mixes urgent practical instruction with the reminiscence that is characteristic of the final period of life, and in v.12, he reflects on what he has learnt – not so much in knowledge but, circling back to chapter 1, in terms of how to live life well. This learning has come out of adversity. Psychological research indicates that adversity is one of the building blocks of wisdom. If the experience of adversity is used well, it enables people to integrate emotion with feeling, to accept human limitation and to tolerate uncertainty. Paul has used his adversity well in all these respects, partly through his determination to rejoice, but also through the fixing of the mind on things that are above (Colossians 3.1).

These 'things' are summarised in the list in v.8. At first sight, they may appear to be abstract qualities or ideals, but in v.13, Paul makes it clear that he is talking about a person. Jesus is true, honourable, just, pure, pleasing, commendable, excellent and worthy of praise. The 'secret' that Paul has learnt is Christ. In the previous chapter, he spoke of being taken hold of by Christ Jesus. Held fast in this loving embrace, he can face anything.

COLLECT

Blessed Lord,
who caused all holy Scriptures to be written for our learning:
help us so to hear them,
to read, mark, learn and inwardly digest them
that, through patience, and the comfort of your holy word,
we may embrace and for ever hold fast
the hope of everlasting life,
which you have given us in our Saviour Jesus Christ,
who is alive and reigns with you,
in the unity of the Holy Spirit,
one God, now and for ever.

Reflection by **Joanna Collicutt**

297

Monday 31 October
Psalms **2**, 146 *or* 123, 124, 125, **126**
Daniel 1
Revelation 1

Revelation 1

'Do not be afraid ...' (v.17)

A bishop used to send a card to new deacons and priests just before their ordination and write in it: 'I wish you a terrifying ordination.' It is indeed a fearful thing to fall into the hands of the living God. This was certainly John's experience as he came face to face in his vision with the one 'like the Son of Man'. But the object of John's vision put out his hand, saying: 'Do not be afraid.'

This is a phrase to carry with us through our navigation of Revelation. As we approach All Saints' tide, we turn a corner in the Christian Year. The weeks before Advent (sometimes called the 'kingdom season') reflect an older tradition of a longer Advent. They offer space to contemplate the traditional themes of the Four Last Things – heaven, hell, death, and judgement – before an over-early anticipation of Christmas crowds them out. Readings in these weeks focus on the coming of God's kingdom, in mercy and in judgement. The calendar (with All Souls and Remembrance) makes us face the pain of loss, and horror of war. But we are not to be afraid.

Like Mary at the Annunciation, the shepherds in the field, and the women at the tomb, our default response to God's intervention is fear. But God meets us with the assurance that, as we move heavenwards, we encounter the one 'who loves us and freed us from our sins by his blood'.

COLLECT

Almighty and eternal God,
you have kindled the flame of love in the hearts of the saints:
grant to us the same faith and power of love,
that, as we rejoice in their triumphs,
we may be sustained by their example and fellowship;
through Jesus Christ your Son our Lord,
who is alive and reigns with you,
in the unity of the Holy Spirit,
one God, now and for ever.

| *Reflection by* **Peter Moger**

Psalms 15, 84, 149
Isaiah 35.1-9
Luke 9.18-27

Tuesday 1 November
All Saints' Day

Luke 9.18-27

'... who do you say that I am?' (v.20)

Peter's confession of Jesus as 'the Messiah of God' jumps off the page; it never fails to hit us squarely between the eyes as if we were hearing it for the first time. For Peter, this appears to have been a 'lightbulb moment' – quite in character for the intuitive apostle who was quick to open his mouth without always engaging the brain. We can easily imagine him scratching his head afterwards and asking, 'Where did that come from?'

Reading this passage on All Saints' Day is a salutary reminder that, if we acknowledge Jesus as the Christ, there will be consequences. The call to follow brings serious conditions: the daily taking-up of the cross, and a willingness to die to self. Set out like this, the vocation to be saints is a daunting prospect.

Peter's place in the story, though, offers us real hope. The picture of him painted in the Gospels is utterly transparent: we see genuine struggles between God's call to holiness and fallen human nature. Peter declares the truth of Jesus the Messiah but tells lies in the High Priest's courtyard. He promises total commitment to Jesus but denies him under pressure. He is a strong leader but is proud and lacks humility. Peter is the archetypal 'work in progress', and it is on him – and on many more like him – that God has chosen to rely to build his Church.

COLLECT

Almighty God,
you have knit together your elect
in one communion and fellowship
in the mystical body of your Son Christ our Lord:
grant us grace so to follow your blessed saints
in all virtuous and godly living
that we may come to those inexpressible joys
that you have prepared for those who truly love you;
through Jesus Christ your Son our Lord,
who is alive and reigns with you,
in the unity of the Holy Spirit,
one God, now and for ever.

Reflection by **Peter Moger**

299

Wednesday 2 November

Psalms **9**, 147.13-end
or **119.153-end**
Daniel 2.25-end
Revelation 2.12-end

Revelation 2.12-end

'To the one who conquers I will also give the morning star' (v.28)

The Galilee Chapel in Durham Cathedral is a remarkable building, not least because it houses the final resting place of the Venerable Bede, monk of Jarrow, scholar and historian. Above Bede's tomb is a quotation from his Commentary on the Apocalypse:

> Christ is the morning star who, when the night of this world is past, brings to his saints the promise of the light of life and opens everlasting day.

Bede, the father of English history, here looks not backward but forward: to eternity, to the resurrection life promised to the saints. That promise – made to those in the Church at Thyatira 'who conquer' (i.e. who overcome the 'works of Satan') – is of the morning star, who turns out to be none other than Christ himself (Revelation 22.16). Christ is both giver and gift, source and goal.

It is a happy coincidence of the Lectionary that the Letter to Thyatira falls on All Souls' Day, a day traditionally observed in commemoration of the faithful departed. The feasts of All Saints and All Souls remind us that we do not journey alone, but as part of the great family of the baptized – a single company that includes the departed and the living, the conquerors and those still striving to conquer. All Souls, despite its focus on the departed, is at root a celebration of the new creation; the risen Christ, the Morning Star, calls us afresh on our journey to everlasting day.

COLLECT

Almighty and eternal God,
you have kindled the flame of love in the hearts of the saints:
grant to us the same faith and power of love,
that, as we rejoice in their triumphs,
we may be sustained by their example and fellowship;
through Jesus Christ your Son our Lord,
who is alive and reigns with you,
in the unity of the Holy Spirit,
one God, now and for ever.

| *Reflection by* **Peter Moger**

Thursday 3 November

Revelation 3.1-13

'... the holy one ... who has the key of David' (v.7)

Keys are symbols of authority. The original key of David was given to Eliakim, Hezekiah's steward, with authority to admit others to the king's presence (Isaiah 22.22). In John's vision, it is now Jesus who has the key of David and with it the authority to 'open the kingdom of heaven to all believers'.

The church at Philadelphia appeared weak but was actually patient and faithful. Because of this, it is assured that its future is secure: it will be spared the tribulation about to come upon the world; no one will remove its crown, and its place in God's temple is guaranteed. But more than that, an open door has been set before it – and will remain open.

There is a danger, in a culture of mission plans and church statistics, that we encourage a culture of 'success', not patience and faithfulness. A faithful church might be small numerically or weak financially, but faithfulness in keeping God's word brings the reward of the open door. A delight of the wonderful multi-valence of Scripture is that Jesus is both keyholder and door (John 10.7). Not only does he unlock the door to the new Jerusalem, but is also himself the gateway to God's presence. A faithful Church stands at the threshold of heaven. As one verse of the great Advent hymn 'O come, O come, Emmanuel' puts it:

O come, thou Lord of David's key!
The royal door fling wide and free;
safeguard for us the heavenward road,
and bar the way to death's abode.

God of glory,
touch our lips with the fire of your Spirit,
that we with all creation
may rejoice to sing your praise;
through Jesus Christ our Lord.

COLLECT

Reflection by **Peter Moger** | 301

Friday 4 November

Psalms **16**, 149 *or* 142, **144**
Daniel 3.19-end
Revelation 3.14-end

Revelation 3.14-end

'I am standing at the door, knocking' (v.20)

As a child in Sunday School, I was given a postcard of *The Light of the World* by the English Pre-Raphaelite artist, William Holman Hunt. The painting – the original of which hangs in the Chapel of Keble College, Oxford – is powerful, if somewhat sentimental, in its appeal. Christ, with crown of thorns and lantern, stands patiently outside a Victorian gothic door and knocks. The door is festooned with weeds and, significantly, has no handle on the outside; only the soul within can open it, that Christ may enter.

The verse thus illustrated is sometimes used effectively in evangelistic appeals: exhorting hearers to open the door of the heart to the waiting Christ. Within its original context, though, this verse challenged not the faithless but those within the church at Laodicea. The Laodiceans had become lukewarm, apathetic and self-satisfied; Christ was effectively 'left out in the cold'.

Moderation (with its avoidance of extremes) is sometimes praised as a virtue. But it is only a short leap from moderation to lukewarmness – a sin requiring repentance. A question for us all to ask is where we draw the line between the two. Christ's reaction to the Laodiceans' behaviour is revulsion (he speaks of 'spitting them out of his mouth'), yet despite this he persists, reproving those whom he loves, desiring that he and they might eat. It is perhaps this patient insistence of divine love that Holman Hunt captures best.

COLLECT

Almighty and eternal God,
you have kindled the flame of love in the hearts of the saints:
grant to us the same faith and power of love,
that, as we rejoice in their triumphs,
we may be sustained by their example and fellowship;
through Jesus Christ your Son our Lord,
who is alive and reigns with you,
in the unity of the Holy Spirit,
one God, now and for ever.

| *Reflection by* **Peter Moger**

Psalms **18.31-end**, 150 *or* **147**   **Saturday 5 November**
Daniel 4.1-18
Revelation 4

Revelation 4

'Day and night without ceasing they sing ...' (v.8)

Singing is good for us! It boosts wellbeing, reduces stress and fosters community. In Scripture, singing marks significant moments in the story of God's people. At the Exodus, Moses and Miriam 'sing to the Lord, for he has triumphed gloriously'. At the Annunciation, Mary sings 'My soul magnifies the Lord'. At the birth of Jesus, angels sing 'Glory to God in the highest'. But in exile, the psalmist writes: 'How shall we sing the Lord's song in a strange land?'

A Scottish Gaelic proverb translates 'Earthly life will end, but love and music will endure' – borne out in the eternal song of the living creatures in Revelation 4. The song resonates with the past – the seraphic song of Isaiah 6 – and present – the Sanctus of the Church's liturgy: 'Holy, holy, holy, Lord God of hosts, heaven and earth are full of your glory.'

'Heaven and earth' – singing helps connect the two: our song joins with that of those around the throne and, as we sing, we catch an echo of divine glory and are caught up into the heart of God and the life of the world to come. Singing is good for our spiritual, as well as physical, health.

It's easy to 'sing the Lord's song' within the confines of the Church. But having caught a glimpse of heaven, we must not forget the 'strange land' beyond the church door. How might we sing the Lord's song there?

God of glory,
touch our lips with the fire of your Spirit,
that we with all creation
may rejoice to sing your praise;
through Jesus Christ our Lord.

COLLECT

Reflection by **Peter Moger**   303

Monday 7 November

Psalms 19, **20** *or* 1, 2, 3
Daniel 4.19-end
Revelation 5

Revelation 5

'And the elders fell down and worshipped' (v.14)

As I left church alone after Morning Prayer, a passer-by asked, 'How many people were at the service?' 'I was there,' I replied, 'but I couldn't count the others.' 'What others?' 'Well, the saints and angels, for a start ...'

It's easy to forget that when we gather for worship, we always share in something far greater than the visible gathering of those assembled. A friend once remarked that earthly worship is about 'logging on to the heavenly broadband' – a sentiment expressed by the eighteenth-century hymn writer Isaac Watts:

> *Come, let us join our cheerful songs*
> *with angels round the throne;*

Whenever worship is offered, it has an eternal dimension, as our prayers and praises join with those offered continually around God's throne. Some see in the earthly sanctuary a replication of the heavenly: the Eucharist as a foretaste of the marriage supper of the Lamb.

Our worship, though, is often a poor echo of its heavenly counterpart, and this has little to do with the number present. Revelation 4 and 5 remind us that the Church triumphant's primary activity is worship, and that at its worship's centre is the Lamb upon the throne. Is that always true of the Church on earth – or is our worship sometimes more a means to an end (evangelism or fellowship, perhaps), and is Christ always at its centre? If it were so, we might then catch a glimpse of those saints and angels.

C
O
L
L
E
C
T

Almighty Father,
whose will is to restore all things
in your beloved Son, the King of all:
govern the hearts and minds of those in authority,
and bring the families of the nations,
divided and torn apart by the ravages of sin,
to be subject to his just and gentle rule;
who is alive and reigns with you,
in the unity of the Holy Spirit,
one God, now and for ever.

Psalms **21**, 24 *or* **5**, 6 (8)
Daniel 5.1-12
Revelation 6

Tuesday 8 November

Revelation 6

'... who is able to stand?' (v.17)

The German painter and printmaker Albrecht Dürer's famous woodcut of the Four Horsemen of the Apocalypse instils terror even 500 years after its creation. The horses of Revelation 6 come alive and gallop diagonally across the page in a relentless and threatening progress. One can almost hear the trampling of hooves and cries of the afflicted.

Each of the horsemen in John's vision brings a disaster upon the earth: conquest, violence, poverty and death. Their impact is limited to a partial destruction of life. Like the plagues that are to follow, these disasters lead not to the annihilation of the earth but serve as a wake-up call. They are the first of several events in Revelation designed to propel readers towards repentance, particularly the self-satisfied and apathetic (personified by the churches of Sardis and Laodicea). For us, almost 2,000 years later, the effect is still profoundly unsettling, forcing us to ask where we place our security – in God, or in the false gods of political power, military might, wealth and personal wellbeing.

The afflicted seek refuge from 'the wrath of the Lamb'. This comes as a shock: we associate the Lamb with gentleness, not wrath. But there is an echo here of 'the kindness and the severity of God' (Romans 11.22). God's wrath is born of love; its ultimate aim is to save the object of its love. Against this wrath, no one can stand – unless God save them.

> God, our refuge and strength,
> bring near the day when wars shall cease
> and poverty and pain shall end,
> that earth may know the peace of heaven
> through Jesus Christ our Lord.

COLLECT

Reflection by **Peter Moger**   305

Wednesday 9 November

Psalms **23**, 25 *or* **119.1-32**
Daniel 5.13-end
Revelation 7.1-4, 9-end

Revelation 7.1-4, 9-end

'... the Lamb at the centre of the throne will be their shepherd' (v.17)

On the Isle of Lewis, where I live, most crofters keep a few sheep. On the west of the island, the terrain is rocky, with steep cliffs along the coast. Despite fencing, sheep often escape, straying across roads or becoming stranded on ledges above the sea, making rescue a dangerous operation. Sheep offer a poor financial return in terms of their wool and their meat, but that is not reflected in the care lavished upon them. The life of the crofter-shepherd is one of constant self-giving and, as such, a potent reminder of the one who 'lays down his life for the sheep' (John 10.11).

Revelation draws extensively on pre-existent Scripture, in both content and theme. Here the writer takes up the biblical image of God as shepherd. This is familiar from Psalms 23 and 80, and from the prophecies of Isaiah and Ezekiel, where the Messianic king is given the title 'shepherd'. Jesus self-identified as the Good Shepherd (John 10.11), and the image resurfaces in 1 Peter (2.25, 5.4) and in the Letter to the Hebrews (13.20).

This helps make sense of a striking confusion of images in Chapter 7, for here the shepherd of the redeemed is none other than the Lamb upon the throne – the one in whose blood the saints' robes are washed and made white. The Lamb-shepherd guides us '... to springs of the water of life'. In the midst of apparently endless godlessness and destruction, his death still prevails as the source of everlasting life.

COLLECT

Almighty Father,
whose will is to restore all things
in your beloved Son, the King of all:
govern the hearts and minds of those in authority,
and bring the families of the nations,
divided and torn apart by the ravages of sin,
to be subject to his just and gentle rule;
who is alive and reigns with you,
in the unity of the Holy Spirit,
one God, now and for ever.

Reflection by **Peter Moger**

Psalms **26**, 27 *or* 14, **15**, 16
Daniel 6
Revelation 8

Thursday 10 November

Revelation 8

'I saw the seven angels ... and seven trumpets were given to them'
(v.2)

The great east window of York Minster was designed and executed by John Thornton of Coventry, master glazier, in only three years (the contract included an early completion bonus!). At its apex sits God the Father – alpha and omega – and below are 108 panels depicting the biblical beginning and end: scenes from Genesis and Revelation. A recent restoration reordered some panels, undoing earlier dubious renovation, one of which – now fully legible – features the seven angels and seven trumpets.

Biblical trumpets are often harbingers of new beginnings. The angels' seven trumpets recall the priests' seven ramshorns at the battle of Jericho; trumpets signalled each new year, and the year of Jubilee. For St Paul, the trumpet heralds resurrection: 'the trumpet will sound, and the dead will be raised' (1 Corinthians 15.52).

Here, the trumpets herald destruction, and signal woe for a world at variance with the ways of God. After each of the first four trumpet blasts, a third of various life forms is afflicted: vegetation, the sea, rivers and springs, and the light of sun, moon and stars. This feels eerily close to home in a world where environmental destruction accelerates at an alarming pace. The plagues, though, are not the last word in judgement, but an encouragement to repent: a warning of danger to come. They stop us in our tracks, call us to attention and action, lest we experience the devastation of the earth in our own time.

God, our refuge and strength,
bring near the day when wars shall cease
and poverty and pain shall end,
that earth may know the peace of heaven
through Jesus Christ our Lord.

COLLECT

Reflection by **Peter Moger** | 307

Friday 11 November

Revelation 9.1-12

'And the fifth angel blew his trumpet' (v.1)

At 11 a.m. today – 104 years after the Armistice – silence will be kept in remembrance of the dead of two World Wars and subsequent conflicts. A bugler will play *The Last Post*: a call that is less a summons to action than a desolate echo of war. War speaks of disintegration; it blows apart nations, alliances and human lives. The fifth angel's trumpet in Revelation announces destruction and torment not unlike that experienced by soldiers in the trenches. The sky is darkened with smoke from the bottomless pit, and locusts inflict such pain that their victims wish only to die. The people of earth hurtle towards disintegration.

Remembrance Day is perhaps less about 'remembering' than 're-membering', an attempt to reassemble pieces blown apart by war and make some sense of them. At its root lies a desire for wholeness, peace and wellbeing. But re-membering leads to re-integration only when set against a backdrop of New Creation in Christ.

A text often sung at Remembrance-tide is *Holy is the true light*. In his setting, Philip Moore makes skilful use of *The Last Post*, its haunting melody carrying words that affirm resurrection hope for the fallen:

> *From Christ they inherit a home of unfading splendour,*
> *wherein they rejoice with gladness evermore.*

And, crucially, woven throughout the entire piece is the insistent repetition of an Easter Alleluia!

> *At the going down of the sun and in the morning,*
> *we will remember them.*

COLLECT

Almighty Father,
whose will is to restore all things
in your beloved Son, the King of all:
govern the hearts and minds of those in authority,
and bring the families of the nations,
divided and torn apart by the ravages of sin,
to be subject to his just and gentle rule;
who is alive and reigns with you,
in the unity of the Holy Spirit,
one God, now and for ever.

| *Reflection by* **Peter Moger**

Psalm **33** *or* 20, 21, **23**
Daniel 7.15-end
Revelation 9.13-end

Revelation 9.13-end

'And they did not repent ...' (v.21)

The angels' trumpets continue to sound, and John's nightmare vision runs its course. But now the devastation moves up a gear. Whereas the fifth trumpet heralded injury and pain, the sixth signals death: we encounter a chilling reversal of the sixth day of creation (Genesis 1.26) when God gave life to humankind. Four avenging angels are unleashed, and a vast cavalry inflicts plagues of fire, smoke and sulphur, killing a third of humanity.

Once again, God's purpose is not to destroy utterly but to warn and encourage repentance. There is a potent echo here of the Passover (Exodus 12.29-30), with its selective sentence of death for some and life for others. But, as Pharaoh and the Egyptians failed to repent following plagues and the death of their firstborn, the remaining inhabitants of the earth do likewise. They persist in an entrenched idolatry, worshipping demons and committing evil deeds – allying themselves with the very forces that threaten their destruction. Nothing, it seems, will turn their hearts.

It is helpful at this stage to remember that Revelation is addressed, not to the world at large, but to the Church. The plagues that follow the sixth trumpet challenge all who follow Christ to confront the stubbornness of our hearts, our idolatries and hostility to God, and our refusal to repent. If the purpose of the angels' trumpets was to bring about repentance, they failed. But God's call – to repent and embrace life – remains.

God, our refuge and strength,
bring near the day when wars shall cease
and poverty and pain shall end,
that earth may know the peace of heaven
through Jesus Christ our Lord.

COLLECT

Reflection by **Peter Moger**   309

Monday 14 November

Psalms 46, **47** *or* 27, **30**
Daniel 8.1-14
Revelation 10

Revelation 10

'Take it, and eat' (v.9)

The book of Revelation is powerful stuff. It is like cask strength whisky: just a little, sipped and savoured, can enliven and enlighten, but the person who takes too much too quickly may easily lose their balance and even lose their mind.

Any one of the awe-inspiring and numinous images offered in this book will be more than enough for a long slow contemplation.

So it is with this command to take just the little scroll and eat it, imbibe it, take it deep within and make it part of ourselves – inwardly digest it, as the collect for Bible Sunday suggests. John may be alluding here not only to Ezekiel eating a scroll (Ezekiel 3.1,3) but also to Psalm 119.10, 'How sweet are your words on my tongue! They are sweeter than honey to my mouth' and, behind both of those, to the lovely Jewish practice of teaching children to recognize and read the letters of Scripture by writing them on the slate in flour and honey and allowing a child to lick the golden letter off the slate once they could pronounce it!

But this little scroll, like this whole book, is bitter-sweet: there is a promise of consolation but there is bitter experience too, as George Herbert witnessed in his little poem 'Bitter-Sweet'. You sometimes have to brace yourself for the first sip of this strong malt – even malt whisky is an acquired taste.

COLLECT

Heavenly Father,
whose blessed Son was revealed
    to destroy the works of the devil
and to make us the children of God and heirs of eternal life:
grant that we, having this hope,
may purify ourselves even as he is pure;
that when he shall appear in power and great glory
we may be made like him in his eternal and glorious kingdom;
where he is alive and reigns with you,
in the unity of the Holy Spirit,
one God, now and for ever.

| *Reflection by* **Malcolm Guite**

Psalms 48, **52** *or* 32, **36**
Daniel 8.15-end
Revelation 11.1-14

Tuesday 15 November

Revelation 11.1-14

'Come and measure the temple of God' (v.1)

There is too much here to take in at one reflection, but we can at least imbibe the small measure of this measuring of the temple. The first thing to grasp is that the temple in Jerusalem had been completely destroyed in John's own lifetime, 20 years before he wrote these words. He is too late! The outward and visible temple has disappeared. In that sense, there is nothing left for him to measure. And yet he is not too late. Ezekiel too was given a vision of an Angel with a measuring Rod, brought up to a vey high mountain, and there, golden and glowing, eternally sure beyond the destructions in Jerusalem, was the true temple, filled with the glory of the Lord (Ezekiel 40 and forward)

In Ezekiel, the angel does the measuring, but here John is called to do it himself, to take such cognizance, such remembrance of what seems to have been lost, that he discovers it has not been lost at all.

So it is with us. What folly, people say, to study theology after 'the death of God', to pore over these old pages of Scripture, when after all, it's all been swept away. But like John in the Revelation, we discover that these two old witnesses, the Old and New Testaments, are not as dead as some suppose, for they have risen again with the risen Lord at their heart, risen with fresh wisdom.

Heavenly Lord,
you long for the world's salvation:
stir us from apathy,
restrain us from excess
and revive in us new hope
that all creation will one day be healed
in Jesus Christ our Lord.

COLLECT

Reflection by **Malcolm Guite**

Wednesday 16 November

Revelation 11.15-end

'The kingdom of the world has become the kingdom of our Lord'
(v.15)

Here, glimpsed for a moment even within the circles of time, even before its time, is the fulfilment of the prayer we make every day, the prayer that marks our time: 'Thy kingdom come, thy will be done on earth as it is in heaven'. Here is our glimpse of 'the end in the middle', the assurance that, even in the midst of apparent destruction and defeat, God has 'begun to reign'.

It is the message of the cross and resurrection, the power of the resurrection working backwards through the cross to wreathe its shame in glory, a message John needed to hear in his time amidst the Domitian persecution, and which we need to hear in ours.

Indeed, this whole chapter is like an interlude in the book of Revelation: we are lifted up and given an epitome of the whole vision, a glimpse of completion, rather as the disciples were lifted up on the mount of transfiguration to see the glory, even though they had still to descend and face their agony and Christ's in Jerusalem. They did so with assurance because, in one sense, they had already seen the resurrection, the joy that was set before them. So it is with us on our dire journey through the book of Revelation: John lets us know that it will come out all right and God 'will reign for ever and ever'.

COLLECT

Heavenly Father,
whose blessed Son was revealed
    to destroy the works of the devil
and to make us the children of God and heirs of eternal life:
grant that we, having this hope,
may purify ourselves even as he is pure;
that when he shall appear in power and great glory
we may be made like him in his eternal and glorious kingdom;
where he is alive and reigns with you,
in the unity of the Holy Spirit,
one God, now and for ever.

Thursday 17 November

Revelation 12

'... a woman clothed with the sun' (v.1)

Now here is a single image worthy of our meditation! Shining out from Scriptures, which seem to so many to have been darkened by the shadows of patriarchy, is this emblem of a woman: not pale and moony, and passively reflective, as earlier archetypes had been, but glorious in 'sun-clad power', as the poet John Milton put it. Who is she? Or perhaps we should ask, 'Who was she then? And who is she now?'

In one sense, of course she is the one through whom Christ is brought into the world. She is therefore God's covenant people, Israel, of whom Isaiah said 'your Maker is your husband' (Isaiah 54.5) and out of whom came the Messiah, not only as the glory of Israel, but also clothed with the sun, a light to lighten the gentiles.

In another, more focused and particular sense, she is Mary, not the shy pre-Raphaelite maiden clutching a lily, but the great prophet in Luke, filled with the Holy Spirit and prophesying just that revolution, that casting-down of the mighty from their seats, which is the story of the book of Revelation. And because Mary herself is the archetype and emblem of the Church, as well as of each believing soul, the woman clothed with the sun is all of us, the believing community right now, still in the anguish of birth pangs but still, in spite of everything, bringing forth Christ to the world.

Heavenly Lord,
you long for the world's salvation:
stir us from apathy,
restrain us from excess
and revive in us new hope
that all creation will one day be healed
in Jesus Christ our Lord.

COLLECT

Friday 18 November

Psalms **63**, 65 *or* 31
Daniel 10.1 – 11.1
Revelation 13.1-10

Revelation 13.1-10

'Who is like the beast, and who can fight against it?' (v.4)

'Who is like the beast?' In one sense, there is a straightforward answer. The symbolic allusions John is making here are to the beasts that came out of the sea in Daniel 7, each representing a successive oppressive empire. John makes it clear that the beast he sees, with its heads and horns corresponding to the Roman emperors, is the oppressive Roman empire, which culminates and somehow includes all those precious alignments of brute force that had oppressed God's people. The wounded head that returns is almost certainly Nero, for many feared the return of an odious and supernatural *Nero redivivus*. What a change this presents from Rome as it was understood and appealed to by Paul, so proud of his Roman citizenship! But the nature of the beast was revealed (for this is a book of revelation) when Christians were commanded to worship the powers of this world and not its maker and redeemer.

And what of us? We too must break our uneasy truce with an old empire that half sheltered us, when we see that the persuasions and powers of this world are making claims on us that only God can make. The key question, though, is who can fight against it and how? And here, at last, John quotes Jesus. We cannot use the weapons of this world. The sword will slay those who take it up. Here only endurance and faith will see us through.

COLLECT

Heavenly Father,
whose blessed Son was revealed
    to destroy the works of the devil
and to make us the children of God and heirs of eternal life:
grant that we, having this hope,
may purify ourselves even as he is pure;
that when he shall appear in power and great glory
we may be made like him in his eternal and glorious kingdom;
where he is alive and reigns with you,
in the unity of the Holy Spirit,
one God, now and for ever.

| *Reflection by* **Malcolm Guite**

Psalm **78.1-39** *or* 41, 42, 43
Daniel 12
Revelation 13.11-end

Saturday 19 November

Revelation 13.11-end

'... to be marked on the right hand or the forehead' (v.16)

Oh dear! With the mark and the number of the beast we have now arrived at conspiracy-theory central. What inane ingenuity has been spent on calculating numbers or on finding little proof-texts that one day we will all wear tattooed barcodes or be vaccinated with microchips!

All that nonsense is a world away from this text. Even the most elementary scholarship reveals that this is a coded description, a veiled unveiling, of what was actually happening in John's day when emperor worship was enforced, when fires were 'kindled from heaven' to burn 'the pinch of dust' – the incense to the emperor – and when the powers of the day did indeed 'cause those who would not worship the image of the beast to be killed'. And it is not far to look for the number: NERON in Latin adds up to 666 and so do the Hebrew letters for Nero Caesar.

The real question is not what happened out there and back then, but what happens in here and right now, and, as John says, 'This calls for wisdom', not ingenuity. What are the forces at work in our world that divert us from giving to God what belongs to him and tempt us instead to give it all to Caesar? Which are those moments when there is a real choice between the right course and a little more personal prosperity? When might we be called to choose between prestige and probity?

Heavenly Lord,
you long for the world's salvation:
stir us from apathy,
restrain us from excess
and revive in us new hope
that all creation will one day be healed
in Jesus Christ our Lord.

COLLECT

Reflection by **Malcolm Guite**

315

Monday 21 November

Psalms 92, **96** or **44**
Isaiah 40.1-11
Revelation 14.1-13

Revelation 14.1-13

'And I heard a voice from heaven' (v.2)

This passage gives us far too full a measure of impossibly strong stuff, the bitter-sweet distillation of Revelation. We can only sip and savour one drop of the heady mix: John's many-layered poetic evocation of the voice of God. He offers one analogy after another to describe the indescribable: each adds something, none is adequate or final by itself, but between them they evoke a little of the mystery.

First there is the sound of many waters. Tradition has it that John was exiled to Patmos, a Roman penal colony. Here perhaps he may be hearing the sea as it breaks on the island's rugged shores, or the rushing of steep cataracts inland, but he is also invoking Psalm 29, recited inwardly perhaps in his forced labour in the mines: 'It is the Lord that commandeth the waters: it is the glorious God that maketh the thunder. It is the Lord that ruleth the sea ... the voice of the Lord is a glorious voice.' Then, after the many murmurs of water, comes the sharp declamation of 'loud thunder', also drawn from that psalm. Then, heartbreakingly amidst that loud multiplicity, is heard the sweet sound of human music, the song of the redeemed, the playing of harps, the very harps that once hung silent on the trees by the waters of Babylon.

Outwardly and audibly, these three sounds could not possibly be combined, but inwardly and spiritually, they suggest what it's like to encounter the living God.

COLLECT

Eternal Father,
whose Son Jesus Christ ascended to the throne of heaven
    that he might rule over all things as Lord and King:
keep the Church in the unity of the Spirit
and in the bond of peace,
and bring the whole created order to worship at his feet;
who is alive and reigns with you,
in the unity of the Holy Spirit,
one God, now and for ever.

Psalms **97**, 98, 100 *or* **48**, 52
Isaiah 40.12-26
Revelation 14.14 – end of 15

Tuesday 22 November

Revelation 14.14 – end of 15

'And the wine press was trodden outside the city' (14.20)

There is a great deal in this passage on the last judgement as a kind of harvest and a *vendange* – a gathering of grapes and pressing of wine – that is gathered and distilled from other apocalyptic literature, from the Old Testament, and from some of the sayings of Jesus. The emphasis on both the grain and the grape gives the whole a strongly eucharistic frame, as with the 'I AM' sayings, which also begin with the bread and end with the vine. What are we to make of it all?

'I have trodden the wine press alone,' says the Lord in Isaiah (63.3). Before Christ, that passage was interpreted as a wine press in which the enemies of God were trampled and their blood flowed like wine, but the crucifixion of the Messiah changes all that. In the press and pressure of Gethsemane and on the cross, it was God himself, in Christ, who was crushed and trampled. And in that wine press instead of *our* blood flowing like wine, it was *his* blood that was pressed to become wine for us, pressed as this passage says 'outside the city'. George Herbert got to the heart of this mystery when, in his poem 'The Agony', he wrote:

> *Love is that liquor sweet and most divine,*
> *Which my God feels as blood, but I, as wine.*

Reflection by **Malcolm Guite** | 317

Wednesday 23 November

Psalms 110, 111, 112
or 119.57-80
Isaiah 40.27 – 41.7
Revelation 16.1-11

Revelation 16.1-11

'... they were scorched by the fierce heat' (v.9)

This appalling, and literally bloodthirsty list of plagues, seems to gather up, with a kind of vindictive exactitude, all the examples of God's wrath that John can remember from the Scriptures he carried in his heart as he brooded in exile on Patmos. Chief among these are, of course, are the ten plagues on Egypt that he would have recited as a child at Passover, but he adds a few of his own for good measure and also returns to the ones he had listed earlier in Revelation at the sounding of the seven trumpets. This is all an understandable response to the trauma of persecution. So many of the images of violence in this book must reflect the traumatized processing of images of state-sponsored violence that he had actually witnessed.

But we must read this differently. Our understanding of the gospel of love will not allow us such fantasies of revenge, and yet there is something for us to ponder here. The plagues in this passage result from human wickedness, and in John's vision, people discover that, as a result of their own actions, the world has changed around them and become hostile and unliveable. Is there a lesson for us? These images of scorching heat, of fouled waters, of rampant disease, seem to reflect to us, as in a dark mirror, some of the consequences of our own environmental degradation. It may not be too late to repent.

COLLECT

Eternal Father,
whose Son Jesus Christ ascended to the throne of heaven
    that he might rule over all things as Lord and King:
keep the Church in the unity of the Spirit
and in the bond of peace,
and bring the whole created order to worship at his feet;
who is alive and reigns with you,
in the unity of the Holy Spirit,
one God, now and for ever.

| *Reflection by* **Malcolm Guite**

Thursday 24 November

Revelation 16.12-end

'... three foul spirits like frogs' (v.13)

Once more we find the nightmare imagery of this dark chapter performing a double function. On the one hand, it is a coded account of the powers at work in John's world and his anticipation of their brief triumph and inevitable demise; on the other hand, they are symbols that still work in our minds and may help us to discern and 'unveil' some truth about the powers at work in our own world.

The dragon, the beast and the false prophet, triple and mutually enfolded powers at work in John's world, represent respectively Satan (the dragon) suborning and empowering Rome (the Beast), organizing the state religion of emperor worship (the false prophet). From the mouth of each of these comes a foul spirit (*pneuma*); *pneuma* also means 'breath' – and sometimes by implication 'word', the speech that is borne on the breath. These frog-like *pneuma* are the constant empty croaking, the noxious flatulence of state-sponsored propaganda.

That much is clear for John, but what about us? The dragon, the beast and the false prophet in our age might well be corrupted and self-serving forms of spirituality, corrupted statecraft and corruption in organized religion. In John's world, these three corruptions infected one another and worked together, and they sometimes do the same in ours. A prosperity gospel, a self-serving politician and a complacent Church might all seem to be singing from the same hymn sheet.

God the Father,
help us to hear the call of Christ the King
and to follow in his service,
whose kingdom has no end;
for he reigns with you and the Holy Spirit,
one God, one glory.

COLLECT

Reflection by **Malcolm Guite**

319

Friday 25 November

Psalm **139** *or* **51**, 54
Isaiah 41.21 – 42.9
Revelation 17

Revelation 17

'So he carried me away in the spirit into a wilderness' (v.3)

It is only from the wilderness that John is able to bring the seductions and luxuries of Babylon/Rome into focus and see them for what they really are. In this he is following in a great biblical tradition. His direct allusion is to Ezekiel – 'The spirit lifted me up and bore me away' (Ezekiel 3.14) – and more specifically in terms of John's specific visionary vocation – 'The spirit lifted me up between earth and heaven, and brought me in visions of God to Jerusalem' (Ezekiel 8.3). But, of course, the motif goes deeper than that, for Moses has his revelation in the wilderness, and it extends into the New Testament for Jesus himself is 'led up by the Spirit into the wilderness' (Matthew 4.1). It is there that Jesus too sees unveiled the essentially cosmic conflict that will define his ministry, a ministry that sees through Satan's offer of wealth and power and chooses instead a radical obedience to and dependence on God alone.

And so it may be with us. While we are in the midst of the luxurious cosseting, the bland blandishments, the sinuous scrolling of all our digital distractions, we cannot see the truth about our life style – the truth that it costs others not only their livelihood but also their lives, and the deeper truth that if we carry on like this, it will kill us all in the end, that we are (in American educator Neil Postman's words) 'amusing ourselves to death'.

COLLECT

Eternal Father,
whose Son Jesus Christ ascended to the throne of heaven
    that he might rule over all things as Lord and King:
keep the Church in the unity of the Spirit
and in the bond of peace,
and bring the whole created order to worship at his feet;
who is alive and reigns with you,
in the unity of the Holy Spirit,
one God, now and for ever.

Psalm **145** *or* **68**
Isaiah 42.10-17
Revelation 18

Saturday 26 November

Revelation 18

'Fallen, fallen is Babylon the great!' (v.2)

All the imagery of this chapter (and indeed of this whole book) and all its power as prophecy are far more clearly understood by our sisters and brothers in the persecuted Church than they are by us. For many of us still live in the heart of Babylon. We send to the four corners of the earth for all our little luxuries and pay scant attention to the lives and working conditions of those who are exploited to keep us pampered and to sate our delicate tastes.

I got my first taste of a different perspective on these verses when I listened to Reggae music in the 70s, blasting out from impromptu 'sound systems' set up under motorway flyovers and in the back-lots and alleyways of London. I was just a white hippy visitor who loved the music and enjoyed an occasional spliff. But when I heard them sing that Babylon was fallen and would fall with such glee and hope, it gradually dawned on me that they were singing about England, and about me and my privilege, my entitlement. Hearing these Scriptures sung back in another accent and with another emphasis was part of my conversion.

We all need yet more conversion if we are to join the song of the saints and not to find that it has been sung against us.

God the Father,
help us to hear the call of Christ the King
and to follow in his service,
whose kingdom has no end;
for he reigns with you and the Holy Spirit,
one God, one glory.

COLLECT

Reflection by **Malcolm Guite** | 321

Seasonal Prayers of Thanksgiving

Advent

Blessed are you, Sovereign God of all,
to you be praise and glory for ever.
In your tender compassion
the dawn from on high is breaking upon us
to dispel the lingering shadows of night.
As we look for your coming among us this day,
open our eyes to behold your presence
and strengthen our hands to do your will,
that the world may rejoice and give you praise.
Blessed be God, Father, Son and Holy Spirit.
Blessed be God for ever.

Christmas Season

Blessed are you, Sovereign God,
creator of heaven and earth,
to you be praise and glory for ever.
As your living Word, eternal in heaven,
assumed the frailty of our mortal flesh,
may the light of your love be born in us
to fill our hearts with joy as we sing:
Blessed be God, Father, Son and Holy Spirit.
Blessed be God for ever.

Epiphany

Blessed are you, Sovereign God,
king of the nations,
to you be praise and glory for ever.
From the rising of the sun to its setting
your name is proclaimed in all the world.
As the Sun of Righteousness dawns in our hearts
anoint our lips with the seal of your Spirit
that we may witness to your gospel
and sing your praise in all the earth.
Blessed be God, Father, Son and Holy Spirit.
Blessed be God for ever.

Blessed are you, Lord God of our salvation,
to you be glory and praise for ever.
In the darkness of our sin you have shone in our hearts
to give the light of the knowledge of the glory of God
in the face of Jesus Christ.
Open our eyes to acknowledge your presence,
that freed from the misery of sin and shame
we may grow into your likeness from glory to glory.
Blessed be God, Father, Son and Holy Spirit.
Blessed be God for ever.

Blessed are you, Lord God of our salvation,
to you be praise and glory for ever.
As a man of sorrows and acquainted with grief
your only Son was lifted up
that he might draw the whole world to himself.
May we walk this day in the way of the cross
and always be ready to share its weight,
declaring your love for all the world.
Blessed be God, Father, Son and Holy Spirit.
Blessed be God for ever.

Blessed are you, Sovereign Lord,
the God and Father of our Lord Jesus Christ,
to you be glory and praise for ever.
From the deep waters of death
you brought your people to new birth
by raising your Son to life in triumph.
Through him dark death has been destroyed
and radiant life is everywhere restored.
As you call us out of darkness into his marvellous light
may our lives reflect his glory
and our lips repeat the endless song.
Blessed be God, Father, Son and Holy Spirit.
Blessed be God for ever.

Blessed are you, Lord of heaven and earth,
to you be glory and praise for ever.
From the darkness of death you have raised your Christ
to the right hand of your majesty on high.
The pioneer of our faith, his passion accomplished,
has opened for us the way to heaven
and sends on us the promised Spirit.
May we be ready to follow the Way
and so be brought to the glory of his presence
where songs of triumph for ever sound:
Blessed be God, Father, Son and Holy Spirit.
Blessed be God for ever.

*From the day after Ascension Day
until the Day of Pentecost*

Blessed are you, creator God,
to you be praise and glory for ever.
As your Spirit moved over the face of the waters
bringing light and life to your creation,
pour out your Spirit on us today
that we may walk as children of light
and by your grace reveal your presence.
Blessed be God, Father, Son and Holy Spirit.
Blessed be God for ever.

*From All Saints until the day before
the First Sunday of Advent*

Blessed are you, Sovereign God,
ruler and judge of all,
to you be praise and glory for ever.
In the darkness of this age that is passing away
may the light of your presence which the saints enjoy
surround our steps as we journey on.
May we reflect your glory this day
and so be made ready to see your face
in the heavenly city where night shall be no more.
Blessed be God, Father, Son and Holy Spirit.
Blessed be God for ever.

The Lord's Prayer and The Grace

Our Father in heaven,
hallowed be your name,
your kingdom come,
your will be done,
on earth as in heaven.
Give us today our daily bread.
Forgive us our sins
as we forgive those who sin against us.
Lead us not into temptation
but deliver us from evil.
For the kingdom, the power,
and the glory are yours
now and for ever.
Amen.

(or)

Our Father, who art in heaven,
hallowed be thy name;
thy kingdom come;
thy will be done;
on earth as it is in heaven.
Give us this day our daily bread.
And forgive us our trespasses,
as we forgive those who trespass against us.
And lead us not into temptation;
but deliver us from evil.
For thine is the kingdom,
the power and the glory,
for ever and ever.
Amen.

The grace of our Lord Jesus Christ,
and the love of God,
and the fellowship of the Holy Spirit,
be with us all evermore.
Amen.

An Order for Night Prayer (Compline)

The Lord almighty grant us a quiet night and a perfect end.
Amen.

Our help is in the name of the Lord
who made heaven and earth.

A period of silence for reflection on the past day may follow.

The following or other suitable words of penitence may be used

**Most merciful God,
we confess to you,
before the whole company of heaven and one another,
that we have sinned in thought, word and deed
and in what we have failed to do.
Forgive us our sins,
heal us by your Spirit
and raise us to new life in Christ. Amen.**

O God, make speed to save us.
O Lord, make haste to help us.

**Glory to the Father and to the Son
and to the Holy Spirit;
as it was in the beginning is now
and shall be for ever. Amen.
Alleluia.**

The following or another suitable hymn may be sung

Before the ending of the day,
Creator of the world, we pray
That you, with steadfast love, would keep
Your watch around us while we sleep.

From evil dreams defend our sight,
From fears and terrors of the night;
Tread underfoot our deadly foe
That we no sinful thought may know.

O Father, that we ask be done
Through Jesus Christ, your only Son;
And Holy Spirit, by whose breath
Our souls are raised to life from death.

The Word of God

Psalmody

One or more of Psalms 4, 91 or 134 may be used.

Psalm 134

1   Come, bless the Lord, all you servants of the Lord, ♦
    you that by night stand in the house of the Lord.

2   Lift up your hands towards the sanctuary ♦
    and bless the Lord.

3   The Lord who made heaven and earth ♦
    give you blessing out of Zion.

**Glory to the Father and to the Son
and to the Holy Spirit;
as it was in the beginning is now
and shall be for ever. Amen.**

Scripture Reading

*One of the following short lessons or another suitable
passage is read*

You, O Lord, are in the midst of us and we are called by
your name; leave us not, O Lord our God.

Jeremiah 14.9

(or)

Be sober, be vigilant, because your adversary the devil is
prowling round like a roaring lion, seeking for someone
to devour. Resist him, strong in the faith.

1 Peter 5.8,9

(or)

The servants of the Lamb shall see the face of God, whose
name will be on their foreheads. There will be no more night:
they will not need the light of a lamp or the light of the sun,
for God will be their light, and they will reign for ever and
ever.

Revelation 22.4,5

The following responsory may be said

Into your hands, O Lord, I commend my spirit.
Into your hands, O Lord, I commend my spirit.
For you have redeemed me, Lord God of truth.
I commend my spirit.
Glory to the Father and to the Son
and to the Holy Spirit.
Into your hands, O Lord, I commend my spirit.

Or, in Easter

Into your hands, O Lord, I commend my spirit.
    Alleluia, alleluia.
Into your hands, O Lord, I commend my spirit.
    Alleluia, alleluia.
For you have redeemed me, Lord God of truth.
Alleluia, alleluia.
Glory to the Father and to the Son
and to the Holy Spirit.
Into your hands, O Lord, I commend my spirit.
    Alleluia, alleluia.

Keep me as the apple of your eye.
Hide me under the shadow of your wings.

Gospel Canticle

Nunc Dimittis (The Song of Simeon)

Save us, O Lord, while waking,
and guard us while sleeping,
that awake we may watch with Christ
and asleep may rest in peace.

1   Now, Lord, you let your servant go in peace:
     your word has been fulfilled.

2   My own eyes have seen the salvation
     which you have prepared in the sight of every people;

3   A light to reveal you to the nations
     and the glory of your people Israel.

Luke 2.29-32

Glory to the Father and to the Son
and to the Holy Spirit;
as it was in the beginning is now
and shall be for ever. Amen.

Save us, O Lord, while waking,
and guard us while sleeping,
that awake we may watch with Christ
and asleep may rest in peace.

Prayers

Intercessions and thanksgivings may be offered here.

The Collect

Visit this place, O Lord, we pray,
and drive far from it the snares of the enemy;
may your holy angels dwell with us and guard us in peace,
and may your blessing be always upon us;
through Jesus Christ our Lord.
Amen.

The Lord's Prayer (see p. 325) may be said.

The Conclusion

In peace we will lie down and sleep;
for you alone, Lord, make us dwell in safety.

Abide with us, Lord Jesus,
for the night is at hand and the day is now past.

As the night watch looks for the morning,
so do we look for you, O Christ.

[Come with the dawning of the day
and make yourself known in the breaking of the bread.]

The Lord bless us and watch over us;
the Lord make his face shine upon us and be gracious to us;
the Lord look kindly on us and give us peace.
Amen.

REFLECTIONS FOR LENT 2022

Wednesday 2 March – Saturday 16 April 2022

This shortened edition of *Reflections* is ideal for group or church use during Lent, or for anyone seeking a daily devotional guide to this most holy season of the Christian year. It is also an ideal taster for those wanting to begin a regular pattern of prayer and reading.

Authors: Christopher Herbert, Philip North, Angela Tilby, Rachel Treweek, *with Holy Week reflections by* Rowan Williams

£4.99 • 64 pages
ISBN 978 1 78140 276 4
Available November 2021

Note: this book reproduces the material for Lent and Holy Week found in the volume you are now holding.

RESOURCES FOR DAILY PRAYER

Common Worship: Daily Prayer

The official daily office of the Church of England, *Common Worship: Daily Prayer* is a rich collection of devotional material that will enable those wanting to enrich their quiet times to develop a regular pattern of prayer. It includes:

- Prayer During the Day
- Forms of Penitence
- Morning and Evening Prayer
- Night Prayer (Compline)
- Collects and Refrains
- Canticles
- Complete Psalter

896 pages • with 6 ribbons • 202 x 125mm

Hardback	978 0 7151 2199 3	**£22.50**
Soft cased	978 0 7151 2178 8	**£27.50**
Bonded leather	978 0 7151 2277 8	**£50.00**

REFLECTIONS FOR DAILY PRAYER
App

Make Bible study and reflection a part of your routine wherever you go with the Reflections for Daily Prayer App for Apple and Android devices.

Download the app for free from the App Store (Apple devices) or Google Play (Android devices) and receive a week's worth of reflections free. Then purchase a monthly, three-monthly or annual subscription to receive up-to-date content.